Blumhouse
PRODUCTIONS

HORROR STUDIES

Preface

Horror Studies is the first book series exclusively dedicated to the study of the genre in its various manifestations – from fiction to cinema and television, magazines to comics, and extending to other forms of narrative texts such as video games and music. Horror Studies aims to raise the profile of Horror and to further its academic institutionalisation by providing a publishing home for cutting-edge research. As an exciting new venture within the established Cultural Studies and Literary Criticism programme, Horror Studies will expand the field in innovative and student-friendly ways.

PRODUCTIONS

THE NEW HOUSE OF HORROR

EDITED BY TODD K. PLATTS, VICTORIA
McCOLLUM AND MATHIAS CLASEN

UNIVERSITY OF WALES PRESS
2022

www.uwp.co.uk

British Library Cataloguing-in-Publication Data

A catalogue record for this book is available from the British Library.

ISBN   978-1-78683-863-6
eISBN 978-1-78683-864-3

Typeset by Chris Bell, cbdesign

Printed by CPI Antony Rowe, Melksham, United Kingdom

Contents

Acknowledgements

TODD K. PLATTS thanks his co-editors Victoria and Mathias for guiding a novice editor through the tedious process of academic publishing. He also wishes to thank his wife and partner in crime, Melanie.

Victoria McCollum wishes to express her most sincere gratitude and appreciation to her kick-ass co-editors, Todd and Mathias, for their support, patience and encouragement. She owes a very important debt this year to the National Health Service. She also wishes to thank her loving and supportive Partner, Gem.

Mathias Clasen would like to thank his co-editors, Todd and Victoria, for an inspiring and productive collaboration, and the Independent Research Fund Denmark (grant number 0132-00204B) for generous research support.

Collectively, the editors thank the contributors of this volume for their diligence during a pandemic.

List of Tables

Notes on the Contributors

Sarah Baker is a senior lecturer in the School of Communication Studies at Auckland University of Technology (AUT) in New Zealand. She is the co-founder of the AUT Popular Culture Centre and a member of the AUT Journalism, Media and Democracy Centre and the AUT Media Observatory Group. Her research interests include political economy, current-affairs television programmes, and popular culture focusing on the Gothic, sexuality and gender.

Mathias Clasen is associate professor of literature and media in the English department at Aarhus University, Denmark. He is the director of the Recreational Fear Lab and associate editor of the journal *Evolutionary Studies in Imaginative Culture*. His research focuses on horror across media, and he has developed a biocultural framework for the analysis of scary entertainment. His recent books are *Why Horror Seduces* (Oxford University Press, 2017) and *A Very Nervous Person's Guide to Horror Movies* (Oxford University Press, 2021).

Fernando Gabriel Pagnoni Berns works as a professor at the Universidad de Buenos Aires, Facultad de Filosofía y Letras, in Argentina, where teaches courses on international horror film. He has published many essays on horror cinema. He has also authored a book about the Spanish horror TV series *Historias para no Dormir* (Universidad de Cádiz, 2020) and has edited a book on Frankenstein's bicentennial. He is currently editing a book on director James Wan and another on Italian *giallo* film.

Zak Bronson is a PhD candidate and instructor at the University of Western Ontario, where he teaches courses on media fandom, technology and horror film. He has previously published essays on the novels of China Miéville, the television show *Fringe*, and has forthcoming essays in several book collections.

Racheal Harris has contributed to several edited collections on popular culture, including chapters on theological concepts in James Cameron's *Terminator* franchise and folklore in the CW series *Supernatural*. Her first single-authored monograph, *Skin, Meaning, and Symbolism in Pet Memorials*, considers contemporary death practices related to mourning and memorialising companion animals. She also has a forthcoming title on the Syfy series *12 Monkeys*, to be published by McFarland Press.

John Kavanagh is a PhD researcher at Ulster University, Magee. His research focuses on the slasher film, myths and misconceptions of the slasher subgenre and the masculinities depicted within these texts. John teaches on the Horror Film: Theory and Practice and Issues of Performance modules in the Cinematic Arts and Drama departments of the Magee campus. His other research interests include late-twentieth century global cinema, exploitation and abject film, and the re-contextualisation of visceral/abject horror.

Craig Ian Mann is an associate lecturer in film and media production at Sheffield Hallam University. He is broadly interested in the cultural significance of popular genre cinema, including horror, science fiction, action and the Western. His first monograph, *Phases of the Moon: A Cultural History of the Werewolf Film* was published by Edinburgh University Press. He has published in *Science Fiction Film and Television*, *Horror Studies* and the *Journal of Popular Film and Television*, as well as a number of edited collections.

Victoria McCollum is a lecturer in cinematic arts at Ulster University (Northern Ireland). Her research tends to centre on how horror films deal with memory, ideology and the often-competing claims of nationalism, American exceptionalism and cultural sorrow. She has authored *Post-9/11 Heartland Horror: Rural Horror Films in an Era of Urban Terrorism* (Routledge, 2016) and edited or co-edited *Make America Hate Again: Trump-Era Horror and the Politics of Fear* (Routledge, 2019), *Alternative Media in*

Contemporary Turkey: Sustainability, Activism and Resistance (Rowman & Littlefield 2019) and *#Resist: Protest and Resistance Media in Brexit Britain and Trump-era USA* (Rowman & Littlefield, 2020).

Shellie McMurdo is a visiting lecturer at both the University of Hertfordshire and Roehampton University. Her most recent publications include an article on true crime fandom and school shooters in the *European Journal of American Culture*, and she has a co-written chapter on late-phase torture horror with Wickham Clayton. Her research interests include a specific focus on the cultural significance of the horror genre and its ability to communicate trauma, as well as extreme horror, cult film and television, and true-crime fandom.

Sotiris Petridis is an adjunct professor of screenwriting and a postdoc researcher at Aristotle University of Thessaloniki, Greece. He holds a PhD in film studies (Aristotle University) and two master's degrees in art, law and economy (International Hellenic University) and in film studies (Aristotle University). His research interests are about film and television genres, screenwriting theory and practice, audiovisual rights and copyright laws, viral marketing and the new ways of film and television promotion. He is a member of the European Film Academy and the Greek Film Academy.

Todd K. Platts is professor of sociology at Piedmont Virginia Community College. He has published numerous articles and book chapters on horror cinema, with his recent scholarship focusing on horror in the twenty-first century.

Amanda Rutherford lectures in the School of Communication Studies and the School of Language and Culture at AUT in New Zealand. She is a member of the AUT Popular Culture Centre, the Gothic Association of New Zealand and Australia, and the Popular Culture Association of Australia and New Zealand. Her interests include mediated popular culture, media communications, fairy tales, the Gothic and horror.

Allison Schottenstein received her PhD in history from the University of Texas at Austin. She specialises in the history of Black-Jewish relations in the United States. She recently published a book entitled *Changing Perspectives: Black-Jewish Relation in Houston During the Civil Rights Era* (UNT Press, 2021). She has also published numerous articles in the genre of pop culture. Her areas of speciality are American history, American and European Jewish history, and race and ethnic studies. She is currently teaching at Cincinnati Country Day School and Gratz College.

Stefan Sereda researches American arthouse and independent cinema, as well as media from Africa and its diaspora. He has previously published analyses of Prince lyrics, Nigerian novels, Nollywood videos and African festival films. He has also published readings of American auteur films including Martin Scorsese's *Mean Streets*, Steven Soderbergh's *The Good German* and Quentin Tarantino's *Inglourious Basterds*. His SSHRC-funded dissertation, 'Cinema in Scare Quotes: Aesthetics and Economics in American Art Cinema', won Wilfrid Laurier University's Graduate Gold Medal for Doctoral Study in the Arts.

Guy Spriggs earned his doctorate in English from the University of Kentucky in 2018, specialising in film studies. He now teaches courses on literature and adaptation at the University of Saint Francis. His research examines the career of Paul Newman as a means for positioning on-screen aesthetic continuity at the centre of our understanding of stardom and star studies. His chapter on the *Friday the 13th* franchise is forthcoming in *The Encyclopedia of Sexism in American Films*, published by Rowman & Littlefield.

Introduction

Victoria McCollum, Mathias Clasen
and Todd K. Platts

IN THE TRADE PRESS, Jason Blum, and his company Blumhouse
Productions, have garnered an impressive array of plaudits – from 'the
new master of horror'[1] to 'master of thrills on a shoestring'[2] to 'horror
movie juggernaut'[3] – since stringing together horror hit after horror hit in
the span of a little more than a decade, from *Paranormal Activity* (2009) to
The Invisible Man (2020). The fortunes of the film industry's top merchant
of the macabre, however, have not always been so bright. After graduating
from Vassar College in 1991, Blum worked in a number of menial jobs in
the entertainment business before becoming the co-head of acquisitions at
Miramax in 1995.[4] Blum stepped down from his Miramax post to found
Blumhouse Productions in 2000, only to toil in Hollywood obscurity
for years, occasionally releasing a quickly forgotten film such as *Griffin
& Phoenix* (2006) and *The Darwin Awards* (2007), and backing several
projects that never finished production such as 'Generation SLUT'[5] and
'My Korean Deli'.[6]

Of course, Blum's string of commercial and critical duds would end
with the release of *Paranormal Activity* in 2009, but the story is not that
simple.[7] The film that had 'already' become 'part of Hollywood folklore'[8]
in the year of its release almost did not happen. *Paranormal Activity* was

conceived and produced in 2007 by computer software programmer Oren Peli, who sent DVDs of the film to every major studio, all of whom passed on the $15,000 film. Eventually, a copy of the film landed in the hands of Blum, who years earlier (while at Miramax) passed on the surprisingly successful *The Blair Witch Project* (1999), and who saw that Peli's found-footage haunted-house film had similar potential. Blum championed the film for nearly two years, but no studio expressed interest. Blum recalls, 'I would not have kept hammering away if it weren't for *Blair Witch* – I would have given up a million times'.[9] Eventually, Paramount agreed to acquire the film, but with an eye to remake it with a bigger budget and recognisable cast under its DreamWorks subsidiary. Blum asked representatives of the company to screen the film in front of a live audience to witness, first-hand, its magic on crowds. During the screening, several audience members walked out of the theatre due to being scared.[10] When DreamWorks left Paramount, president of Paramount production Adam Goodman urged studio top brass to release the film.[11] *Paranormal Activity* was then screened in select cities, including Los Angeles whose crowd reactions were included in trailers as it went into wide release.[12] After being one of the first films to leverage social media for marketing, *Paranormal Activity* exploded at the box office, surpassing *Saw VI* (2009) – the latest entry in the torture porn stalwart – and helped to usher in a new wave of horror.[13]

With a *bona fide* hit under his belt, Blum attempted emulate what he had done with *Paranormal Activity*. 'I decided that now that I did something that worked, I was going to try to repeat the model',[14] he recalls. The next significant film he backed, *Insidious* (2011), did more than this. Both *Paranormal Activity* and *Insidious* were low-budget haunted-house films, but *Insidious* opened the industry's eyes to Blum's potential by jettisoning the found footage aesthetic and replacing it with standard modes of mainstream film production.[15] The success of both films landed Blumhouse a first-look deal with Universal, which allowed the company to perfect its production model.[16] Since then, Blumhouse Productions has emerged as an increasingly central player in the production of cinematic horror with a library of more than 100 films and counting.

Indeed, Blumhouse has rapidly achieved a remarkable degree of success in a relatively short time,[17] eclipsing $4 billion of box-office receipts after the mostly critically applauded reboot of the *Halloween* franchise (1978–present).[18] In addition to the aforementioned *Paranormal Activity* (2009–present) and *Insidious* (2011–present) series, the company has been behind the resuscitation of Universal's 'Dark Universe' with *The*

Invisible Man, other high-profile franchises such as *The Purge* (2013–present), critically lauded films as in *Split* (2017) and *Get Out* (2017), box-office draws as *Happy Death Day* (2017) and *Truth or Dare* (2018), and the potential company behind the rebooting of several dormant horror franchises.

At its core, Blumhouse Productions operates on a simple formula discovered and refined with *Paranormal Activity* and *Insidious*: making scary movies on tight budgets under a first-look deal with Universal that has enabled an era of micro-budget, filmmaker-driven genre films. Until recently, Blumhouse's model entailed producing original films for no more than $5 million and sequels for no more than $10 million. More recent releases, however, have carried slightly upgraded budgets, including $7 million for original productions of *The Invisible Man* and *Fantasy Island* (2020), $13 million for the franchise film *The First Purge* (2020), and $15 million for the prestige film *BlacKkKlansman* (2019) and *The Hunt* (2020). Blumhouse has even diversified into drama such as *Whiplash* (2014), while earning Best Picture nominations at the Academy Awards for *Whiplash*, *Get Out* and *BlacKkKlansman*.

Along with the non-Blumhouse films *The Babadook* (2014), *The VVitch* (2015) and *Hereditary* (2018), Blumhouse's *Get Out* and *The Invisible Man* have been named as torch-bearers for 'elevated horror', a type of horror preoccupied with de-emphasising genre tropes, poetically prolonging a sense of dread and exhibiting visual constraint over shock and gore.[19] Although the history, characteristics, terminology and labelling of 'elevated horror' is subject to intense debate, several critics, including Graeme Virtue[20] and Laura Bradley,[21] credit Blumhouse for inaugurating a new golden age of horror predicated on the command of traditional genre tools such as suspense and pacing, but updated for contemporary audiences.

Not content with broadcasting nightmares on the silver screen solely, Jason Blum's energy and unique business model allowed him to seal a first-look deal with Lionsgate TV in 2012, which resulted in the short-lived series *The River* (2012) and *Stranded* (2013).[22] Two years later, when Blumhouse re-upped its first-look deal with Universal, the contract included partnerships with multiple NBCUniversal ventures, including Universal Television and Universal Cable Productions.[23] The deals, however, did not prove lucrative for Blumhouse. As company president Charles Layton explains, the television division operated as for-hire producer, only receiving fees for each episode produced: 'we made $35,000 to $45,000 per episode. If you are trying to build a company, it's almost nothing'.[24]

This changed in early 2017, when Blumhouse Television entered into a deal with UK broadcaster ITV who purchased a 45 per cent stake in Blumhouse Television. The deal afforded Blumhouse Television 'the ability to be a true independent studio with the ability to finance and producing original scripted and unscripted "dark" genre programming aimed at global audiences'.[25] Since inking the deal, Blumhouse has backed several television series and miniseries with multiple distributers, including a small screen adaptation of *The Purge* (2018–19) for the USA Network; a Roger Ailes (of Fox News fame) miniseries entitled *The Loudest Voice* (2019) for Showtime; horror anthology series *Into the Dark* (2018–present) for Hulu; drama series *Sacred Lies* (2018–present) for Facebook Watch; and another horror anthology, *Welcome to the Blumhouse* (2020–present) for Amazon Prime, to name a few. The new arrangement proved successful enough for Blum to claim in 2020 that he evenly splits his time between films and television.[26] It is also significant to note that in 2015 Blumhouse bought an interest in Crypt TV, a company involved in the production of short horror-based digital media.[27]

Blumhouse is even trying its hand at book publishing through a partnership with Doubleday, an imprint of Penguin Random House.[28] The deal provides 'another way for the writers and directors [Blum] works with to tell a story'.[29] So far, Blumhouse has published eight books, including *Feral* (2017), *Haunted Nights* (2017) and *Final Cuts: New Tales of Hollywood Horror and Other Spectacles* (2020).

While Blumhouse is justly celebrated for its groundbreaking contributions to horror, the company has also been embroiled in controversies over politics and ideology, not least in 2018 when controversy erupted over Jason Blum's statements about a lack of female horror movie directors. Following that public controversy, Blumhouse seems to have put renewed efforts into finding and cultivating female talent in the genre. In 2019, Blumhouse was embroiled in another controversy when the then-upcoming *The Hunt* attracted conservative condemnation. The film, which was rumoured to be about a gang of murderous liberal elites savagely hunting down Republican voters, was publicly condemned by President Trump. Following the controversy, the film was pulled from the studio's release schedule. It was eventually released, in March 2020, with the new tagline 'The Most Talked About Movie of the Year is One that No One's Actually Seen', showcasing Blumhouse's willingness to engage with controversial material (as well as demonstrating Blum's daring business sense).

Despite the challenges faced by Blumhouse in an era of political firestorms and outrage culture, not to mention profound technological change with its wide-ranging effects on the movie industry, the small studio's low-budget/high-return business model has allowed it to sustain its position as one of the most low-key yet highly influential production companies in Hollywood. While the COVID-19 pandemic of 2020 and 2021 has delayed large-scale film production globally, causing profound challenges for the industry as it grapples with how to bring film back to both audiences and cinemas, Blumhouse has responded by shooting low-budget, small-scale production under new coronavirus safety protocols. Indeed, the studio's long-established low-budget model could become a blueprint for pandemic-era productions.[30] Should Blumhouse's efforts succeed, it is likely that the studio will change the way that horror films are made in the future as it remains poised to generate new industry standards, thus shepherding in a cutting-edge era for the horror genre driven by more accessible and inclusive indie filmmaking.[31]

Although Blumhouse Productions has grown in prominence and commands significant attention from the business and trade press, the company has largely escaped the purview of academic scrutiny. To date, there exists a small scattering of studies that only partially focus on Blumhouse and its films, despite the company representing, in the words of horror scholar Murray Leeder, 'the most visible force in American horror'.[32] This volume endeavours to fill this void by collecting the work of scholars from varying academic traditions in one place. The result is a collection that will serve as essential reading for academics of modern horror cinema as well as interested lay readers. The book simultaneously contributes to the growing body of horror studies by bringing into focus recent theoretical and methodological developments in the field of horror cinema by focusing on one of the genre's most prolific producers.

The chapters that follow are broken into three sections: the economic influences on Blumhouse's productions; content themes that span across individual films and franchises; and key films and franchises. It is significant to note that due to the nuance and complexity of the scholarship, many of the chapters can be justifiably included in more than one of the sections.

The first section begins with a chapter by Todd K. Platts, who examines the performance of Blumhouse films at the box office while also accounting for the company's unusual business model. Platts emphasises Blumhouse's strong reliance on haunted-house films during the company's early history before diversifying its horror offerings, including investment in new properties and resurrecting dormant franchises. Stefan Sereda's chapter on *Get Out* unpacks Jordan Peele's mobilisation of signifyin' – a practice that co-opts the language of oppressors to derive subversive meanings. Notably, Sereda highlights how Peele uses signifyin' to not only critique the myth of post-racialism, but also the industrial and economic underpinnings of independent film. That is, how Hollywood has commodified black anguish for cinematic profit, as subtly and ingeniously lampooned in *Get Out*.

The second section covers thematic content of Blumhouse horror films. It commences with Racheal Harris's chapter on how contemporary representations of traditional haunted-house themes are increasingly employing the human body in the role of house and home. She argues that, unlike traditional haunted-house narratives, it is an individual or family unit that becomes the subject of the haunting in films like those of the *Paranormal Activity* and *Insidious* franchises, both *Sinister* films (2012, 2015), both *Ouija* films (2014, 2016) and *Amityville: The Awakening* (2017). Fernando Gabriel Pagnoni Berns's chapter spotlights the union of 'toxic masculinity' with 'Gothic sensibility', which he labels 'gothixity', across films such as *Paranormal Activity, Paranormal Activity 2* (2010), *Sinister, The Purge, The Boy Next Door* (2015) and *The Gift* (2015). In such films, Berns posits that men are responsible for letting malignant or supernatural forces into the lives of their families by refusing to heed the warnings of other family members. Craig Ian Mann's chapter documents how many of Blumhouse's films post-*Paranormal Activity* have foregrounded economic concerns linked to the 2008–9 financial crisis. Mann shows that such themes were not limited to haunted-house films but are also present in *Dark Skies* (2013), a hybrid of horror and science fiction. Mann further argues that the science-fiction elements of the film augment its sociopolitical commentary. The second section closes with Shellie McMurdo's chapter on Blumhouse's continual reliance on found footage. McMurdo makes the case that the critically derided subgenre is more intimately connected to contemporaneous societal anxiety than scholarship has otherwise suggested. She links the first three films of *Paranormal Activity* to the ubiquity of surveillance technology and security in the wake of the terrorist attacks on 11 September 2001. Similarly, *Unfriended* (2015), which takes place mostly on computer screens, speaks to internet shaming and cyberbullying.

The third section focuses on select Blumhouse films and franchises. Todd K. Platts, Victoria McCollum and Mathias Clasen's chapter synthesises research connecting broadly felt social trauma to horror cinema content, shifts in the popularity of certain subtypes of horror to changes in the business of filmmaking and the continual appeal of stock horror antagonists to humans' evolved psychology, arguing that their integrated framework can comprehensively account for the popularity of the *Insidious* franchise while historicising its significance. Amanda Rutherford and Sarah Baker's chapter attends to use of authoritarian religious ideology witnessed throughout *The Purge* franchise. Rutherford and Baker draw parallels between *The Purge*'s religious and political New Founding Fathers of America and the Trump-era Republican party. Sotiris Petridis's chapter argues that *Happy Death Day* disrupts typical slasher formulas through an emphasis on the social and psychological maturation of its 'final girl'. Although the film proved popular with audiences and inspired a sequel – *Happy Death Day 2U* (2019) – Petridis cautions against crediting *Happy Death Day* for inspiring a new wave of slasher tropes. Zak Bronson examines *Unfriended* and *Unfriended: Dark Web* (2018) for their engagement with digital anxieties that he calls 'haunted networks', wherein characters are terrorised by mysterious and unknown forces who have access to personal information and the ill will to use that information to achieve horrific ends. The films' employment of haunted networks dramatise fears associated with social media in which sensitive information is under continual threat of becoming publicly exposed to strangers. Guy Spriggs tracks the evolution of empathy in slasher films from *Halloween* (1978) to *Halloween* (2018), arguing that slasher remakes of the late 2000s and early 2010s transitioned antagonists from evil incarnate to past victims of suffering and trauma. *Halloween* (2018) reverts Michael Myers back to being simply evil while elevating Laurie Strode to a full-blown protagonist. According to Spriggs, this narrative recalibration privileges the psychology and humanity of female victims rather than apologising for the violence of its male antagonists. John Kavanagh takes on Blumhouse's remake of *Black Christmas* (2019), a film made relevant and controversial due to Blum's erroneous comments on the dearth of female horror directors and its unabashed feminist messaging. Kavanagh maintains that the remake updates the themes, subtext and narrative elements of the original, but adapts to the MeToo era with a greater awareness of how institutions help to produce and justify patriarchal violence. The section and the book conclude with one of Blumhouse's most high-profile non-horror films – *BlacKkKlansman*. Here, Allison Schottenstein maintains that the film demonstrates that real life can be scarier than horror cinema. *BlacKkKlansman* ends with footage from the Unite the Right Rally in Charlottesville, Virginia to communicate that we are in the midst of a crucible moment in history. For Schottenstein, the film sounds a clarion call for Blacks, Jews and those concerned with human rights to stand together.

Collectively, the chapters in the pages ahead demonstrate not just the vitality and diversity of current scholarship on the horror film, but also – by emphasising the importance of one production company in the landscape of horror filmmaking – the need for such research to attend closely to the many facets of the horror movie, including its industrial context. Despite being a young production company, Blumhouse has already had a crucial impact on the shape of the horror genre, demonstrating through its various ventures (into films, television and books, so far) that it truly has become the new house of horror.

Notes

1. J. Crucchiola, 'The New Master of Horror', *Vulture* (3 March 2017), *www. vulture.com/2017/03/get-outs-jason-blum-is-the-new-master-of-horror.html/* (accessed 30 January 2021).

2. M. Garrahan, 'Master of Thrills on a Shoestring', *Financial Times* (31 May 2011), *www.ft.com/content/bc7bc3e6-8baf-11e0-a725-00144feab49a/* (accessed 30 January 2021).

3. J. Guerrasio, 'Horror Movie Juggernaut Blumhouse is Jumping into Podcasting with a Series for iHeartRadio', *Business Insider* (10 October 2019), *www. businessinsider.com/blumhouse-making-original-horror-podcasts-for-iheartradio-details-2019-10/* (accessed 30 January 2021).

4. A. Elberse, 'Jason Blum's Blumhouse Productions', *Harvard Business Review* (18 May 2018), 2.

5. I. Mohr, 'Par Drawing a Blum Role', *Daily Variety* (20 May 2005), 1, 26.

6. D. McNary, '"Deli" on Plate with Pic Pair', *Daily Variety* (8 May 2006), 1, 13.

7. For further details concerning Blum's acquisition and release of Paranormal Activity, see T. Platts, 'Cut-Price Creeps: The Blumhouse Model of Horror Franchise Management', in M. McKenna and W. Proctor (eds), *Horror Franchise Cinema* (New York: Routledge, 2021), pp. 115–16.

8. P. McClintock, 'Mega-Profits for Micro-Pic', *Daily Variety* (26 October 2009), 23.

9. Quoted in Elberse, 'Jason Blum's Blumhouse Productions', 3.

10. J. Horn, 'The Haunted History of *Paranormal Activity*', *Los Angeles Times* (20 September 2009), *www.latimes.com/zap-haunted-history-paranormal-activity-story.html/* (accessed 30 January 2021).

11. McClintock, 'Mega-Profits for Micro-Pic', 23.

12. M. Cieply, 'Thriller on Tour Lets Fans Decide on the Next Stop', *New York Times* (20 September 2009), *www.nytimes.com/2009/09/21/business/media/21paranormal.html/* (accessed 30 January 2021).

13. McClintock, 'Mega-Profits for Micro-Pic', 23; M. Cieply, 'Film on a Tiny Budget Earns Big Money', *New York Times* (26 October 2009), C2.

14. Quoted in Elberse, 'Jason Blum's Blumhouse Productions', 3.

15. For more on the significance of *Insidious* in Blumhouse's history, see '*Insidious* Patterns: An Integrative Analysis of Blumhouse's Most Important Franchise' in this volume.

16. M. Fleming Jr, 'Universal Makes First-Look Deal with Jason Blum of *Paranormal Activity* and *Insidious*', *Deadline* (29 June 2011), *https://deadline.com/2011/06/universal-in-first-look-deal-with-paranormal-activity-and-insidious-producer-jason-blum-144401/* (accessed 30 January 2021).

17. B. M. Murphy, '"It's Not the House That's Haunted": Demons, Debt, and the Family in Peril Formula in Recent Horror Cinema', in M. Leeder (ed.), *Cinematic Ghosts: Haunting and Spectrality from Silent Cinema to the Digital Era* (New York: Bloomsbury, 2015), p. 236.

18. R. Rubin, 'How Blumhouse Got Everything Right About Making a *Halloween* Sequel', *Variety* (22 October 2018), *https://variety.com/2018/film/box-office/halloween-box-office-analysis-horror-1202987761/* (accessed 30 January 2021).

19. David Church, *Post-Horror: Art, Genre and Cultural Evolution* (Edinburgh: Edinburgh University Press, 2021), pp. 27–57.

20. G. Virtue, 'Why Smart Horror is Putting the Fear into Sequel-Addicted Hollywood', *Guardian* (12 April 2018), *www.theguardian.com/film/2018/apr/12/horror-quiet-place-get-out-hollywood/* (accessed 30 January 2021).

21. L. Bradley, 'This was the Decade Horror Got "Elevated"', *Vanity Fair* (17 December 2019), *www.vanityfair.com/hollywood/2019/12/rise-of-elevated-horror-decade-2010s/* (accessed 30 January 2021).

22. N. Andreeva, 'Feature Producer Jason Blum Signs First-Look Television Deal with Lionsgate', *Deadline* (14 February 2012), *https://deadline.com/2012/02/feature-producer-jason-blum-signs-first-look-television-deal-with-lionsgate-231013/* (accessed 30 January 2021).

23. M. Fleming Jr, 'Universal, Blumhouse Extend to Decade-Long Film, TV Production Pact', *Deadline* (20 July 2014), *https://deadline.com/2014/07/universal-blumhouse-extend-to-decade-long-production-pact-806978/* (accessed 30 January 2021).

24. Quoted in Elberse, 'Jason Blum's Blumhouse Productions', 5.

25. M. Fleming Jr, 'Blumhouse Launches Indie TV Studio With ITV; *The Purge* becomes Series, Roger Ailes Fox News Series Lands at Showtime', *Deadline* (4 April 2017), *https://deadline.com/2017/04/blumhouse-the-purge-roger-ailes-fox-news-tv-series-showtime-itv-1202060793/* (accessed 30 January 2021).
26. J. Giroux, '*You Should Have Left* Producer Jason Blum on the Future of Movie Theaters and which Filmmakers Fit the Blumhouse Mold [Interview]', *Slash Film* (25 June 2020), *www.slashfilm.com/jason-blum-interview/* (accessed 30 January 2021).
27. M. Shields, 'Jason Blum-backed Crypt TV Thinks the Next Freddy Krueger Will be Launched on Mobile Phones', *Business Insider* (31 October 2017), *www.businessinsider.com/jason-blum-backed-crypt-tv-sees-next-freddy-krueger-launched-on-mobile-2017-10/* (accessed 30 January 2021).
28. Quoted in Elberse, 'Jason Blum's Blumhouse Productions', 5.
29. B. Lee, 'Why Horror Super-producer Jason Blum has Turned to Publishing', *Guardian* (1 July 2017), *www.theguardian.com/books/2017/jul/01/jason-blum-horror-publishing-get-out-purge-feral/* (accessed 30 January 2021).
30. K. Masters, 'Blumhouse Plans Film Shoot on Universal Lot Despite Insurance Risks', *Hollywood Reporter* (18 May 2020), *www.hollywoodreporter.com/news/blumhouse-plans-film-shoot-universal-lot-insurance-risks-1294936* (accessed 30 January 2021).
31. B. Ramella, 'Blumhouse is on the Brink of Changing Horror Movies', *Screen Rant* (20 May 2020), *https://screenrant.com/blumhouse-horror-movie-changes-small-budget-after-coronavirus/* (accessed 30 January 2021).
32. Murray Leeder, *Horror Film: A Critical Introduction* (New York: Bloomsbury Academic, 2018), p. 84.

1

Blumhouse at the Box Office, 2009–2018

Todd K. Platts

ACROSS A SPAN of ten years, starting with the release of *Paranormal Activity* (2009) and concluding with *Halloween* (2018), Blumhouse Productions rode a near 'decade-long hot streak'[1] that helped to establish the company as 'one of the most bankable players in the [film] business',[2] with a production model that is 'singlehandedly shaping modern horror'.[3] So successful has the company been that a 2018 *Harvard Business Review* profile revealed it was 'responsible for thirteen of the top 25 most profitable films in the last five years in the US and ten of the top 25 worldwide – more than any other producer – when measured by box-office grosses as a percentage of production budgets'.[4] Blumhouse does more than churn out cheap, but profitable horror films, however. With the release of highly regarded (and lucrative) films such as *Split* (2017), *Get Out* (2017), *BlacKkKlansman* (2018) and *The Invisible Man* (2020) – films sometimes called 'social thrillers' due to their unflinching critiques of social ills – it has established itself as a *bona fide* brand.[5]

With the commercial and critical triumphs of Blumhouse Productions in mind, the aim of this chapter is to chart the mechanisms driving the company's success, including its business model, reliance on established horror formulas and willingness to experiment with those formulas. This chapter will cover Blumhouse's horror and non-horror outings and will touch upon its hits and misses. The chapter divides Blumhouse's cinematic output into subtypes to decipher how Blumhouse's calculus of success has altered since becoming the new house of horror. In so doing, this chapter will properly profile one of the companies most responsible for the elevation of horror in the 2010s.[6]

The Blumhouse Model

Blumhouse's success can be traced to its unusual business model, which, since *Paranormal Activity*,[7] has been to produce (mostly) horror movies on strict budget constraints.[8] Until recently, those constraints were $5 million or less for an original picture[9] and $10 million or less for sequels.[10] Recent efforts, though, have carried slightly higher budgets, including $13 million for *The First Purge* (2018), $15 million for the *BlacKkKlansman* and *The Hunt* (2020) and $7 million for both *Fantasy Island* (2020) and *The Invisible Man*.[11] Although representing markups for Blumhouse, these price tags are still far below the average $60 to $70 million budget of a Hollywood motion picture.[12] Company founder and CEO Jason Blum explains the reasoning behind the paltry budgets:

> The three-to-five million is not a random picked number. That amount is about what we are able to recoup on the movies if we don't get a wide release. In a worst case scenario, we break even and maybe lose a little money but not very much, and everyone gets paid scale.[13]

The low budgets allow for the production of numerous films. Blum notes, 'we make a ton of movies for a production company of our size. The way to get profitable movies is to make a lot of them'.[14] This allows Blumhouse to test the waters with non-traditional films such as *Get Out* and *Whiplash* (2014), as Blum posits, 'the movies that are done for low budgets are actually very edgy . . . the higher the budget gets, the fewer storytelling risks you're able to take'.[15]

Blumhouse employs numerous measures to keep costs low. All talent works on scale, only making money if or when a movie turns a profit. Blumhouse also keeps aspects of the production process in-house, including editing, colour correcting and mixing and producing visual effects.[16]

Shooting locations, sets, special effects and speaking roles are also min-imised, with most films shot in the Los Angeles area within twenty to twenty-five days.[17] Blumhouse also has a unique vetting process for theatrical releases. Minus sequels, films never enter production with an established release date.[18] Wide release is granted only when films are deemed 'market-competitive', which is defined as movies that have a shot at earning at least $25 million (the receipts needed to break even on budget and market-ing).[19] 'Market-competitive' films are then fished out to Universal under a first-look deal.[20] If Universal passes, Blumhouse can shop the film out to rival studios. Strikingly, many of Blumhouse's completed pictures never make it to theatres,[21] with Blum confirming 'about half of our movies get a wide theatrical release'.[22] Many of the films not getting theatrical release find quiet release on streaming services or home video.[23]

Ratings figure into the Blumhouse Model as well. Here, the calcula-tion is simple: if the protagonists are under eighteen, the movie must be accessible to younger audiences. In other words, it must be rated PG-13. According to Blum:

> If someone gave me a great scary movie all about high school kids, and they said it was R-rated, we wouldn't make it. PG-13, we'd make it . . . You can't make a movie about kids, and then tell those kids they can't go see it without their parents.[24]

Similarly, the Blumhouse model contains a logic behind franchise man-agement, ensuring that the creative personnel behind a particular series are also involved in its sequels.[25] Blum explains, 'I really like to have the people who create the movies that turn into franchises to be as involved as possible'.[26] In exchange for keeping costs low, directors are given cre-ative control.[27]

The Blumhouse model is undeniably successful; it 'reliably creates profits that exceed production budgets by more than 2,000 percent'.[28] Critic Eric Benjamin argues, 'the genius of Blumhouse's model is that when a movie flops, there's minimal loss due to the low budget. When a film works, though, the gains can be huge'.[29] The resulting output has a distinctive character that is 'artistically unique without carrying a whole lot of financial risks, making them easier to sell to the major studios as well as to theaters across the country'.[30] As demonstrated below, Blumhouse routinely pulls from established horror formulas, but spreads the risk of film production by not only thinly capitalising new films, but also offering a variety of subtypes. Before getting to this analysis, however, it is important to pause and consider the data and methods used in this chapter.

Data and Methods

Data for this chapter is drawn from several sources. Box-office totals, domestic and international, as well as film budgets and other descriptive data (e.g., ratings) are derived from The Numbers, which tabulates the performance of every theatrically released in the United States. Classification of a film's subtype was determined through consulting the reviews from *Variety*, the *Los Angeles Times* and the *New York Times*. As with any classificatory scheme, contentions are 'unavoidable' because, as Peter Hutchings observed, 'there can be no fixed once-and-for-all list of horror films',[31] much less a fixed list of subtypes. Nonetheless, the subtypes do represent distinct, if somewhat overlapping, styles and categories of film.

Films were included for analysis only when budget and box-office revenue were available, which excluded four films from the final sample.[32] Moreover, movies distributed by BH Tilt, Blum's company designed to give films a limited release,[33] but not produced by Blumhouse, are also excluded – a step that took away another five pictures.[34] Finally, movies produced prior to *Paranormal Activity* were not included, as these predate the model of production that has characterised Blumhouse since. In sum, a total of forty-six films, released between 2009 and 2018, were included for analysis. The movies informing the analysis below can be found in Table 2 of this chapter. The following section gives a brief descriptive overview of the films analysed, while the following sections give separate consideration to each subtype.

The Shape of Blumhouse Productions

Across the films analysed in this chapter, Blumhouse Productions has earned $3.86 billion in ticket sales against a combined $231.6 million in budgets for a 3,027.5 per cent return on investment per movie, which is an average budget of $5 million and an average of box office of

$83.9 million. Blumhouse's success, it seems, hinges on its mobilisation of various subtypes of horror and some dabbling outside the genre, which is shown in Table 1. Blumhouse has relied mostly on horror films, constituting 87 per cent of the movies that it has theatrically released, with 37 per cent of its output being ghost/haunted-house films. Blumhouse repeatedly turns to ghost/haunted-house films in part because of the success of *Paranormal Activity*, but also because their costs can be easily contained.

In an era dominated by PG-13 horror films,[35] the majority of Blumhouse's films carry an R-rating, or films with content deemed unsuitable for children (just under 61 per cent). Perhaps no other genre is as prone to sequels as horror, and Blumhouse is no different, with nearly half of its movies (45.7 per cent) being sequels or films that produced sequels, a figure Blum himself quotes: '[production output is] about 50 percent franchises and 50 percent original movies'.[36]

Table 1: Cinematic Output by Subtype

	Number	Per cent
Horror	40	87
Ghost/haunted house	17	37
Thriller/psychological	7	15.2
Possession	5	10.9
Action	3	6.5
Slasher	2	4.3
Other	6	13
Non-horror	6	13

Below, the production trends of Blumhouse Productions are briefly considered. Given the total number of films included in the analysis, it is unfeasible to provide the in-depth discussion necessary to leverage the complex meanings of each. This important task is left to other contributors in this volume.

Ghost/haunted-house films

As noted above, ghost/haunted-house films dominate Blumhouse's production coffers, accounting for seventeen films in the sample. In such pictures, vengeful and/or malicious spirits or demons terrorise members of a family inside (and even outside) their homes. Most of the examples in this subtype emanate from popular series, including the six films from the *Paranormal Activity* (2009–present) series, the four films of the *Insidious* franchise, and both *Sinister* films. Six of seventeen films in this subtype procured a PG-13 rating, each instalment of *Insidious*, *Jessabelle* (2014) and *The Darkness* (2016). Ghost/haunted-house films witnessed an uptick in production in response to the 2008–9 financial recession because they could effectively dramatise the fears associated with home loss and foreclosure.[37] While similarities between Blumhouse's ghost/haunted-house cycle and those that appeared in the 1980s have been noted,[38] scholars have also documented key discontinuities. Bernice Murphy, for instance, suggests that in recessionary-era ghost films families cannot simply escape their haunted abodes because, like bad credit history, the ghost or demon will follow.[39] In this volume, Racheal Harris suggests that Blumhouse's ghost movies switch the source of the haunting from the home to the body, which she argues more frighteningly bears witness to the emotional trauma wrought by the decline of middle-class stability.

These pictures, which scholars have shown to be metaphorically rich and intimately connected with the zeitgeist, are the ones that built Blumhouse into the juggernaut that it has become. Average budgets for ghost/haunted-house films ran to a meagre $4.8 million, while the average box office for films in this sample was $103.2 million. As media reporter Todd Gilchrist noted, Blum 'created an empire for himself over the past seven years with a series of (comparatively) microbudget productions modeled on the success of *Paranormal Activity*'.[40] Since 2016, however, Blumhouse has only theatrically released two ghost/haunted-house films – *The Darkness* and *Insidious: The Last Key* (2018). Industry reporter Richard Newby made note of the pull away from ghost/haunted-house films: 'while it is still the house that *Paranormal Activity* built, its horror movies have largely left behind the trend of found-footage features and traditional demonic possession films for high-concept originals that are rewarded for their risks and relevant social commentary'.[41]

The shift away from ghost/haunted-house films can be explained, in part, due to their diminishing returns. While new additions to the *Insidious* franchise have retained their profitability, new movies in the *Paranormal*

Activity series and the sequel to *Sinister* earned significantly less than films released earlier in the cycle. By way of illustration, *Paranormal Activity: The Ghost Dimension* (2015), the latest of the *Paranormal Activity* franchise (at the time of writing this chapter), took only $77.9 million in ticket sales, nearly $13 million less than the next lowest outing of the series. The trend of diminishing returns holds true for Blumhouse's later ghost/haunted-house examples such as *Oculus* (2014), which received favourable reviews, *Jessabelle*, *The Gallows* (2015) and *The Darkness* (the latter three of which were given limited release). Despite the recent struggles of ghost/haunted-house films, Blumhouse is planning a seventh instalment of the *Paranormal Activity* series.

Thriller/psychological horror

Thriller/psychological horror films build suspense and tension through a focus on deranged individuals or groups and/or the use horrific themes while usually maintaining a rationalistic or secular worldview. This subtype represented seven films, or nearly one-sixth (15.2 per cent) of the sample, with over half appearing in 2017 and 2018. If the analysis were extended to 2019, two more films would have been added – *Ma* (2019) and *Glass* (2019). All but two films in this subtype received R-ratings, with those being *Split* and *The Visit* (2015). The average budgets of $4.3 million and average box office of $101.3 million are comparable to Blumhouse's ghost/haunted-house films, but the figures are skewed by *Get Out* and *Split*, the company's top and third highest box-office performing films. *Get Out* pulled in a worldwide box office of $255.4 million on a $4.5 million budget, while *Split* earned just under $279 million against a $9 million budget.

Since their release, *Get Out* and *Split* have been the subject of much scrutiny. Where the former has been extensively analysed for its skewering of contemporary racial dynamics, the latter has been derided by scholars for its stereotypical portrayal of dissociative identity disorder. Importantly, for the operations of Blumhouse, Blum sees the films as underwriting 'a Blumhouse 2.0 – a new act in the company'.[42] This seems to be a migration away from ghost/haunted-house films towards more difficult to categorise films such as *Ma* and *BlacKkKlansman*, but also a turn towards the seemingly more formulaic such as *Halloween* and the company's plans to remake many other horror films, including *Dracula*, *The Craft*, *Spawn*, *The Thing* and *Wolfman*.

Although two of Blumhouse's most critically and commercially successful films come from the thriller/psychological horror subtype, it also
houses two pictures that lost money at the box-office – *13 Sins* (2014) and
Delirium (2018). It is important to note that both received limited releases.
Of the remaining thriller/psychological horror films in the sample, only
The Visit earned close to $100 million, while the *The Gift* returned $59
million and *Unfriended: Dark Web* (2018) made $16.4 million.

Possession films

A close cousin to ghost/haunted-house films, possession films, which
feature characters who have their bodies and/or minds infiltrated by an
external force or personality, comprised a small (five films or 10.9 per
cent) but significant portion of Blumhouse's cinematic output. All Blumhouse's possession films are clustered in the last five years of the analysis,
with one, *Exeter* (2015), receiving a PG-13 rating. Movies in this subtype
returned an average box office of $58.1 million against average budgets of
$4.5 million – seemingly making it one of the least reliably lucrative sub-
types for Blumhouse. Having noted that, three films in the subtype reached
or nearly reached $100 million in sales. *Ouija* (2014) earned $103.3 million, *Ouija: Origin of Evil* (2016) made $81.8 million and *Truth or Dare*
(2018) took in $95.3 million at the box office. *Exeter* and *Incarnate* (2016)
each made under $10 million on limited releases, dragging down the aver-
age of the small sample. Although the movies in this subtype are seen as
foregrounding possession, it is important to note that possession is a key
plot point in some of Blumhouse's most successful films such as the *Insidious* series explored in Platts, McCollum and Clasen's chapter.

Blumhouse's possession films stray from the formula established by
The Exorcist (1973). According to Christopher Olson and CarrieLynn
Reinhard, the typical possession narrative presents (often fatherless) pubes-
cent females who are exorcised (made good) by holy men.[43] Where possession movies in the vein of *The Exorcist* usually involve a static (one-person)
possession, Blumhouse's possession films tend to see the possessing force
bounce from host to host. As well, the company's possession films also feature the possession of men and women from varying age groups, with the
role of religion often in the background of the film. Though not critically
acclaimed, *Truth or Dare* arguably embellished the possession narrative the
most by featuring set-piece deaths associated with slashers, supervised by
a possessing force.

Action horror

All Blumhouse's action horror films are made up of the three entries of *The Purge* (2013–present) series, a franchise that initially started as a home invasion narrative in the vein of *The Strangers* (2008). Action horror films spotlight sequences of action over the more brooding aspects of the genre. As one of Blumhouse's flagship franchises, the three *Purge* instalments have earned an average of $122 million at the box office against comparatively high (for Blumhouse) average budgets of $10.7 million, with each carrying an R-rating. *The Purge* even resulted in a spin-off television series that aired on the USA Network for two seasons. Since *The Purge: Anarchy* (2014), a new instalment has been released during each midterm and presidential election. *The Forever Purge* (2021) was initially set for a July 2020 release until COVID-19 caused a global shutdown of productions and most theatrical releases. With its impeccable political timing coupled with the rightward shift of the Republican party under Donald Trump, the franchise has been seen as a parable of contemporary politics,[44] which is explored more deeply in this book's chapter by Amanda Rutherford and Sarah Baker. The series can, thus, be seen as providing a glimpse into the potential future of the United States under President Trump, while standing as one of the most 'important horror franchise[s] of the decade'.[45]

Slasher films

Slashers, those films portraying a usually blade-wielding shadowy killer stalking sexually promiscuous teenagers, constitute only two movies in this sample – *Happy Death Day* (2017) and *Halloween*. Despite the small number, it is worth considering Blumhouse's involvement with slashers, as the company has started to pursue the subtype in the period after this sample, with *Happy Death Day 2U* (2019), *Black Christmas* (2019), *Halloween Kills* (2021) and *Halloween Ends* (2022), among others. Significantly, *Happy Death Day*'s box office of $125 million far exceeded the company's average of $83.9 million. Meanwhile, not only was *Halloween*'s box office of $255.5 million the highest earning film in the *Halloween* franchise,[46] it is also Blumhouse's second highest box-office performing film behind *Split*. Recent Blumhouse slashers, however, have not experienced the same success, despite receiving wide release. *Happy Death Day 2 U* returned a seemingly impressive $64.7 million at the box-office – only slightly more than half of *Happy Death Day*'s returns and $19.2 million short of the company average. *Black Christmas* fared worse, netting only $18.5 million against its $5 million budget.

Where prior slashers have been criticised for their punishment of female sexuality,[47] Blumhouse seems to have blazed a new trail as suggested by several entries in this volume. Sotiris Petridis' chapter, for instance, argues that *Happy Death Day* flips the script of prior slashers by focusing on the story of the final survivor. Guy Spriggs' chapter articulates how *Halloween* grapples with the trauma caused by male-perpetrated violence against women. *Black Christmas*, with its predominantly female cast, female director and open lampooning of campus rape culture, has been called 'a slasher movie for the #MeToo movement',[48] which is examined in John Kavanagh's chapter. In short, where prior slashers were seen as regressive, Blumhouse has tapped into the progressive potential of the subtype.

Other horror releases

Six of Blumhouse's horror theatrical releases do not fit in the subtypes above. These include: *The Bay* (2012); *Dark Skies* (2013); *The Lords of Salem* (2013); *The Purge* (2013); *The Lazarus Effect* (2015); and *Area 51* (2015). The films in this catch-all category have the lowest average budgets ($3.3 million) and the lowest average box office ($26.7). *The Purge* was the most successful, turning in $64.5 million, while *The Lazarus Effect* and *Dark Skies* can be considered moderate hits, the former making $38.4 million and the latter $27.7 million. *Area 51* and *The Bay* each returned less than $40,000 at the box office. *Area 51* was released exclusively in Alamo Drafthouse theatres and was directed by Oren Peli, the man behind *Paranormal Activity*. *The Bay* was released in only twenty-three theatres before entering the ancillary market. Within these errata films, *Dark Skies* and *Area 51* can be classified as science-fictional horror films, the former of which Craig Ian Mann demonstrates has affinities with the company's haunted-house films, *The Bay* and *The Lazarus Effect* as outbreak films, and *The Lords of Salem* an occult film. Had any of these films become a runaway hit, it is likely that Blumhouse would have followed them up with similar films or sequels. With the small number of errata films, Blumhouse's reliance on established, bankable subtypes is further underscored. Although Blumhouse has diversified its cinematic output lately, the company has yet to tackle zombies, big monsters, sharks, torture porn and vampires – all staples of the horror genre. Of these subtypes, Blumhouse is currently developing a new adaptation of *Dracula*.[49]

Non-horror

Although Blumhouse is rooted firmly in horror cinema, they have produced six theatrically released non-horror films since 2010. These include, *Plush* (2013), *Whiplash*, *The Boy Next Door* (2015), *Jem and the Holograms* (2015), *Lowriders* (2017) and *BlacKkKlansman*. Blumhouse's non-horror films carry the cheapest average price tag ($2.5 million) and the lowest average grosses ($16.6 million). Three films from this category stand out as worthy of separate consideration: *Whiplash*, *Jem and the Holograms* and *BlacKkKlansman*. *Whiplash* tells the story of the relationship between a drumming student at a prestigious conservatory and his abusive instructor. The movie netted many accolades, including Best Editing and Best Sound Mixing from the Academy Awards, Top Ten Movies of the Year from the American Film Institute, Best Independent Film from the Saturn Awards, and the Grand Jury Prize (Dramatic) from the Sundance Film Festival, to name a few. Despite its accolades, Blum has spoken dismissively of *Whiplash*, stating it 'was a disaster theatrically' and 'it was one of the lowest-grossing Oscar-winning movies of all time'.[50] Despite Blum's downplaying, *Whiplash* managed to make a respectable $38.9 million.

By far, *Jem and the Holograms* represents Blumhouse's biggest failure. The film was based on the 1980s animated children's series and popular toy line *Jem* (1985–8) that featured an adolescent female and her holographic alter ego, Jem, the leader of a rock band called the Holograms. Production of the film was inspired by successes of other live-action adaptations of 1980s children's shows and toy lines – most notably *Transformers* (2007) and *G.I. Joe* (2009). Unfortunately, *Jem and the Holograms* holds the distinction of having lowest opening weekend gross for a wide release film ever at $1.4 million. Blum recalls: 'Universal lost money on that . . . I was totally convinced it was going to be a big film'.[51]

BlacKkKlansman, based on police officer Ron Stallworth's memoir of the same name, tells the story of a black police officer who managed to infiltrate the Ku Klux Klan in Colorado Springs, Colorado during the 1970s. The Spike Lee directed film drew many accolades, including Best Director from AARP's Movies for Grownups Award, Best Adapted Screenplay from the Academy Awards, Best Screenplay and Actor from the African American Film Critics Association, and Top 10 Films of the Year from the American Film Institute, among others. Though not a horror film, Allison Schottenstein's chapter suggests the film demonstrates that real life is often scarier than horror cinema. For her, the film sounds a clarion call for Blacks, Jews and those concerned with human rights to stand together. Despite the commercial and critical failures of films such as *Jem and the Holograms*, commercial and critical successes such as *Whiplash* and *BlacKkKlansman* encourage Blumhouse to continually venture outside the horror genre.

Conclusion

On the surface, thinly capitalising horror films for theatrical release seems an easily replicable formula for potential competitors. Blumhouse's success, however, is not that simple. Its model is 'nearly impossible to emulate',[52] in part, because no one has taken the same chances on films as Blum. Many Blumhouse films, including *Get Out*, *Happy Death Day* and *The Purge* floated around Hollywood for years before Blum gave them the greenlight. Blumhouse's ten-year first-look deal with Universal is highly unusual, as the average first-look deal is only two years. This gives Blumhouse more leeway to experiment compared to similar production companies (e.g., A24). While Blum keeps risks low for his company, the same is not true for the talent who work on industry minimums. Creative personnel reap rewards only when films hit big, a feat which almost always requires a wide theatrical release – something that applies to only half of Blumhouse's films.[53] No other company can put itself in the same situation. Hence, its unusual features and market position enable Blumhouse to be one of the most innovative and profitable purveyors of horror in the modern cinematic landscape.

Although Blumhouse is at the forefront of modern horror cinema, Blum has expressed concerns over the future of the genre in terms of market glut and coronavirus. On the former Blum noted that 'there's going to be a depression in the horror market real soon, because when you get a bunch of hit scary movies, everyone wants to make them. The market can't expand too much. If there's a horror movie every two weeks, all horror is going to be hurt'.[54] On the latter he quipped, 'The consumer is going to be more used to staying at home. Something is going to give, there has to be something that's going to happen post-corona. The movie business will look different after the coronavirus'.[55] Specifically, Blum sees a long-term decline in theatre attendance as consumers demand shifts to video-on-demand.[56] In response to the virus, Blum has had to lay off several workers, halt several productions and delay the release of several films.[57] While Blum also remains steadfast in his desire to not produce a film dramatising the pandemic,[58] several films using the virus as a backdrop such as Deon

Taylor's *Don't Fear* are already in the works.[59] In light of these concerns, however, Blum's company has an ambitious list of films lined up for the next year several years.

Notes

1. A. Bhattacharji, 'How Producer Jason Blum is Disrupting Hollywood', *Wall Street Journal Magazine* (16 July 2018), *www.wsj.com/articles/how-producer-jason-blum-is-disrupting-hollywood-1531750907/* (accessed 7 February 2020).
2. J. Guerrasio, '*Us* and *BlacKkKlansman* Producer Jason Blum's Plan to Take Over Hollywood is Simple: Stay Independent', *Business Insider* (16 April 2019), *www.businessinsider.com/jason-blum-on-staying-independent-in-hollywood-2019-4/* (accessed 7 February 2020); N. Summers, 'Timeless Wisdom from a Chiseling Skinflint', *Forbes* (April 2014), 64.
3. D. Taylor, '*Happy Death Day 2U* Producer Jason Blum Wants to Make 10 More *Halloween* Movies', *Moviefone* (13 February 2019), *www.moviefone.com/2019/02/13/happy-death-day-2u-jason-blum-interview/* (accessed 7 February 2020).
4. A. Elberse, 'Jason Blum's Blumhouse Productions', *Harvard Business Review* (18 May 2018), 1.
5. S. Mendelson, 'Box Office: After *Split* and *Get Out*, *Happy Death Day* may get a Blumhouse Bump', *Forbes* (9 October 2017), *www.forbes.com/sites/scott mendelson/2017/10/09/box-office-after-split-and-get-out-happy-death-day-may-get-blumhouse-bump/#6fe7ace36051/* (accessed 7 February 2020).
6. L. Bradley, 'This was the Decade Horror Got "Elevated"', *Vanity Fair* (17 December 2019), *www.vanityfair.com/hollywood/2019/12/rise-of-elevated-horror-decade-2010s/* (accessed 30 January 2021).
7. Prior to finding a winning formula with *Paranormal Activity*, Blumhouse dabbled in a variety of films, including the romance drama *Griffen & Phoenix* (2006), the dramas *The Fever* (2006) and *Graduation* (2008), and the comedies *The Darwin Awards* (2007), *The Accidental Husband* (2009) and *Tooth Fairy* (2010).
8. C. Ryan, 'Scare Tactics', *The Ringer* (2 November 2016), *www.theringer.com/2016/11/2/16077310/blumhouse-new-hollywood-success-paranormal-activity-the-purge-74dc38852ac5/* (accessed 7 February 2020).
9. J. Horn, 'Trying to Make a Killing for Less', *Los Angeles Times* (6 June 2013), D10.
10. J. Guerrasio, 'How the Company Behind 2 of the Year's Biggest Movies is Blowing Up the Hollywood Playbook', *Business Insider* (1 March

2017), *www.businessinsider.com/blumhouse-productions-get-out-split-2017-2/* (accessed 7 February 2020); *Business World*, 'Horror on a Shoestring: The Blum Manifesto', (19 September 2017), *www.bworldonline.com/horror-shoestring-blum-manifesto/* (accessed 7 February 2020).

11. Recode Staff, '*Get Out* Producer Jason Blum Talks about Netflix, Low-Budget Movies and the Oscars', *Vox* (15 March 2018), *www.vox.com/2018/3/15/17118460/get-out-producer-jason-blum-talks-about-netflix-low-budget-movies-and-the-oscars/* (accessed 7 February 2020).

12. Elberse, 'Jason Blum's Blumhouse Productions', 1.

13. R. Lincoln, 'Blumhouse and the Calculus of Low Budget Horror – Produced By', *Deadline* (30 May 2015), *https://deadline.com/2015/05/blumhouse-panel-produced-by-conference-1201435034/* (accessed 7 February 2020).

14. Elberse, 'Jason Blum's Blumhouse Productions', 5.

15. J. Crucchiola, 'The New Master of Horror', *Vulture* (3 March 2017), *www.vulture.com/2017/03/get-outs-jason-blum-is-the-new-master-of-horror.html/* (accessed 7 February 2020).

16. Crucchiola, 'The New Master of Horror'.

17. *Business World*, 'Horror on a Shoestring'; Elberse, 'Jason Blum's Blumhouse Productions', 6; Summers, 'Timeless Wisdom from a Chiseling Skinflint', 64.

18. *Business World*, 'Horror on a Shoestring'.

19. E. Benjamin, 'Buy Low, Sell High: How Blumhouse Does Horror Films the Right Way', *Daily Orange* (11 April 2018), *http://dailyorange.com/2018/04/buy-low-sell-high-blumhouse-horror-films-right-way/* (accessed 7 February 2020).

20. Elberse, 'Jason Blum's Blumhouse Productions', 2, 4.

21. K. Masters, 'Jason Blum's Crowded Movie Morgue', *Hollywood Reporter* (7 March 2014), *www.hollywoodreporter.com/news/jason-blums-crowded-movie-morgue-683212/* (accessed 7 February 2020).

22. Elberse, 'Jason Blum's Blumhouse Productions', 6.

23. Masters, 'Jason Blum's Crowded Movie Morgue'.

24. E. Eisenberg, 'How Horror Studio Blumhouse Decides Whether or Not a Movie Will be R-Rated', *Cinema Blend* (12 January 2018), *www.cinemablend.com/news/2063170/how-horror-studio-blumhouse-decides-whether-or-not-a-movie-will-be-r-rated/* (accessed 7 February 2020).

25. Recode Staff, '*Get Out* Producer Jason Blum Talks about Netflix, Low-Budget Movies and the Oscars'.

26. H. Foutch, 'Jason Blum on *The First Purge*, the Future of the Franchise and *Halloween*'s R Rating', *Collider* (2 October 2018), *https://collider.com/jason-blum-interview-first-purge-halloween/* (accessed 7 February 2020).

27. Horn, 'Trying to Make a Killing for Less', D10; *Business World*, 'Horror on a Shoestring'; Recode Staff, '*Get Out* Producer Jason Blum Talks about Netflix, Low-Budget Movies and the Oscars'.

28. Summers, 'Timeless Wisdom from a Chiseling Skinflint', 64.

29. Benjamin, 'Buy Low, Sell High'.

30. J. Humphreys, 'The Haunted House That Blum Built – How an Indie Producer Saved Horror and Changed Hollywood', *Cineramble* (20 October 2018), *http://cineramble.com/2018/10/the-haunted-house-that-blum-built-how-an-indie-producer-saved-horror-and-changed-hollywood/* (accessed 7 February 2020).

31. Peter Hutchings, *The Horror Film* (New York: Pearson, 2004), p. 9.

32. These films include *Visions* (2015); *Viral* (2016); *In a Valley of Violence* (2016); and *Amityville: The Awakening* (2017).

33. M. Fleming Jr, 'Blumhouse Launches Multi-Platform Arm BH-Tilt', *Deadline* (9 September 2014), *https://deadline.com/2014/09/blumhouse-launches-multi-platform-arm-bh-tilt-831985/* (accessed 7 February 2020).

34. These films include *The Green Inferno* (2015); *The Resurrection of Gavin Stone* (2017); *The Belko Experiment* (2017); *Sleight* (2017) and *Birth of the Dragon* (2017).

35. D. Bukszpan, 'Here's Why R-Rated Horror Movies are Making a Comeback on the Big Screen', *CNBC* (28 October 2017), *www.cnbc.com/2017/10/28/heres-why-r-rated-horror-movies-are-making-a-comeback-on-the-big-screen.html/* (accessed 7 February 2020).

36. B. Kit, '*Get Out* Producer Jason Blum on Hollywood's Leadership Crisis and Missing Out on *La La Land*', *Hollywood Reporter* (16 March 2017), *www.hollywoodreporter.com/heat-vision/get-producer-jason-blum-hollywoods-leadership-crisis-missing-la-la-land-985861/* (accessed 7 February 2020).

37. C. I. Mann, 'Death and Dead-End Jobs: Independent Horror and the Great Recession', in P. Bennett and J. McDougall (eds), *Popular Culture and the Austerity Myth: Hard Times Today* (New York: Routledge, 2017), pp. 175–9.

38. B. M. Murphy, '"It's Not the House That's Haunted": Demons, Debt, and the Family in Peril Formula in Recent Horror Cinema', in M. Leeder (ed.), *Cinematic Ghosts: Haunting and Spectrality from Silent Cinema to the Digital Era* (New York: Bloomsbury, 2015), p. 235.

39. Murphy, 'It's Not the House That's Haunted', pp. 241–2.

40. T. Gilchrist, '*Paranormal Activity*, *The Purge*'s Jason Blum on Fixing a Film Series – Even When It's a Hit', *Forbes* (7 April 2014), *www.forbes.com/sites/toddgilchrist/2014/04/07/paranormal-activity-purge-jason-blum-blumhouse-marked-ones-blu-ray/#2816694f67bc/* (accessed 7 February 2020).

41. R. Newby, 'Why *Truth or Dare* Feels Like a Step Back for Blumhouse', *Holly-wood Reporter* (15 April 2018), *www.hollywoodreporter.com/heat-vision/truth-dare-movie-is-a-step-back-blumhouse-1102803/* (accessed 7 February 2020).

42. Guerrasio, 'How the Company Behind 2 of the Year's Biggest Movies is Blow-ing Up the Hollywood Playbook'.

43. Christopher J. Olson and CarrieLynn D. Reinhard, *Possessed Women, Haunted States: Cultural Tensions in Exorcism Cinema* (Lanham MD: Lexington Books, 2017), pp. 1, 29–36.

44. C. Frederick, 'How *The Purge* Became the Most Unexpectedly Important Horror Franchise of the Decade', *Slash Film* (4 July 2018), *www.slashfilm.com/evolution-of-the-purge/* (accessed 7 February 2020).

45. Frederick, 'How *The Purge* Became the Most Unexpectedly Important Horror Franchise of the Decade'.

46. R. Rubin, 'How Blumhouse got Everything Right About Making a *Halloween* Sequel', *Variety* (22 October 2018), *https://variety.com/2018/film/box-office/halloween-box-office-analysis-horror-1202987761/* (accessed 7 February 2020).

47. For a review and empirical critique see, A. D. Ménard, A. Weaver and C. Cabrera, '"There are Certain Rules that One Must Abide by": Predictors of Mortality in Slasher Films', *Sexuality and Culture*, 23/2 (2019), 624–33.

48. R. Ito, 'A Slasher Film for #MeToo', *New York Times* (15 December 2019), AR17.

49. T. Siegel and B. Kit, 'New *Dracula* Movie in the Works as Universal Remakes Its Monsterverse (Exclusive)', *Hollywood Reporter* (10 March 2020), *https://www.hollywoodreporter.com/heat-vision/new-dracula-movie-works-as-universal-remakes-monsterverse-1283635/* (accessed 7 April 2020).

50. C. Barfield, 'Jason Blum Calls *Whiplash* a "Disaster Theatrically" and Says the Days of Low-Budget Dramas in Theaters are Over', *The Playlist* (20 June 2019), *https://theplaylist.net/jason-blum-whiplash-theatrical-disaster-20190620/* (accessed 7 February 2020).

51. Elberse, 'Jason Blum's Blumhouse Productions', 4.

52. K. Konda, 'Box Office: Blumhouse's Secret to Success is Astonishingly Simple, yet Nearly Impossible to Emulate', *We Minored in Film* (17 October 2017), *https://weminoredinfilm.com/2017/10/17/box-office-blumhouses-secret-to-succcess-is-astonishingly-simple-yet-nearly-impossible-to-emulate/* (accessed 7 February 2020).

53. Masters, 'Jason Blum's Crowded Movie Morgue'.

54. B. Lang, 'Building Blumhouse', *Variety* (12 June 2018), 64.

55. G. Bolling, 'Jason Blum Thinks Moviegoing Will be Very Different After the Coronavirus', *JoBlo* (24 March 2020), *www.joblo.com/movie-news/*

jason-blum-thinks-moviegoing-will-be-very-different-after-the-coronavirus/ (accessed 7 April 2020).

56. M. Redmon, 'Blumhouse Founder Jason Blum Believes the Coronavirus Will Have a Permanent Effect on How We Watch Movies', *Uproxx* (24 March 2020), *https://uproxx.com/movies/jason-blum-coronavirus-vod-movie-theater-release-window/* (accessed 31 August 2020).

57. M. Donnelly, 'Blumhouse Productions Hit with Layoffs, Pay Cuts for Senior Leadership (EXCLUSIVE)', *Variety* (10 April 2020), *https://variety.com/2020/film/news/blumhouse-productions-layoffs-coronavirus 1234577187/* (accessed 31 August 2020).

58. M. Prigge, 'Blumhouse Head Jason Blum Says He's Definitely Not Making Any Virus Horror Movies After the Pandemic Ends', *Uproxx* (11 April 2020), *https://uproxx.com/movies/jason-blum-moviegoing-coronavirus/* (accessed 31 August 2020).

59. E. Sacks, 'Hollywood's COVID Pandemic Disruption Storyline Desperately Needs a Rewrite', *NBC News* (9 August 2020), *www.nbcnews.com/pop-culture/movies/hollywood-s-covid-pandemic-disruption-storyline-desperately-needs-rewrite-n1235823/* (accessed 31 August 2020).

Table 2: Blumhouse's Theatrical Releases

Year	Title	Release Date	Budget ($)	International Box Office	Genre	Subtype	Rating	Return on Investment ($)
2009	Paranormal Activity	25 September	450,000	194,183,034	Horror	Ghost/haunted house	R	43,051.79
2010	Paranormal Activity 2	22 October	3 million	177,512,032	Horror	Ghost/haunted house	R	5,817.07
2011	Insidious	1 April	1.5 million	99,870,886	Horror	Ghost/haunted house	PG-13	6,558.06
2011	Paranormal Activity 3	21 October	5 million	207,039,844	Horror	Ghost/haunted house	R	4,040.8
2012	Sinister	12 October	3 million	87,727,807	Horror	Ghost/haunted house	R	2,824.26
2012	Paranormal Activity 4	19 October	5 million	142,817,992	Horror	Ghost/haunted house	R	2,756.36
2012	The Bay	2 November	2 million	1,545,308	Horror	Outbreak	R	-22.75
2013	Dark Skies	22 February	3.5 million	27,704,111	Horror	Abduction	PG-13	691.55
2013	The Lords of Salem	19 April	1.5 million	1,541,131	Horror	Occult	R	2.74
2013	The Purge	7 June	3 million	91,266,581	Horror	Home invasion	R	2,942.22
2013	Insidious: Chapter 2	13 September	5 million	161,921,515	Horror	Ghost/haunted house	PG-13	3,138.84
2013	Plush	13 September	2 million	28,864	Erotic thriller	N/A	R	-98.56
2014	Paranormal Activity: The Marked Ones	3 January	5 million	90,904,854	Horror	Ghost/haunted house	R	1,718.10
2014	Oculus	11 April	5 million	44,115,496	Horror	Ghost/haunted house	R	782.31
2014	13 Sins	18 April	4 million	44,552	Horror	Ghost/haunted house	R	-98.89
2014	The Purge: Anarchy	18 July	9 million	111,534,881	Horror	Action	R	1,139.28
2014	Whiplash	10 October	3.3 million	38,969,037	Drama	N/A	R	1,088.88

Year	Title	Release Date	Budget ($)	International Box Office	Genre	Subtype	Rating	Return on Investment ($)
2014	Ouija	24 October	5 million	103,300,632	Horror	Possession	PG-13	1,966.01
2014	Jessabelle	7 November	4 million	6,998,359	Horror	Ghost/haunted house	PG-13	74.96
2015	The Boy Next Door	23 January	4 million	53,401,938	Erotic thriller	N/A	R	1,235.05
2015	The Lazarus Effect	27 February	5 million	38,359,310	Horror	Outbreak	PG-13	667.19
2015	Unfriended	17 April	1 million	64,364,198	Horror	Ghost/haunted house	R	6,336.42
2015	Area 51	15 May	5 million	7,556	Horror	Sci-fi	R	-99.85
2015	Insidious: Chapter 3	5 June	10 million	120,453,155	Horror	Ghost/haunted house	PG-13	1,104.53
2015	Exeter	2 July	25,000	489,792	Horror	Possession	NR	1,859.17
2015	The Gallows	10 July	100,000	41,656,474	Horror	Ghost/haunted house	PG-13	41,556.47
2015	The Gift	7 August	5 million	58,978,477	Horror	Thriller/psychological	R	1,079.57
2015	Sinister 2	21 August	10 million	54,104,225	Horror	Ghost/haunted house	R	441.04
2015	The Visit	11 September	5 million	98,677,816	Horror	Thriller/psychological	PG-13	1,873.56
2015	Paranormal Activity: The Ghost Dimension	23 October	10 million	77,959,374	Horror	Ghost/haunted house	R	679.59
2015	Jem and the Holograms	23 October	5 million	2,368,937	Drama	N/A	PG	-52.62
2016	The Darkness	13 May	4 million	10,898,293	Horror	Ghost/haunted house	PG-13	172.46
2016	The Purge: Election Year	1 July	10 million	118,514,727	Horror	Action	R	1,082.15
2016	Ouija: Origin of Evil	21 October	9 million	81,831,866	Horror	Possession	PG-13	809.24

Year	Title	Release Date	Budget ($)	International Box Office	Genre	Subtype	Rating	Return on Investment ($)
2016	Incarnate	2 December	5 million	9,731,036	Horror	Possession	PG-13	94.62
2017	Split	20 January	9 million	278,964,806	Horror	Thriller/psychological	PG-13	2,993.94
2017	Get Out	24 February	5 million	255,408,115	Horror	Thriller/psychology	R	5,008.16
2017	Lowriders	12 May	916,000	6,188,421	Drama	N/A	PG-13	575.59
2017	Happy Death Day	13 October	4.8 million	125,010,260	Horror	Slasher	PG-13	2,504.38
2018	Insidious: The Last Key	5 January	10 million	172,811,971	Horror	Ghost/haunted house	PG-13	1,628.12
2018	Truth or Dare	13 April	3.5 million	95,292,744	Horror	Possession	PG-13	2,622.65
2018	Delirium	22 May	1 million	454,481	Horror	Thriller/psychological	R	-54.55
2018	The First Purge	4 July	13 million	137,054,597	Horror	Action	R	954.27
2018	Unfriended: Dark Web	20 July	1 million	16,434,588	Horror	Thriller/psychological	R	1,543.46
2018	BlacKkKlansman	10 August	15 million	93,411,426	Crime	N/A	R	522.74
2018	Halloween	19 October	10 million	255,485,178	Horror	Slasher	R	2,454.85

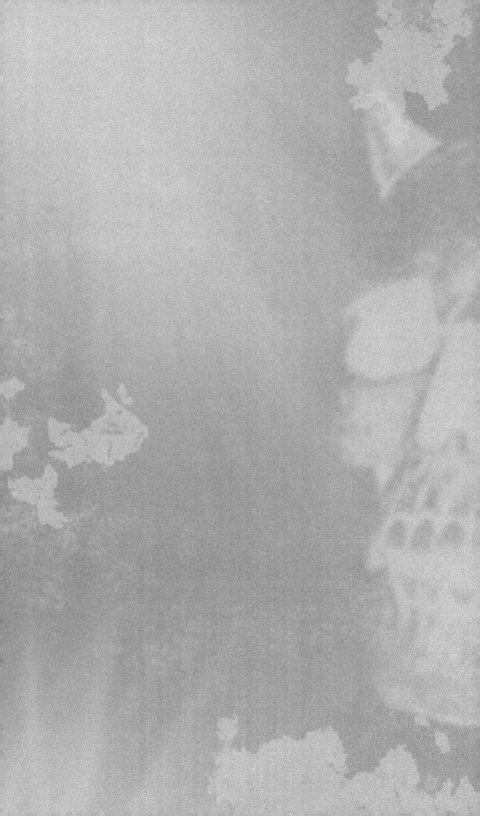

2

'Those Things You See Through'

Get Out, Signifyin', and Hollywood's Commodification of African-American Independent Cinema

Stefan Sereda

JORDAN PEELE'S 2017 debut feature film, *Get Out*, revolves around a science-fiction device wherein minds are transferred between bodies via a combination of medical science and hypnosis. This procedure acts as a metaphor that satirises slavery's pervasive legacy of racism in the supposedly 'post-racial' United States. The film's victim-protagonist is Chris Washington, a New York photographer who finds himself lured to an affluent suburban enclave where he meets his white partner Rose's family. There, the hero faces impending enslavement as a brainwashed physical vessel to be colonised and driven by a white host's mind. Although Chris's captors initially claim magnanimity, as their veneer slips it appears that they objectify 'blackness' for familiar reasons, putting forth seemingly benevolent racist clichés – for example, that black men make better lovers and superior athletes.

Yet when a blind art dealer, Jim Hudson, purchases Chris at auction, he explains that Chris's value to him is not based on genetic assumptions. Instead, Hudson, who initially appears sympathetic to Chris's plight, sees him as a cultural commodity and expresses admiration for Chris's photographs.

As they converse via an onscreen video feed, Hudson asks Chris not to lump him in with the other slavers, and tells him: 'I could give a shit what color you are. No, what I want is deeper. I want your eye, man. I want those things you see through.' Notably, Hudson wants Chris's 'eye' – not his eyes, plural, but his perspective. 'Those things' that Chris sees America through cannot be reduced to organs, but are instead the culminating symptoms of racism and 400 years of African-American slavery. In this admission, Hudson reveals that he commoditises Blackness along with the other whites he accuses of 'ignorance', most of whom also deny their racism. That this confession occurs in a meta-cinematic screen-to-screen conversation should, in the vernacular of Chris's astute friend Rod Williams, 'rankle' audiences. This self-reflexive alienation effect calling attention to the screen medium provokes the viewer to interrogate their own experience of the film: while the story unfolds from Chris's perspective, is it not Hudson, at this point in the film, who best reflects the audience's taste for Black miserabilism?

Hudson's disclosure, especially because it involves a play on words between the 'eyes' audiences expect the blind man to covet, and the more metaphysical 'eye' that he desires, constitutes a deployment of the rhetorical strategy Henry Louis Gates Jr terms *signifyin'*. A quintessential African-American semantic practice and resistance strategy, signifyin' redirects the oppressor's language and symbols to connote subversive meanings.[1] By means of this device, Peele critiques the myth of 'post-racial' America and the American film industry's racist history. Moreover, the film's subtext demonstrates Peele's awareness of how studios commoditise Blackness and diversity. Ultimately, Peele critiques audience and industry expectations of African-American independent films as narratives of Black suffering to be consumed by a bourgeois film-going public. In effect, Peele likens the studio system to Hudson, who co-opts and consumes Chris's perspective on Black tribulation. The extratextual irony in the film's enthusiastic reception by critics and award-giving bodies, despite some of *Get Out*'s characters finding the plot laughably outrageous, further underscores the film's argument that Black anguish is commoditised in American cultural circles.

Signifyin', or What We Mean When We Say 'Get Out!'

Signifyin', or signifyin(g), is a type of wordplay often deployed as a subversive rhetorical strategy, wherein a word or phrase's connotative (as opposed to literal) meanings speak to those belonging to the same discursive community.[2] A discrete example of such wordplay in *Get Out* is the name that Peele gives the film's sole science-fiction device: the 'Coagula Procedure'. 'Coagula', which in Latin means 'it joins', denotes a coagulated or gelled mass, but the word's sound connotes 'Count Dracula'. Here the film implies that the white Armitage family are bloodsuckers. The humourist Cecil Adams provides an early, equivocal definition of signifyin':

> to some it means any kind of ritual insult; to others, it must include an element of indirection – i.e., the victim doesn't realize he's being insulted, you egg the victim into a fight with somebody else, or in general you just lay on the BS.[3]

Whereas Adams notes that signifyin' 'isn't an exclusively African American occupation',[4] literary theorist Henry Louis Gates Jr deems it 'a strategy of black figurative language use' and traces signifyin(g)'s African-American roots to the signifyin' monkey, a trickster figure of African-American folk tales.[5] Gates calls signifyin' the 'slave's trope' and the 'trope of tropes', which 'subsumes the master tropes': metaphor, metonymy, synecdoche, irony and the like.[6] In other words, it is a manner of speaking in the dominant language to subvert hegemonic authority.

Gena Dagel Capoli applies signifyin' to the arts – specifically music – as she contends:

> Signifyin(g) is also a way of demonstrating respect for, goading, or poking fun at a musical style, process, or practice through parody, pastiche, implication, indirection, humor, tone- or word-play, the illusions of speech, or narration, and other troping mechanisms . . . Signifyin(g) shows, among other things, either reverence or irreverence toward previously stated musical statements and values.[7]

While Caponi limits her discussion to music, *Get Out* demonstrates how films signify, employing both pastiche and parody while calling forth genre tropes from horror, science fiction and melodrama. The film's pitch-dark opening where a masked assailant stalks and attacks his victim in a white suburban enclave borrows its iconography from *Halloween* (1978). Its credit sequence, where blue titles roll as a car drives through wilderness, pays homage to *The Shining* (1980). *Get Out*'s plotting draws inspiration from *Guess Who's Coming to Dinner* (1967), *Rosemary's Baby* (1968) and *The Stepford Wives* (1975). As with *Guess Who's Coming to Dinner*, the inciting incident is a Black man visiting his white partner's family. Similar to *Rosemary's Baby*, one member of a couple begins to suspect – correctly – that their partner is part of a cabal plotting against the protagonist. Inevitably, the film resembles *The Stepford Wives*, only instead of women being replaced with docile, domesticated duplicates, Black bodies are colonised by white minds. Within the narrative proper, the characters themselves display their cinephilia, likening Chris's situation to both *The Hills Have Eyes* (1977) and *Eyes Wide Shut* (1999). Elsewhere, the film references *Dirty Dancing* (1987), as Rose listens to '(I've Had) The Time of My Life' through earbuds after imperilling Chris. The latter reference is an apt example of how signifyin' redirects a pre-existing symbol's meaning to effect criticism: for Rose, her affair with Chris has been less a whirlwind romance than her 'favourite' foray into slave poaching.

In more cinematic terms, signifyin' is comparable to Kristen Hoerl's concept, *cinematic jiujitsu*, a term she coined to describe how films:

> that adopt the formal structures of dominant hegemony can convey controversial political ideas. Like the martial art, cinematic jujitsu uses counter techniques that draw upon the strength of an opposing force in order to achieve a more dominant position.[8]

In light of *Get Out*'s jiujitsu motif, Hoerl's metaphor is an apt description of how the film counter-appropriates Hollywood tropes, such as genre conventions and African-American caricatures, to level a racial critique.

The title *Get Out* exemplifies signifyin' in practice, as it has multiple connotative meanings. In the context of a thriller, 'get out' encapsulates the anxiety the audience feels while experiencing the narrative. The viewer might shout these words at the screen as the scenario closes in around Chris. Indeed, two characters in the film – Rod and Andre – tell Chris to 'get out'. A more indirect connotation pertains to the film's engagement with US race history and melodrama. *Get Out* exists in dialogue with the aforementioned *Guess Who's Coming to Dinner*, wherein a white woman brings her Black fiancé to meet her supposedly liberal but initially disapproving parents, who are eventually won over. *Get Out* opens as a pastiche of the earlier film's premise before the film mutates into a thriller that parodies its source material. Viewers can read the title as an alternative – and perhaps more likely – response in the *Guess Who's Coming to Dinner* scenario: rather than embracing their African-American guest, the white family might say, or at least think, 'get out'. This connotation is in keeping with the history of *sundown towns* in the United States: segregated all-white municipalities where signs warned African-Americans (as well as other racial and ethnic minorities) to 'get out' before sundown.[9]

A third more comedic meaning is a colloquial response for when someone says something unbelievable, as in, '*get out of here!*' This expression is itself akin to *signifyin'*, as its meaning depends less on the denotative and more on tonal connotations. 'Get out of here' is Chris's attitude for the first half of the film, which he holds in check in the presence of white liberals who claim they are not racist while simultaneously acting in a bigoted manner. It is also easy to imagine 'get out' encapsulating Chris's response to seeing Andre, an urban African American, wearing a straw hat and behaving like a stereotype in a classical Hollywood film. In this sense, 'get out' becomes a response that calls into question Hollywood's history of onscreen race relations. This connotative meaning is also self-satirising, as it corresponds to the authorities that laugh at Rod when he discloses his fear that Chris has been kidnapped into suburban white slavery. If the title is understood to be signifyin', then this *double entendre* serves as an alienation effect to provoke the audience into a counter-reading of the film as having a ridiculous plot that should cause the viewer to reflect on their own participation in Hollywood's trafficking in Black miserabilism. Peele's critique is perhaps most devastating when it appraises Hollywood's history of racism and contemporary commodification of diversity.

'They are not Racist': Get Out's Re-evaluation of Hollywood History

Film scholar Ed Guerrero contends that, 'blackness has always been in vogue in the mainstream culture industry,' but it remains 'framed and controlled by an overdetermining sense of white hegemony'.[10] *Get Out* signifies against how white hegemony has historically framed Blackness in the Hollywood culture industry. Peele affirms that *Get Out* is a rebuttal to sociocultural sentiment that the United Sates became a post-racial society with Barack Obama's election to the presidency, calling this myth a 'post-racial lie'.[11] The film dissects this myth by persistently undermining its white characters' contention that they are not racist. Indeed, '*they are not racist*' is the film's central thematic premise, a governing irony spoken by the deceitful Rose in act one. The film ultimately decimates this statement, the 'post-racial lie', and Hollywood's complicity in this lie.

The film situates itself firmly in the contemporary post-Obama era, as Rose states and her father Dean repeats that he 'would have voted for Obama a third time'. This is an early instance of signifyin' in the narrative: the savvy viewer will note that Rose and Dean are not being entirely honest, but running lines from a script. The first act presents Chris and Rose as a liberal couple similar to John and Joanna in *Guess Who's Coming to Dinner* or Guy and Rosemary Woodhouse in *Rosemary's Baby*. As a pair, they are model 'progressives' in an egalitarian relationship where Rose drives the car and supposedly does not see why Chris's race would need to be raised as an issue with her family. Chris, for his part, finds it 'hot' when Rose defends him from a police officer, suggesting that he is attracted to her taking charge. Rose's parents have a similar dynamic, where Dean jokes in front of Missy that Chris should get used to saying Rose is 'right'. The Armitages appear matriarchal, with Missy giving orders and Dean deferring. In another play on words, Dean says 'fruck' instead of 'fuck' in front of Missy, who prefers that her family mind their language and topics of conversation. After introducing Chris to the servants, Walter and Georgina, Dean makes two statements that are loaded with hidden meaning. Dean, embarrassed to have Black servants, says, 'I hate how this looks', and explains that they were his parents' servants, and after they died, 'we couldn't bear to let them go'. Dean tries to convince Chris that he hates to appear racist, evoking the post-racial America myth, where some Americans might deny the country's problems with racism, even if this denial comes from a place of guilt and shame. Still, Dean is ironically referring to the truth: that his parents occupy the bodies of their former servants, meaning Dean could not bear to let his parents go. Since Dean hates how it looks, the film is providing a clue to his racism: he hates that his once white parents now have black skin. Moreover, the dialogue also connotes that what the Armitages could not bear to let go of are the perks for whites of African-American slavery. The Armitages only pretend that they are post-racial progressives to lull Chris into ignoring their underlying racism.

Yet Chris, who Hudson notes for his eye, witnesses the Armitages' progressive veneer slip almost immediately. Chris notices Missy rudely dismiss Georgina and endures Rose's brother Jeremy's barely concealed desire to fight him, but keeps any opinion that he has on their racism to himself until Rose recalls these encounters in private. Another incident entails Dean's fondness for the phrase 'my man' when addressing Chris. Ostensibly, Dean says this to appear familiar with Chris, but Chris and Rose find it cloying, as though Dean is trying too hard not to appear racist. There are further connotations to this dialogue: for one, Dean is engaging in a sort of cultural appropriation by adopting an urban Black vernacular. Furthermore, every time Dean says this, he implies ownership over Chris, as the viewer might imagine a plantation owner saying this to a house slave. Other aspects of the family's racism seem to escape Chris but are implied in his introduction to the house. To keep Chris from discovering the basement where a fate worse than death awaits him, Dean warns of 'black mold', connoting a loathing for Blackness. Ironically, this comment is offered as an aside after Dean shows off trinkets he picked up in Bali. Dean attempts to minimise his colonial tendencies with self-awareness, stating, 'it's such a privilege to be able to experience another person's culture'. This is, essentially, the same attitude of disavowed racism that Hudson brings to colonising Chris's body and mind, and integral to the film's most self-reflexive commentary on blackness in the culture industry. Peele's *mise-en-scène* also offers an implied critique of how the Armitage family abuses their privilege: Missy controls minds with a silver spoon that she uses as a focal point for her hypnosis.

Get Out's commentary on latent racism extends beyond Peele's characters to an examination of race in Hollywood film. In 'The Uncanny', Sigmund Freud hypothesises that people experience dread through a return of the repressed.[12] Although Freud writes in strictly psychoanalytical terms related to individual tensions between the conscious and unconscious mind, he provides a useful framework for interpreting horror media and the sociocultural histories with which it frequently reckons. *Get Out* reckons with the ghosts of Hollywood history by resurrecting maligned representations of African Americans from its past. In so doing, the film metaphorises how the post-racial myth is intended to occlude America's racist history and present, so as to sedate African Americans and have them behave according to the whims of white hegemony. Guerrero notes:

> in one sense, contemporary Hollywood has broken with its openly white supremacist origins. Mostly gone are the obvious caricatures: the stern Mammies, bug-eyed Sambos, grunting Tontos, and pidgin-speaking Charlie Chans of the past.[13]

Get Out resurrects these caricatures to demonstrate a United States that is not in fact post-racial, but instead haunted by this history of representations, which metonymise white supremacy. Through the brainwashed and colonised Black bodies, Peele calls attention to and mocks Hollywood's racist history of African-American stereotypes.

Chris's acquaintance Andre, for example, has transformed into 'Logan King', who acts like a relic of an earlier era. Andre has become a 'Tom': a 'kind hearted and submissive black man' stock character common in the classical Hollywood era, who is 'well liked and willing to endure white domination'.[14] Andre resembles the Tom characters Bill 'Bojangles' Robinson portrayed alongside Shirley Temple in films such as *Rebecca of Sunnybrook Farm* (1938), where he plays a straw-hatted farmhand, and *The Littlest Rebel* (1935), in which he stars as a devoted slave in the antebellum South too ignorant to understand the impending Civil War or what it means for his own freedom. Once Andre has been brainwashed, his style, including a straw hat, harkens to the first half of the twentieth century, while his behaviour and vernacular are similarly anachronistic. Viewed through Chris's and Peele's eye, as well as a twenty-first century lens, Andre, and through him, the Tom stereotype, appears ridiculous.

By contrast, the film likens Chris to a 'Bad Buck'. Another dated Hollywood stereotype, the Bad Buck is a physically strong Black man with 'pent up rage' who is 'especially threatening to whites'.[15] *Get Out* makes this connection early in the film when Chris takes a moment to empathise with a deer struck by his girlfriend's car. Upon arriving at the Armitage residence and reporting the buck, Dean exclaims, 'one down, a couple hundred thousand to go'. The film implies that African-American males beyond white control threaten Dean. When Chris is bound in the Armitage's basement, a buck's head is mounted on the wall. Moreover, Chris has pent up rage that he keeps in check, but which erupts from him in the climax when he impales Dean with the stuffed buck's antlers. Indeed, Jeremy Armitage's attitude towards Chris betrays how the Bad Buck is in fact a valuable stereotype for white culture. During their first meeting, Jeremy sizes up Chris's potential for MMA fighting, stating, 'with your frame and your genetic body . . . no pussyfooting around, you'd be *a fucking beast*'. Antlers appear in the background behind Chris during this scene. Yet Chris is not a one-dimensional lumbering villain, and he resists this stereotype, refusing to grapple with Jeremy. Later, Chris jokes about being a 'beast' before sex with Rose, but afterward turns a stuffed lion away so it does not face him; with this gesture, Chris resists the Armitage's attempts to dehumanise him and treat him as chattel. Meanwhile, Andre, Walter and Regina come across as automatons in their conforming to white expectations. Peele simultaneously resists African-American stereotypes while offering them up for ridicule, as the Armitage residence becomes a haunted (plantation) house, where the repressed legacy of slavery returns to reflect on present race relations. Indeed, Hollywood's African-American stereotypes never disappeared, but reformed: the Tom has become the 'magical negro' trope, and the Bad Buck the generic 'scary black man'.

Get Out's critique of Hollywood race relations proffers a self-reflexive meditation on how studios and audiences commoditise African-American authorship in a process akin to cultural appropriation. To revisit Hudson's reason for purchasing Chris, the film posits that whites see African-American perspectives on racial strife as an object for commodification and consumption. This theme pervades the film, which introduces Chris through the photographs on his wall: a Black woman's pregnant stomach, a bunch of balloons, a dog pulling at its chain, a bird flying through an alley and a boy wearing a mask. Meanwhile, sad music plays, bestowing a sense of tragedy. Taken together, these images create meaning through their juxtaposition: to Chris, the African-American life cycle from birth onward involves learning at an early age to attempt assimilation through mimicking the white majority, as symbolised through the photos of a pregnant stomach and a boy in a mask.[16] The film's premise puts Chris in a position where he is expected to 'fit in' with a white family. The photos of the dog and the balloons suggest tethering and restraint, standing in for African-American confinement. By contrast, the bird flying through an alley suggests a conflict between freedom and the urban environment, or perhaps Chris finds freedom in the urban environment, whereas he will be forced to compromise elements of his identity in the white suburbs.

Throughout the film, Chris photographs those things that catch his eye: most often, African Americans suffering. Chris first trains his photo on Walter, the family's gardener and a host for their grandfather, who is isolated from the group. Later, Chris takes a picture of Andre, now transformed into the Tom, Logan. Although Chris never articulates any such sentiment aloud, the viewer might surmise that he sees in Walter and Andre/Logan the destructive effects that conforming to white American expectations (and the impossibility thereof) has on the African-American psyche. It is this ability that gives Chris value to Hudson as a cultural commodity: Chris has an eye for Black America's existential predicament.

Get Out grapples with African-American suffering in an industry that invests in films about African-American tribulation so that it can exploit and profit from those hardships. It anticipates and avoids becoming an exercise in African-American miserabilism akin to, for example, *Precious*

(2009), through humour, self-reflexivity and subverting racist tropes. One of these tropes is the 'white saviour' who rescues Blacks. In *Get Out*, every white character is compromised by racism, and a fellow African American saves Chris. The film flouts its humour and self-reflexivity in a scene typical of horror films reliant on social paranoia, as Rod relates Chris's plight to the doubtful Detective Latoya and her two colleagues. Rod explains:

> they're probably abducting black people, brainwashing them and making them slaves . . . or sex slaves. Not just regular slaves, but sex slaves and shit. See? I don't know if it's the hypnosis that's making them slaves or what not, but all I know is they already got two brothas we know and there could be a whole bunch of brothas they got already.

In a more traditional horror film, such as *Rosemary's Baby*, the paranoiac's audience typically views the speaker as being insane or is themselves 'in' on the plot: either result ends with the protagonist further endangered. Yet in *Get Out*, Rod's audience registers his diatribe for a beat . . . and laughs. Latoya mocks, 'oh, white girls . . . they get you every time!' The scene is played for laughs, which disrupts the narrative proper's tone: the audience knows Chris is in danger. Still, the viewer sympathises with Latoya: Rod's enthusiastic delivery of his paranoid yarn is laughable. Here, the viewer comes to a paradox: *Get Out* is at once a deadly serious investigation of race relations in so-called 'post-racial' America, with a plot that no sensible person should take seriously – or, at least, as the film suggests, no sensible *African-American* person. Latoya and her colleagues belong to the film's milieu of savvy urban African Americans, and they find Rod's story of African Americans turned into slaves through hypnosis hysterical. Their response betrays Peele's own understanding that his narrative is ludicrous, and also his own foresight in anticipating such a critical response.

Get Out's production and distribution classify it as a horror film focusing on the African-American plight. The film's production company, Blumhouse, is reputed for its horror releases; its distributor, Universal, marketed *Get Out* around a master shot of Chris's crying eye. Chris's exchange with Hudson suggests that it is reasonable to argue that Peele anticipated Blumhouse and Universal would be eager to traffic in Black miserabilism, as such exploitation is symptomatic of a greater pattern in Hollywood. For example, the previous decade witnessed a cycle of mostly critically acclaimed films dedicated to African strife, among them *Blood*

Diamond (2006), *Tears of the Sun* (2003), *Hotel Rwanda* (2004) and *The Last King of Scotland* (2006). In *12 Years a Slave* (2013) and *Moonlight* (2016), both of which won Academy Awards for Best Picture, their respective protagonists endure a kind of suffering reminiscent of saintly patience literature. Meanwhile, Blumhouse greenlit *Get Out* in a cultural climate of mounting social pressure on Hollywood to increase diversity among its onscreen performers and behind-the-scenes personnel, especially directors. A year before *Get Out*'s release, the Academy Awards were embroiled in the #OscarsSoWhite controversy.[17] The world's largest media conglomerate, Disney, designed 2016's second-highest grossing film, *Rogue One: A Star Wars Story* (2016), as a vehicle for diversity casting, where a multicultural group of rebels led by a white woman take on an almost exclusively white male evil Empire. Peele likely understood that as a first-time writer-director of a feature film, his *Blackness* made him a commodity in Hollywood. When Hudson declares 'I want your eye', there is another level of connotation: if the listener takes 'eye' for its homonym, 'I', then Hudson is harvesting Chris's identity and subjectivity. Taken this way, the statement becomes Peele's method of signifyin' against Hollywood's cultural appropriation of Black identity.

Yet despite this indictment and Latoya's meta-reception to the story – or perhaps *because* of such postmodern self-awareness, which remains in vogue – the critical establishment lauded *Get Out*, and its reception is further testament to the film's prescience.[18] *Get Out* succeeded with audiences, critics and award-giving bodies. The film was a global box-office success, earning more than $255 million on an indie film budget of $4.5 million.[19] At the time of writing this chapter, the film holds a 98 per cent Fresh rating on the fan site *Rotten Tomatoes*, which speaks to its mass appeal.[20] Review aggregator site *MetaCritic* averages *Get Out*'s rating among 48 different reviews as 85 per cent positive, citing one mixed review and zero negative reviews, which by their metric indicates 'universal acclaim'.[21] Moreover, the film garnered 219 award nominations from sixty-four different film societies, winning eighty-three.[22] The Academy of Motion Picture Arts and Sciences nominated *Get Out* in the Best Picture, Actor and Director categories, and awarded Peele Best Original Screenplay.

Get Out's critical lauding betrays a desire on the part of independent and Hollywood circles to celebrate Jordan Peele as a maverick filmmaker. After fourteen years of climbing from being an ensemble cast member on cable television to co-starring in his own show to co-starring in a movie vehicle, *Get Out* provided a career catapult to critical acclaim and set up

Peele as the next A-list *auteur*. Counting the Best Picture awards Peele shared with his co-producers, he himself won sixty-three awards. Among Peele's awards were nine awards for directing, twenty-four for writing, and twenty-one naming *Get Out* the year's best film or debut film or placing it among the top ten films selected by that committee. At the 2017 Independent Film Awards, Peele won the Bingham Ray Breakthrough Director Award. The Writers Guild of America awarded Peele Best Original Screenplay and the Directors Guild nominated him for Best Director. A year after protesters declared '#OscarsSoWhite', Peele became the first African-American screenwriter to win the Oscar for Best Original Screenplay. In a system that routinely commoditises *auteurs* for studio profit, it was as though the independent and Hollywood establishments were slapping Peele on the back and exclaiming, 'my man'![23] As the art dealer purchased Chris, so too did the film establishment invest in Peele as a vehicle for profit and legitimacy, thereby reinforcing *Get Out*'s argument regarding cultural appropriation in the arts. Going forward, film scholars might look to Peele as a model for *diversified authorship*.

A Last Laugh

The so-called 'post-racial' Obama years have given way to a period of pronounced racial strife under the Trump administration, characterised by travel and immigration restrictions, deportations of undocumented immigrants, a human rights crisis on the border with Mexico, a surge in white nationalist extremism and hostilities against people of Asian descent in the wake of a trade war against China and the COVID-19 pandemic. The police killing of George Floyd in Minneapolis renewed anti-racism protests by the Black Lives Matter movement across the country. The protests – now considered the largest in US history – prompted national dialogue on systemic racism and police brutality, provoked further police brutality and a militaristic response from the federal government, and at the time of writing have not abated. Griffin Sims Edwards and Stephen Rushin argue, 'Donald Trump's election in November of 2016 was associated with a statistically significant surge in reported hate crimes across the United States', hypothesising that it 'was not just Trump's inflammatory rhetoric throughout the campaign that caused hate crimes to increase', but that 'Trump's subsequent election as President of the United States . . . validated this rhetoric in the eyes of perpetrators and fueled the hate crime surge'.[24]

Whereas Trump's rhetoric and election might have emboldened this surge, his racist motivations in fact gestated earlier, in an era when Americans could point to an African-American president as an argument that the country was no longer racist. Similar to the Armitage clan, Trump has repeatedly refuted that he is a racist. *Get Out* opened in the Trump era to stellar success. In the rush to laud Peele as a necessary new voice whose film offered a scathing indictment of the post-racial myth, some outlying award-giving bodies saw *Get Out* less as a horror film than a comedy. The Hollywood Foreign Press Association's announcement that *Get Out* would be eligible in the Best Comedy or Musical Category at the Golden Globes met with controversy. As Graeme Virtue summarised the pushback in the *Guardian*:

> while it might have originated from a particularly sharp comic mind, to label *Get Out* a comedy – even if it is just to give it a strategic awards edge – seems unforgivably lazy, sanding off the spikier edges of a film that engages with the precarious state of US race relations in a year where it could not be more timely. By repositioning it in the public consciousness as a comedy . . . we're in danger of short-changing *Get Out*'s achievements and the tough questions it raises. Are we trying to LOL ourselves into a false sense of security?[25]

No matter how hard Detective Latoya laughed at the film's plot, Virtue and other industry pundits insist it must be taken seriously. In light of this debate over the film's genre and the context of escalating racial tensions in which it was released, Peele signified, in cryptic, arch-satirical fashion: '*Get Out* is a documentary'.

Notes

1. See, Henry Louis Gates, *The Signifying Monkey: A Theory of African-American Literary Criticism* (Oxford: Oxford University Press, 1988).
2. Hence the word's spelling as signifyin' or signifyin(g) – this linguistic practice signifies meaning, but with a difference.
3. C. Adams, 'To African-Americans, What Does "Signifying" Mean?', *The Straight Dope* (28 September 1984), *www.straightdope.com/columns/read/498/to-african-americans-what-does-signifying-mean/* (accessed 2 April 2020).
4. Adams, 'To African-Americans, What Does 'Signifying' Mean?'.

5. Gates Jr, *The Signifying Monkey*, p. 84.

6. H. L. Gates Jr, 'The "Blackness of Blackness": A Critique of the Sign and the Signifying Monkey', *Critical Inquiry*, 9/4 (1983), 686.

7. Gena Dagel Caponi, *Signifyin(g), Sanctifyin', & Slam Dunking: A Reader in African American Expressive Culture* (Amherst MA: University of Massachusetts Press, 1999), p. 141.

8. K. Hoerl, 'Cinematic Jujitsu: Resisting White Hegemony through the American Dream in Spike Lee's *Malcolm X*', *Communication Studies*, 59/4 (2008), 358.

9. For a history of sundown towns, see James W. Loewen, *Sundown Towns: A Hidden Dimension of American Racism* (New York: Touchstone, 2005).

10. Ed Guerrero, 'A Circus of Dreams and Lies: The Black Film Wave at Middle Age', in J. Lewis (ed.), *The New American Cinema* (Durham NC: Duke University Press), p. 332.

11. D. Raymos, '*Get Out* Director Jordan Peele on Divisiveness, Black Identity and the "White Savior"', *Deadline* (22 October 2017), *https://deadline. com/2017/10/jordan-peele-get-out-film-independent-forum-keynote-speaker-diversity-inclusion-1202192699/* (accessed 10 May 2020).

12. S. Freud, 'The Uncanny', in V. B. Leitch *et al.* (eds), *Norton Anthology of Theory and Criticism* (New York: W. W. Norton & Company, 2001), pp. 929–52.

13. Guerrero, 'A Circus of Dreams and Lies', p. 331.

14. Catherine A. Luther, Carolyn Ringer Lepre and Naeemah Clark, *Diversity in U.S. Mass Media* (Hoboken NJ: Wiley-Blackwell, 2017), p. 53.

15. Luther, Lepre and Clark, *Diversity in U.S. Mass Media*, p. 53.

16. On colonial mimicry, see Frantz Fanon, *Black Skin, White Masks* (New York: Grove Press, Inc, 1967).

17. See R. Ugwu, 'The Hashtag that Changed the Oscars: An Oral History', *New York Times* (11 February 2020), *www.nytimes.com/2020/02/06/movies/oscars-sowhite-history.html* (accessed 14 May 2020).

18. So as not to suggest the film's success was entirely the result of a metajoke at white film critic's expense, it is worth noting that *Get Out* dominated the major award categories at the Black Reel Awards and the African American Film Critics Association Awards, while winning three of the major NAACP Image Awards.

19. *Box Office Mojo*, '*Get Out*', *www.boxofficemojo.com/release/rl256280065/* (accessed 15 May 2020).

20. See chapter 'Blumhouse at the Box Office, 2009–2018', this book.

21. *Meta Critic*, 'Critic Reviews for *Get Out*', *www.metacritic.com/movie/get-out/critic-reviews* (accessed 15 May 2020).

22. See, *Wikipedia*, 'List of Accolades received by *Get Out*', *https://en.wikipedia. org/wiki/List_of_accolades_received_by_Get_Out* (accessed 15 May 2020).

23. For a discussion of commodified authorship, see T. Corrigan, 'Auteurs and the New Hollywood', in J. Lewis (ed.), *The New American Cinema* (Durham NC: Duke University Press, 1999), pp. 38–63.

24. G. S. Edwards and S. Rushin, 'The Effect of President Trump's Election on Hate Crimes', *Social Science Research Network* (14 January 2018), *https:// papers.ssrn.com/sol3/papers.cfm?abstract_id=3102652* (accessed 12 May 2020).

25. G. Virtue, 'Is *Get Out* a Horror Film, a Comedy . . . or a Documentary?', *Guardian* (17 November 2017), *www.theguardian.com/film/filmblog/2017/ nov/17/get-out-golden-globes-race-horror-comedy-documentary-jordan-peele* (accessed 16 May 2020).

3

Haunted Bodies, Haunted Houses

Racheal Harris

HORROR FILMS ARE ALWAYS intimately linked to the culture and time in which they were made and, in many instances, the very basis for their appeal lies in the fact that they allow audiences to grapple with and overcome social or cultural ills, which in lived experience seem insurmountable or unsolvable.[1] This is equally as true of older films as it is of new. In engaging with a specific film or franchise, audiences may note that the subgenre into which it falls is also invariably recognisable as having been deeply influenced by the social psyche and fears of a specific era. This does not necessarily change how scary a film is for an audience at any given time or place, though *why* the film is considered scary may shift to mirror the social concerns and subconscious terrors of differing audiences and the cultural milieu in which they find themselves. As such, debates around canon films will frequently focus on alternating themes and characters in their discussion of what even makes a film canon or 'classic' among the horror-film audience. The fears or malaise of the past, it seems, are always in a state of flux, a process of metamorphosis that invokes terror in the present. Turning to the films of the past with a critical eye then, we can learn a great deal about the communal history of fear, and of the impact of world events and social upheaval on our engagement with the horrific, supernatural or sublime. In undertaking such an assessment, we will also perhaps see a direct link between the past and the present, perhaps even an echo towards the future.

Since its inception in 2000, Blumhouse Productions has not only become a powerhouse within the horror-film market broadly, but has focused to address the specific desires of a niche market of the horror genre in its re-imagining of the haunted-house and possession film. It has achieved this by distinctively merging the traditional haunted-house narrative with the idea of possession, creating a subgenre of film in which the haunted home transitions from a literal bricks-and-mortar structure to the human body. For audiences, this is not only a twist of one of horror's cornerstone tropes, but a new avenue through which they might investigate many of the cultural and liminal fears that prompt them to engage with the horror genre in the first place. Films such as *Paranormal Activity* (2009), *Paranormal Activity 2* (2010), *Insidious* (2011), *Paranormal Activity 3* (2011), *Sinister* (2012), *Insidious: Chapter 2* (2013), *Ouija* (2014), *Sinister II* (2015), *Ouija: Origin of Evil* (2016), *Amityville: The Awakening* (2017) and *Insidious: The Last Key* (2018) have all been released by Blumhouse in the past two decades. Each film deals explicitly with this theme and, to some degree, has been important to the metamorphosis of this genre of horror film. The relationship between hearth and home that takes place within these narratives is not only one of horror, but a reflection on a range of social ideas and phobias pertaining to the body and its appearance in present-day society. This chapter looks to these examples with an eye towards how traditional ideas, such as gender and the family, are present. It examines how the films pay tribute to some traditional horror concepts, while reinvigorating others.

Before discussing the metamorphosis of the current breed of haunted-house/possession film, it is imperative to consider the role of haunting and possession narratives within the horror genre historically. Examples of titles that we can look to as canon include *The Haunting* (1963 and 1999), *The Exorcist* (1973), *The Amityville Horror* (1979) and *Poltergeist* (1982). Throughout the late 1970s and particularly into the early 1980s, the focal point of the haunted-house narrative was the comment that they made on economic insecurity and the frailty of the domestic setting. As Douglas Kellner argues, franchise films such as *Poltergeist* and *Poltergeist II* (1986) were each a comment on the crisis of the working class and the destruction of the American Dream.[2] In the second film in particular, this narrative extends beyond the bricks-and-mortar structure to focus on the role of the father (the breadwinner and therefore the financial foundation of the home) and his inability to provide financial stability and protection for his wife and children.[3] Although his choice of family over wealth is seen as a triumphant moment at the conclusion of the first film, the sequel makes it apparent that families cannot flourish purely on love and devotion. The precarity and perceived failure of the father's ability to financially provide or secure a home becomes the avenue through which evil is again able to lay siege against them. What each has in common is a narrative that begins with a series of disturbances, suggesting an apparent haunting within the family dwelling. Growing in frequency and violence over time, it is revealed that a possessing entity of some description is responsible, the power of which is strong enough that it threatens to possess the human body of one of the homes' inhabitants. The ensuing battle over the site of home, and ownership of the body, then becomes the focus of the unease and fear that the narrative compels in its audience. After all, when we think about the places where we feel most safe, and over which we are most protective, the home in which we dwell and the body that sustains us are the most sacrosanct.

Horror has a history of treating the physical body as something outside culture.[4] In taking over the physical form in the confrontational and often visceral way that it does, the haunted/possession horror speaks to an innate fear of loss over the functions of our own body, of our own selves. It is specifically this idea of self as something that is contained within the body, more so than the home, that makes the merging of these two themes fascinating and horrific. For instance, in the case of *The Haunting*, it is the whispering voices of a cacophony of spirits, rather than a singular force, which lead to Eleanor's emotional and spiritual decline. Although hers is not a physical possession, her loss of autonomy, along with the response patterns of those around her, have much in common with more traditional possession stories. I count the film as a type of possession narrative specifically because, as audience members, we are terrified over Eleanor's dislocation from all that she knows and understands about herself. Although the symptoms of her torment commence within the home that she is visiting, over time they invade and transform her psyche and the relationship that she shares with her physical self. To question one's own sanity or to lose trust in the body in which we dwell is a timeless fear that appeals to many on a very deep, often spiritual, level.

Carol J. Clover suggests that all horror is representative of the evolution of the audience and responds explicitly to the needs, interests or (hidden) desires of that audience.[5] A sense of fear is among the primary reasons why audiences persistently engage with the horror film. While some researchers have questioned the validity of this fear, its authenticity and the relationship that it shares (if any) with the primal 'fight or flight' response, audiences show no concern over such trivial matters.[6] This complements Dumas' argument, who, discussing a similar theme from a Freudian viewpoint, concludes that we do not go to horror films in order to be afraid, but because they appeal to interests and behaviours that are inherently fascinating to us. He suggests that these are distinct forms of dark and morbid desire, which, most of us, would never have the will or the moral shortcomings to carry out in real life.[7] Over time, it has become necessary for filmmakers to investigate new methods for storytelling and what has become evident is that the delivery of the haunted-home/possession narrative has undergone a subtle but constant transformation. Specifically, the setting for the haunting is now increasingly turning away from the domestic or bricks-and-mortar dwelling, to embrace the setting of the human body as home.

Within the genre itself, there are a range of thematic tropes that appear time and again. Each one has a different relationship to the fear and fascination that it commands of its audience. As such, we might conclude that it is precisely because the genre has such firmly established narrative cues, which leave little if any room for unpredictable twists and turns to enter the narrative, that it maintains its foothold within contemporary popular culture. In the opinion of James B. Twitchell, whose work informed Clover's,[8] this is the precise reason why the genre is so well-recognised for long-running franchises such as *A Nightmare on Elm Street*, *Halloween* and *Friday the 13th*, which are also considered some of the most popular franchises to come from contemporary horror.[9] It suggests that audiences are not particularly interested in anything 'new'. Instead, the constant repetition of a specific type of death (often in a succinct and formulaic order among characters) makes the horror film attractive. As the following sections of this chapter will discuss, this is equally true of the haunted/possession horror. Although it may examine new ways to challenge traditional ideas of home and self, as we shall see, it continues to engage with 'old' issues related to family, gender and childhood, issues that have long been the staple elements of the subgenre.

One complaint that could be levelled against the argument that horror reflects the concerns of its audience might be that contemporary viewers are progressively less involved with organised religion (and may even be antagonistic towards it) and, thus, horror narratives motivated by religious possession are out of step with the demands of current popular culture. Instead, I suggest that it is because audiences are falling away from organised religious beliefs that religion, specifically some of its more obscure concepts, are becoming more attractive. As for possession, a diabolical spirit need not represent fear of the devil or damnation in an audience member. Rather, what it indicates is a loss of autonomy, a loss of power. These are primary, instinctual fears – and they will never go out of fashion. Religion helps audiences cope with the horror that possession films instil in them, while horror confronts helplessness in the face of a force much bigger and older than humankind.[10] Religion-based horror, as with horror that draws on religious iconography in the discussion and treatment of haunting and exorcism, does not necessitate that audiences have a specific faith belief. It is often more effective when specific church dogmas retain their air of mystery, as it makes the audience question whether the events unfolding might, perhaps, be possible.

Although the physical aspects of the haunting/possession film transition from home to body, in each example the physical dwelling remains the geographical locus of the action, a physical focal point for the events that cause psychological horror and upset to both characters and audiences. In some instances, the structures become characters themselves. This is especially true of *The Amityville Horror*, where the property at 112 Ocean Avenue has left a far more enduring legacy than any individual character from the films. Owing to the visually arresting presence of the home, another commonality to haunted-home narratives and possession films has been that the protagonist is generally trapped there. This may be owing to a relatively remote location (such as *The Haunting* or *The Amityville Horror*) or because to leave would be to endanger a member of their family or group. In either case, the geographical isolation reflects the psychological isolation soon to be experienced by the victim, while melding the identity of the home and the body together. In many cases, much of how we see ourselves is measured against where we live; as such, it is important to link the home (a physical representation of status and personality) with the self. To do so makes the act of possession more terrifying, as the possessing forces shatter the identity on more than just a bodily level.

For audiences, a remote locale will also act as a cue, alerting them to the fact that social and emotional isolation will follow. This remains a significant part of the subgenre, although the significance of the foreshadowing has changed. For instance, contemporary society is lived largely free of isolation, with the online world allowing us access to the never-ending sphere of the cyber community. What this is has done is heighten anxiety around being 'cut off' – geographically or technologically – from the world around us. It is interesting that, while characters within the haunted-home/haunted-body film will turn to the online world for assistance in tracing the cause of paranormal disturbance, their online identities rarely figure in the plot in a meaningful way. This can be read as a comment on the idea that despite increasingly living in the online world, audiences remain anxious for human connection. Alternatively, we can view this as compounding the sense of identity construction discussed above. If the home is a physical extension of the inner self, then the online persona should be seen in a similar way. To corrupt, remove or distance the individual from this to truly to isolate them on all fronts, dislocating them from the very creature comforts that make them feel the most connected to the world.

When we consider the purpose of a specific location within the home it is also apparent that the geography of disturbance is indicative of inter-familial tensions or relationship discord. These manifestations precipitate the haunting and possession of the body to come. They may even be a conduit between place and the space occupied by the human body. For example, the attic and basement share equally detailed histories as prime places for haunting and possession. In all the examples discussed within this chapter, the initial disturbances within the home take place here. It is these spaces that the audience then equates as the entry point of the 'entity'. They are hence the haunted rooms, with their status as storage spaces ensuring that the gathering energy of the nefarious entity is not immediately evident to family members. Like the emotional and spiritual problems that we are disinclined to address, the attic and the basement are rooms in which we hide things that we would prefer to avoid. In most cases, emotional conflict between the physical bodies within the dwelling acts as an additional distraction, while also feeding the power of the entity.

Considering the religious themes that are common to the possession narrative, it is perhaps unsurprising that in most instances the initial interaction between the living and the haunting entity takes place from above, usually the attic. For instance, both *The Changeling* (1980) and *Hellraiser* (1987) use the attic as a conduit between realms and it is here that the object of the haunting/possession makes contact with the supernatural realm. Similarly, comedic and dramatic horror variants, such as *Beetlejuice* (1987) and *The Skeleton Key* (2005), employ the use of the attic as a place where spirits dwell. From here, spirits can transcend into the living world, while also communing with the energy of the afterlife. As Cleaver Patterson highlights, the attic, while once a place of safety and comfort, has become in the modern home the storage space for that which should be hidden from the world.[11] In much the same way, religious beliefs in general, but specifically those that deal with the topic of possession, have become a point of contention in much modern-day belief, with any ritual or ceremony related to them hidden from the minds and thoughts of adherents.

As seen in *Sinister* and *Ouija*, it is the attic that produces both the box or Super 8 film and the Ouija board that become the doorway though which the entity enters the home and eventually the body. Both examples depict the room as a forgotten storage space. *Ouija* specifically describes it as a junk space, which Debbie is cleaning when she rediscovers the Ouija board from her childhood. In breaking the primary rule of the game (not to play alone), Debbie is soon tormented by the restless spirt of Doris. Upon investigating her death, it is in the attic where Laine also encounters the spirit of Doris and her mother. The manhole that leads from the attic into the home is located in Debbie's bedroom and we see Laine fall through this space (transitioning from the forgotten to the familiar) after being scared by the image of Doris. After this encounter, Doris is more actively present within the home, giving the audience the sense that Laine has pulled the negative energy from the hidden recesses of the home out into the open. Here, it will run amok.

In the case of *Insidious*, it is in the attic where Dalton falls from the ladder after being scared by a spectral vision entering the living realm. The interaction precipitates his vanishing into the astral plane, which leaves his body open to possession. As they cannot enter the human shell immediately, in this case, spirits of the dead begin to enter the home. Again, a fall in the attic creates an entry point to the rest of the home. This results in the destruction of the sense of safety felt by other family members, fracturing the parental relationship. Even though the family attempt to move dwellings, because it is the body that is haunted, the spirits are brought forth into the new setting. In *Insidious: The Last Key*, audiences witness Elise, entering the attic (in the form of a traveller) through a door from The Further. Here, she witnesses Dalton and becomes aware that she will soon need to engage with the family to save him. That Elise witnesses the event in the attic rather than any other room, and is herself in astral form, enhances the idea that the spirit realm exists above, in a forgotten space.

Although the physical possession in *Paranormal Activity 2* takes place in the basement, it is the attic (or crawl space) that again functions as the site of communion between the spiritual (or forgotten) supernatural realm and the living world. After a violent encounter with the demonic entity, it is here (in the first film) that Micah locates the photograph of Katie that, as the second film later demonstrates, has been used in the transference ritual that shifts the possession from one sister to the other. This ritual, enacted by Katie's brother-in-law, Daniel, is one hidden from the family.

The only exception to this rule comes from *Amityville: The Awakening*. Based on an existing franchise, and the real-life murders that inspired them, the possession takes place in the basement. It is here, under the earth and the structure, where the restless entities dwell. As they pervade the home and body from beneath, what they symbolise in this instance is the destruction of the family unit from its foundation. In many versions of the Amityville tale, the attic is the scene for the gruesome murder of a small child. This act in itself seems particularly godless, highlighting that while it might be the closest point in the home to Heaven, it is often the furthest from God.

Haunted Bodies and the Nuclear Family

The 'nostalgic' nuclear family of the 1950s no longer exists, while the concept of family itself has ceased to be synonymous with the idea of an emotional or physical safe haven. This is not a new concept within the horror genre, as several films of the 1980s highlight by drawing on ideas related specifically to the untrustworthiness of parents and to the questioning of adult authority. In these examples, the protagonist of the plot (usually a teenager) is left with no one to count on except their friendship group.[12] It is in overcoming trauma and attack together that the group are bonded into relationships that are often more relevant or meaningful to the protagonist (and viewer) than the fractured family unit. In a way that mirrors the transition from adolescence into adult life, friends and partners come to function as a surrogate family. In contemporary horror however, we might go so far as to say that not only family, but also peer groups and partners are of little use to the protagonist's struggle. This is particularly true of films in which haunting and possession are the focal point. Unlike their predecessors, what horror films, particularly those with the spiritual influence evident in most possession narratives, are increasingly revealing is that we are ultimately alone in the dark.[13] For instance, in the case of *Ouija*, although it is a group of friends who accidentally summon Doris (thus engaging with the possessing entity as a collective), once her demonic spirit has been brought forth, they are powerless to help each other escape its clutches. Each must confront her in their own battle, which takes place away from the group, often with fatal consequences.

Similarly, in the first three films of the *Paranormal Activity* franchise (which focus on relationships within the familial home), as well as both *Sinister* and *Ouija: Origin of Evil*, although members of the family unit are aware that something is amiss within the home, by the time they discover the truth it is impossible to render assistance to the victim. For *Paranormal Activity*'s Micah and Katie, the love and protectiveness that Micah displays are hopeless in his efforts to rid Katie (or the home) of the intrusive entity. Similarly, in *Ouija: Origin of Evil*, Mrs Zander (Elizabeth Reaser) cannot see past the 'gifts' that Doris's possession gives her, even when it becomes apparent that her daughter's soul has been consumed by an ungodly force. At that point, the maternal love that she feels for Doris is similarly useless in subverting her daughter's physical and spiritual destruction.

Just as parents were either absent or untrustworthy in films of the 1980s, fathers are traditionally troubled characters in Blumhouse horrors, with distraction or wilful ignorance of the family patriarch frequently leading to the decline of the larger family unit. In *Sinister*, Ellison is distracted by the narcissistic endeavour to reclaim past fame as an author. As Bernice Murphy argues, this preoccupation sets the scene for the impending possession and destruction of the family unit, while also speaking to the economic anxiety existing in American society.[14] Finding a box of Super 8 films in his attic, Ellison is enticed into watching them because of their seemingly idyllic titles. Named 'yard work', 'BBQ' and 'pool party', among other innocuous things, what each name suggests is the type of wholesome family activity traditionally associated with the domestic space. Upon watching the home movies, however, it becomes quickly apparent that the films capture anything but traditional family activities. Witnessing the fracture and subsequent decimation of the family in these movies is what begins the mental and physical fracturing of Ellison's own family, albeit in ways that he refuses to see.[15] Over the course of the film, his role as patriarch is further thrown into question, as his self-interest places the safety of his family into continued jeopardy. The viewer gets the sense that Ellison has long been the absent father, an idea confirmed during a vitriolic exchange between husband and wife, in which she accuses him of being in the home physically but not engaging on an emotional or mental level with his family. It is this absence that will ultimately leave them open to destruction. Kimberly Jackson discusses Ellison's role in *Sinister* as being metaphorical of the 'challenge to the patriarchal order' that has taken place throughout western culture since the first wave of 1960s feminism,[16] a theme also evident in the first two *Insidious* films. As the following section of this chapter will discuss, this ties in closely with Clover's assertion that most possession narratives are, at their heart, the story of manhood in crisis.[17] Unlike older examples, however, what is becoming increasingly apparent is that it is not the figure of the wife/mother or lover who is the object of the possession, but the child. While diabolical children will also be discussed at a later stage in this chapter, in this instance it is important to highlight that the child suffers for the ignorance of the parent more often than a spouse.

In another particularly telling scene in *Sinister*, Ellison's daughter Ashley takes him his morning coffee. For her, this is an act of care and pride. Distracted by the phone call that he is on, however, he slams the door in her face, without acknowledging her at all. It is precisely this sort of thoughtlessness that causes a relationship rift that ultimately allows for the possession of the child. For audiences, it mirrors the sense of guilt that many feel about the demands of work and the division of time within their own families. For others, it is perhaps a difficult reminder of their own upbringing. Although we are not possessed in the same way that Ashley becomes possessed, the anger and disappointment she feels, the growing bitterness from being overlooked and made to feel unimportant are certainly aspects of teen and adolescent life that form unpleasant memories for many of us.[18]

Sinister II presents a similarly difficult view of the family patriarch. Whereas Hawke's father was self-interested and emotionally absent, in this example the father is brutally abusive to both his wife and children. The effect of this is that the audience fails to feel any empathy towards him. In a side plot, the mother, Courtney, develops feelings for Ex-Deputy So & So, who is now investigating the death of Ellison's family (which concluded the first film). This consumes much of the narrative, placing both family unit and the son's possession in the background. In a sense, it is indicative of the idea of the crumbling or fractured family unit, but it also highlights the issue of parental preoccupation, although through the lens of the female-gendered parent. The abused wife represents the issue of domestic violence that continues to be endemic in society. As the victim, her focus is removed from nurturing and turned to protection of the children, something that they cannot understand. The entry of another male further complicates this dynamic, as the mother wrestles with her romantic feelings. From the perspective of her sons, this man is an interloper within the home, challenging the status of the existing male parent. Although he attempts to assume the role of surrogate father (thus putting the established order back to rights), Ex-Deputy So & So is too late to prevent the possession of the son, just as he was too late to prevent the violent outbursts of the father, which are the cause of the rupture within the family to begin with. This only confirms the deeply fractured state of the nuclear family today. In this instance, fear is not derived from emotional neglect or absence, but from the overpowering presence of the violent adult. As the audience views the violence within the home, particularly at the dinner table, the same sense of powerlessness and loss of control that pervades the possession horror is evident.

Haunted Bodies and Gender

Unlike other horror subgenres, haunted-body/possession narratives feature both men and women in lead roles – although their motivations for doing so often differs. For instance, the use of a male protagonist is frequently a comment on maleness and masculinity in crisis.[19] This is frequently evident in family-centred films through the patriarchal figure. Interestingly, in these cases, the male will, traditionally, not actually be the victim of the possession, his role instead hinges on the relationship that he shares with a possessed female counterpart. Throughout the plot, it thus becomes the role of the male to save the female from her demons (figurative and literal) but also to rediscover himself in the process.[20] Gender dynamics between men and women in this setting can also be read as a symbol of masculinity under threat from uncontrollable female agency (as in *Paranormal Activity* when all of Micah's efforts are useless in saving Katie, so much so that she actually berates him for this), or as a comment on the lack of male dominance (as in the case of *Sinister* or *Insidious*, where the father of the house is constantly jostling for authority with his wife). In both examples, the male persona struggles with a specific element of his female counterpart. Her possession is both symptomatic of the discord in their union, and a punishment for her challenge to some element of his personality. Were he able to save her, traditional gender constructs would be restored, with the husband/father/boyfriend reclaiming his identity as head of the family – although that is rarely the outcome in modern horror cinema. Returning to *Paranormal Activity*, it is clear that Micah is both the owner of the home in which he and Katie live and the primary breadwinner. During her possession, he loses control of his dominant position within the partnership, causing friction between them as she steadily falls under the influence of the entity. The entrance of another male (the medium) is viewed as a direct challenge to his authority and Micah resists his advice. As Katie also tries to warn him against antagonising the entity (through the use of a Ouija board and the video camera), he refuses to heed her advice. This will ultimately lead both to his death and to Katie's.

Similarly, in *Insidious*, Josh is threatened by the appearance of a priest in his home and berates Renai for looking outside the family for assistance. Unlike the scenario between Micah and Katie, the intervention of Josh's mother, Lorraine, leads to the engagement of the less-threatening female medium. Although Josh initially resists her presence, too, he comes to accept her help after receiving a signal from Dalton. It is the voice of the oldest male child that trumps that of the wife and the expert, but this is perhaps also symptomatic of Josh's feelings of castration by the domineering females in his life. As the plot of the second film details, Josh is removed of the authority to 'astral project' because his mother engages Elise to hypnotise him during adolescence, rendering him unable to travel or to remember that he once had the ability to do so. While she has acted for his own good, in both cases the actions of the mother in these films can be viewed as a form of mental castration. In the case of Josh, as his latent abilities begin to reassert themselves in his adult life, his lack of authority and the challenges that Renai, his mother and Elise pose to his masculinity also reassert themselves with incredible dominance and, in the case of Elise, fatal consequences. Still, it is only through the intervention of Elise (and her reversal of his initial hypnosis) that Josh is able to save his son (and, in the second film, himself), but without engaging the services a female to do this, he is unable to reassert his role as the undisputed head of the family. This leaves him in a catch-22 situation, in which he resents Renai and his mother for challenging his inherent masculinity, but without whom he is unable to fulfil his role as father and family patriarch.[21]

Finally, in *Sinister*, Professor Jonas is Ellison's intellectual superior, but the fact that he is removed from the location of the haunting allows their relationship to appear equal. Although both men are clearly successful, Jonas is the more intelligent of the pair, but his appearance over videocall removes the challenge seen in the above examples by the entrance of another man into the home. Similarly, only Ellison and Jonas communicate with each other, there is no female involvement in their meeting. Ultimately, it is the assistance of the Sheriff's deputy that is the intervention that is important. When Ellison rejects the calls of Deputy So & So, it delays his discovery of Bughuul's continued presence within the home, which in turn leads to his destruction and that of his family.

Comparatively, the use of a woman in the lead role can be read as a (usually negative) comment on the female psyche, or the female body as the inverted, alien other.[22] There are two threads of Clover's discussion on possession horror that are important to revisit. The first being that there has been an abundance of new styles or narratives that have entered the canon since her book was published, not least being 'found footage' (invoked in all the *Paranormal Activity* films), along with the fact that gender roles and identity have also undergone a radical shift throughout most of western society. It is not only male characters who have issues with gender and sexuality in the horror film of course. In many cases, women fulfil the role of the psychic medium or spiritual doorway. As much criticism of the genre has highlighted, this is problematic for the comment that it makes on the idea of women being spiritually compromised in comparison to their male counterparts.[23] Such thinking seems to support patriarchal ideas of the female body as 'monstrous' and more vulnerable to possession (often in the form of demonic penetration) than their male counterparts. Indeed, women are equally depicted as being morally, spiritually and physically compromised, perhaps never more so than in the possession film. Traditionally, we might see this at its most evident when it is the woman who has become the object of a haunting. In much the same way as an evil entity will infest and corrupt a home, slowly unpicking the seams of the family unit, the haunting of the mother figure unavoidably leads to the same outcome. In this aspect, one of the most interesting examples among Blumhouse films is *Amityville: The Awakening*.

Although it adopts many of the same themes as the original group of films that take on the Amityville home and the story of its possession, I classify this as an attempted reboot of the franchise for the fact that it removes itself from an association with the Lutz family. There is still a connection to the DeFeo family, and it is through this that the possessing entity of the original films is able to integrate into the home and the body of an ailing child once more. In this instance, the child is a young adult son, James, who has been left in a vegetative state following an accident. The discord within the home lies in the fact that it was while trying to protect the moral integrity of his sister Belle, who had been the victim of revenge porn from an ex-boyfriend, that this incident took place. In this sense, the narrative invokes the concept of the 'good child/bad child', in which the injured child (the son) was favoured over his twin (the daughter). That it was his life that was ruined despite his moral goodness is a fact that becomes intolerable to the mother, causing the breakdown of her marriage and incredible friction between her and the other children (there is also a younger daughter in the narrative).

In this case, the domineering and evil feminine are seen in the relationship that develops between mother and son. It is the mother who is the force behind her son being kept alive by machine, even when his body is failing, and it is the mother who is the witness to his gradual (and miraculous) recovery. This is a consequence of the possession that she refuses to see (in much the same way as Doris's possession is ignored in *Ouija: Origin of Evil*). As the body of her son recovers and he begins to show more positive signs of life, a sexual interaction takes place between the two. This idea of incest remains among the ultimate taboos and becomes the primary motivator for her son's revenge once the possessing entity has restored him to health.

It is important to recall that all Amityville films link to the real history of the dwelling. Unlike the true story of the DeFeo home, the absence of the father in *Amityville: The Awakening* leaves the mother as the central point of the castration narrative. Not only is it she who has mollycoddled her son, denying him the nobility of his sacrificial death, in her sexual engagement with his vegetative body, she victimises him, highlighting the removal of his autonomous and masculine identity. It is hardly surprising that her death is the most confrontational of the film.

The monstrous feminine and the abusive mother also recall *Insidious: Chapter 2*, in which Parker Crane's mother forces him to live as a female before encouraging him, in his adulthood, to kill young brides. In much the same way as *Insidious: Chapter 2*, the audience is left wondering whether the complete absence of the paternal figure is linked directly with a predisposition towards abuse of the male child. In these instances, the possessed becomes the direct product of nurture, not nature.

Haunted Bodies and the Terrible Child

Where the haunted body belongs to an adult, audiences are suitably terrified by the destruction that the possessing entity deems fit to heap onto the victim. When the body belongs to a child, however, there is an added element of terror or the uncanny – and this has become a staple motif of contemporary horror cinema, particularly in haunting or possession narratives. Jessica Balanzategui's study covers this angle from a range of perspectives and, like Clover's work before her, a large portion of the discussion around the possessed body considers the role of the child.[24] Whereas Clover is concerned with *The Exorcist* and *Poltergeist* (the dominant possession films of the time) and their female protagonists, Balanzategui's discussion looks largely at male children in films such as *The Shining* (1980) and *The Changeling* (1980). In both examples, the age and suggested innocence of the child compose a significant part of the films' sickening qualities, specifically because the idea of diabolical possession is such an invasive, visceral process. What we have seen in more recent haunted-body films, however, is confirmation that children are not out of bounds for the demonic. In fact, they are often employed as agents of evil in horrors narrative where gender plays even less of a pivotal role.

While uncanny children are present, to varying degrees, in all the films under discussion, I look at the role of sibling bonds and the feminine as they appear in Blumhouse films. This theme is present in both *Ouija* and *Ouija: Origin of Evil*, albeit in different characters. Similarly, sisterly bonds and the transference of the possession entity from one vessel to another is at the core of the first three *Paranormal Activity* films. Finally, *Sinister* considers the role of the terrible child in its depiction of the neglected daughter, whose strained relationship with an emotionally absent father has starkly different consequences from the fractured father/son relationship discussed above.

In the first of the *Ouija* films, absent parents play a major role in the infestation narrative. So too, the physically absent mother and the emotionally absent father are a point of contention between sisters Laine and Sarah, with Laine, the older of the two, feeling responsible for the policing of her younger sister's bad behaviour. This dynamic becomes a mirror of the relationship between the sisters in the second film (a prequel). We are introduced to Paulina Zander (the older of these two siblings) towards the end of *Ouija*, when she is visited in an asylum by Laine. Whereas the first film uses the sibling bond as a source for the triumph of good over evil (which is also present in *Amityville: The Awakening*), in the second film, however, it is the strength of sisterly love that becomes a conduit for the persistent presence of the possessing entity in the living realm. As the final scene of that film demonstrates, through the use of the Ouija board, the sisters (both now suffering from varying forms of possession) are able to keep in contact, with Doris returning in spirit to cause havoc within the walls of the hospital. The viewer is given little option other than to assume that this is at the behest of her living sibling.

Sisters working in league with and against each other is a theme also evident in the *Paranormal Activity* franchise, which, like the *Ouija* films, delivers the narrative in reverse. The impact of this being that audiences know before going into the second and subsequent films, that the lead characters have already died. Whereas the first two *Paranormal Activity* films show Katie and Kristi as adult women, the third shows their childhood. As the older sibling, Katie (like Paulina Zander) becomes aware that something has attached itself to Kristi, yet she is unable to do anything to prevent the slow decline of her sister. Unlike *Amityville: The Awakening*, there is no opportunity for sibling love to overcome the demonic power, as in the case of the sisterhood narratives, the older of the two sisters will kill her younger sibling. This is not the end of their torment of course, as in both films the possessing spirits remain either in possession of the older sibling (Katie) or tormenting her until she goes insane (Paulina).

The fact that their fate has already been sealed puts them in a backseat compared to the exploration of how the demonic entity infiltrates and infests the home and multiple members of a family line. This is where the true horror of the narrative lives. As a nameless, formless entity, the demonic presence does not exist explicitly within the narrative world of this franchise, in fact, it bears many similarities to demonic entities that are present in other films (including productions by the same studio). Further, the relationship that the possession shares with the superstition of biblical belief is integral to audience perception. Regardless of individual religious ideologies or adherence within a specific faith community, most audiences have grown up in a culture that is drenched to the core in religious mythology, iconography and dogma. It is difficult to draw the line between what is possible and what is not. Linking the demonic form (no matter how tenuously) to recognisable religious tradition empowers the entity within the film to come to life. When the primary characters are two-dimensional, it does not take a big narrative leap to place ourselves into the story – or the demonic creature into our living world.

Conclusion

Blumhouse continues to be at the forefront of horror movie production, with several successful film franchises to its name, many of which continue to produce sequels. What this chapter has outlined are some of the ways in which the haunted house and haunted body has been used within modern horror as a means of commenting not only on the crumbling state of the nuclear family, but on the shifting definitions of gender and their associated gender roles. In large part, it has done this by considering the link that these concepts share with religious belief and the contemporary turn from religious rigidity towards a spiritually fluid society. It is at the nexus of these points where viewers feel a profound uncertainty and tension, which translates readily from the real world to the screen. It has been suggested that much of what modern audiences find horrific about the haunted or possessed body in horror films, is the lingering sense of possibility that many of these films promote. One need not believe in hell or the Devil to become an object of possession by his minions and, once the body's physical realm becomes haunted by an external entity, there is usually little that can be done to escape. Such a sense of isolation and powerlessness is one with which we are all infinitely familiar. It is this sense of unease that lingers long after the film's final credits have rolled.

Notes

1. Bruce F. Kawin, *Horror and the Horror Film* (London: Anthem Press, 2012), p. 16.
2. D. Kellner, 'Poltergeists, Gender, and Class in the Age of Reagan and Bush', in D. E. James and R. Berg (eds), *The Hidden Foundation: Cinema and the Question of Class* (Minneapolis MN: University of Minnesota Press, 1996), pp. 218–9.
3. Kellner, 'Poltergeists, Gender, and Class in the Age of Reagan and Bush', p. 232.
4. Catherine Driscoll, *Teen Film: A Critical Introduction* (New York: Berg, 2011), p. 95.
5. Carol J. Clover, *Men, Women, and Chainsaws: Gender in the Modern Horror Film* (Princeton NJ: Princeton University Press, 2015), p. 11.
6. A. Smuts, 'Cognitive and Philosophical Approaches to Horror', in H. M. Benshoff (ed.), *A Companion to the Horror Film* (London: Wiley-Blackwell, 2014), p. 11.

7. C. Dumas, 'Horror and Psychoanalysis: A Primer', in Benshoff, *A Companion to the Horror Film*, pp. 23–5.
8. Clover, *Men, Women, and Chainsaws*, p. 11.
9. Wheeler Winston Dixon, *A History of Horror* (New Brunswick NJ: Rutgers University Press, 2010), p. 125.
10. Jason Zinoman, *Shock Value: How a Few Eccentric Outsiders Gave Us Nightmares, Conquered Hollywood, and Invented Modern Horror* (London: Penguin Books, 2012), p. 92.
11. Cleaver Patterson, *Don't Go Upstairs! A Room-by-Room Tour of the House in Horror Movies* (Jefferson NC: McFarland, 2020), p. 145.
12. T. S. Kord, *Little Horrors: How Cinema's Evil Children Play on Our Guilt* (Jefferson NC: McFarland, 2016), pp. 52–4.
13. See Clover, *Men, Women, and Chainsaws*, p. 67.
14. B. M. Murphy, '"It's Not the House That's Haunted": Demons, Debt, and the Family in Peril Formula in Recent Horror Cinema', in M. Leeder (ed.), *Cinematic Ghosts: Haunting and Spectrality from Silent Cinema to the Digital Era* (New York: Bloomsbury, 2015), pp. 240–1.
15. Kimberly Jackson, *Gender and the Nuclear Family in Twenty-First-Century Horror* (New York: Palgrave Macmillan, 2016), p. 104.
16. Jackson, *Gender and the Nuclear Family*, p. 102.
17. Clover, *Men, Women, and Chainsaws*, p. 65.
18. This concept is discussed at length in Kord's book, *Little Horrors*. Sinister features extensively in the text, along with a range of other contemporary horror titles, not limited to the haunting/possession subgenre.
19. Jackson, *Gender and the Nuclear Family*, pp. 101–2.
20. Clover, *Men, Women, and Chainsaws*, pp. 107–8.
21. Jackson, *Gender and the Nuclear Family*, p. 66.
22. Clover, *Men, Women, and Chainsaws*, p. 107.
23. Clover, *Men, Women, and Chainsaws*, pp. 73–4.
24. Jessica Balanzategui, *The Uncanny Child in Transnational Cinema: Ghosts of Futurity at the Turn of the Twenty-First Century* (Amsterdam: Amsterdam University Press, 2018).

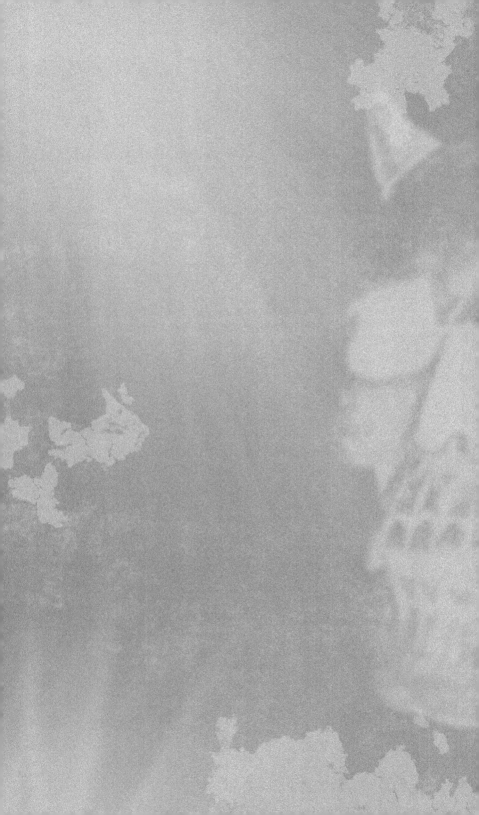

4

Gothixity

Evoking the Gothic through New Forms of Toxic Masculinity

Fernando Gabriel Pagnoni Berns

PARANORMAL ACTIVITY (2009) is considered to be the film that launched Blumhouse as the new 'house of horror'. Blumhouse produced movies before this film, but it was the story of a young couple who, after moving into a suburban home, become increasingly disturbed by nightly demonic interventions that put the studio on the global map. The film contains many blueprints of things to come: intimate dramas taking place in urban and suburban areas; the supernatural intruding into the domestic space; and the small budget and emphasis on subtle horror rather than spectacle. One of the less discussed trademarks that was already present in *Paranormal Activity*, is the union of toxic masculinity with a Gothic sensibility. Indeed, Blumhouse favours gendered horror, meaning films that illustrate, via a fantastic lens, gender issues.

Still, the presence of toxic masculinity goes further than the presence of the generic male killer in horror films. In many Blumhouse films, the toxic man is not the main villain. Sometimes, he is not a villain at all, as represented by Micah in *Paranormal Activity*. In the film, Katie begs her boyfriend Micah to stop fooling around with the camera and the Ouija board that he bought home to communicate with the demons that are slowly invading the family. According to Katie, Micah's attitude 'invites' the demon into the house, rather than helping her to get rid of the supernatural beings. Micah dismisses his girlfriend but, actually, *she is right*. The demon is following Katie, and it is Micah's incapacity to heed his girlfriend's warnings that welcomes the demon. Micah, however, cannot be defined as 'evil' since, by no means, is he trying to hurt Katie on purpose. It is his prerogative as the 'reasonable' (i.e., male) voice that brought horror to the household.

Accordingly, for this chapter, toxic masculinity is defined as 'the heart of the culture of popular misogyny' and 'involves a sense of entitlement in all realms of culture, economy, and social life'.[1] This kind of masculinity positions all things male as superior to all things female. It informs *Paranormal Activity*, but also frames other Blumhouse films such as *The Purge* (2013), *Sinister* (2012) and *The Gift* (2015), reaching its apex with the studio's latest efforts, the remake of *Black Christmas* (2019) and Leigh Whannell's *The Invisible Man* (2020). Regarding this latter film, Sara Stewart celebrated that 'this version of H.G. Wells' classic is fueled by toxic masculinity', finding the premise 'inspired'.[2] The new version of *Black Christmas*, in turn, has been lauded (even if the film suffered poor box office and negative reviews) as 'a modern manifesto against toxic masculinity'.[3]

The concept of 'toxic masculinity' is new and has been gaining predominance and analysis in only the past few years. These representations of the real-world phenomenon of toxic masculinity, however, are deeply embedded in the Gothic narrative from its inception. Traditional forms of the Gothic were sustained, in part, by the domineering structures of patriarchal oppression that imprison women,[4] mostly through the figure of a creepy, sadistic villain who desires to hunt down and punish young ladies[5] through forced marriage or imprisonment in the domestic space.

In the #MeToo era, these archetypal villains have shifted into more subtle, but still oppressive, forms of damaging masculinity that I call 'gothixity', a portmanteau linking 'Gothic' and 'masculine toxicity'. In the films mentioned above, men are exclusively responsible for letting the horrific enter their lives and the lives of their family and friends. Their refusal to accept warnings from women invites the horror in. Blumhouse critically engages with negative models of masculinity, but the studio does so by evoking the male roles of classic Gothic texts. Rather than villains, the oppressive masculine figures are the heroes or, at least, characters that cannot be defined simply as 'villains'. Blumhouse's ideological position is ambiguous as well. Some films explicitly condemn this kind of negative masculinity (*Black Christmas*, *The Invisible Man*) while others, such as *Paranormal Activity*, signal how social models of masculinity are so embedded into the cultural fabric that they are not even discussed as 'negative' even when they certainly are. In other words, audiences may read Micah as an irritating man and not as the modern counterpart of the classic Gothic figure of the oppressive, poisonous husband that silences his wife's voice. It is this obliterated link existing between toxic masculinity and the classical Gothic mode that I try to underline with my examination of many Blumhouse's films.

Gothixity

Although the term 'toxic masculinity' has become widely used in both academic and popular discourses, its definition is unclear. It has been used to describe 'the need to aggressively compete and dominate others and encompasses the most problematic proclivities in men'.[6] Toxic masculinity's definition is inextricably attached to the notion of 'hegemonic' masculinity. Rather than being 'natural', masculinity is a social and cultural construction that simply 'passes' for natural, obscuring the fact that gender is produced and reproduced through the social arena. In Western society, some masculinities are more favoured than others that are considered 'weak' or 'deviant'. Culturally dominant forms of masculinity are referred to as 'hegemonic masculinity', a term that positions masculinity through univocal characteristics passing for essential: aggressiveness, intelligence, sexual prowess and physical power, among others. Sentimentality, shyness or politeness are seen to 'feminise' men. For R. W. Connell, this form of hegemonic masculinity oppresses and suppresses (in themselves and in others) any behaviour that escapes the 'normal'.[7] Even if the concept has been 'historically and contextually mobile',[8] hegemonic masculinity 'refers to the most culturally exalted forms of masculinity configurations that justify dominance and inequality'[9] over women and deviant masculinities.

Toxic masculinity – an extremely negative derivation of hegemonic masculinity – rejects any opening to new, more nuanced experiences of being a man, leading to toxic effects on the lives of others: rape and domestic violence and abuse against women (including a sense of 'possession' of the female body), homophobic hostility and racism. Toxic masculinity lies at the foundation of domestic violence and femicide. Still, this form of masculinity does not necessarily involve murder and criminality. The pejorative gaze and the paternalist attitude towards women are common issues also sustained by toxic masculinity.

This form of being a male has ties with the gendered Gothic. The Gothic heroine was an exploration of female selfhood, as the inquisitive female gaze denied the passivity and domestic nature associated with the feminine. Trapped within the domestic space, the Gothic heroine actively searched for an escape. This entrapment, in turn, was forced by the figure of the hero and the villain, one and the other almost indistinguishable in traditional Gothic tales. In the Gothic mode, the domestic space 'has the power to unnerve, fragment, and even destroy its inhabitant',[10] a situation especially sensitive to women, the latter more attached to the domestic sphere.

The Gothic tale is, basically, the plot of the search of masculine control and the struggles of women to get free of it. The classical Gothic book's cover of a woman running away in the middle of the night, wearing just a see-through white dress, an ominous castle in the background, represents not the flight of women from supernatural occurrences but from male oppression. Like contemporary toxic masculinity, Gothic manliness means the emphasis on 'the system of patrilineal inheritance where the boy's passage into manhood involves the murderous repression of the feminine within himself',[11] forcing the man to act as 'macho' as possible to avoid any form of contagion with 'weaker', sensible forms of being male.

For the Gothic mode, 'what is particularly interesting about sensibility is its relationship to gender. Insofar as it has been seen as a democratising force (everyone has feelings), sensibility might be seen as a potential means of levelling the ground between men and women'.[12] Thus, it is interesting to note that *Paranormal Activity* is informed by two 'villains': a poltergeist attacking the couple (especially, Katie); and Micah, whose lack of sensibility is the real source of the invading horrors.

Paranormal Activity and Toxic Masculinity: Unhearing the Woman

Paranormal Activity begins with Micah addressing the fact that his girlfriend is haunted by a demon that has followed her since her childhood. Micah finds the story fascinating, so he mounts a camera in their bedroom to register any paranormal occurrences taking place at night.

Katie is not interested in being filmed and studied, not even by her boyfriend. It is clear that Micah bought the expensive camera without consulting her first, an issue that Katie brings up repeatedly in the film's first scenes ('How much this did cost you?'). Micah simply ignores her questions. Katie's discomfort increases when Micah uses the camera to film her from behind in the hope of spicing up their sex life. The camera is Micah's omnipresent, masculine point of view. Katie calls the machine 'big and impressive' and a 'giant-ass camera'. The camera becomes an extension of Micah's masculinity, a surrogate of his penis. When Micah shows the camera to Katie, he wants her to 'kiss the camera'; Katie is disgusted and quickly rejects the idea. She mentions that the 'really bright light' of the camera blinds her; thus, Katie has no voice (she tells the camera what Micah wants her to say) and, further, she is blinded. As such, Katie is depowered, an object to be studied, not the owner of the story.

Katie's fears, however, revolve around how useful the camera will be to stop the supernatural. Micah wants to have any supernatural occurrence captured on camera, and so he pushes Katie to accept this new status quo – having their lives constantly recorded. Since Micah manages the camera, he is also the narrator – a subtle form of control. He asks Katie to narrate for the camera all her past encounters with the poltergeists that have haunted her since childhood. Katie's discomfort is clear, but Micah insists. Curiously, when Katie brings in Dr Fredrichs (Mark Fredrichs), an expert on ghosts to help her, Micah (who, arguably, believes in Katie's allegations of being molested by a supernatural presence as his intention in recording the paranormal activity testifies) adopts a derisive, sarcastic attitude towards the man. He questions Katie: 'is the psychic gonna give me some stock tips while he's here? Haven't bet on the horses in a while.' He also mocks the psychic's punctuality. When the psychic finally arrives, Micah asks him if he can predict traffic jams, dismissing Katie's embarrassment. Micah's uneasiness stems from the fact that another man may be of greater help to Katie. Furthermore, Dr Fredrichs feels that the use of the camera could make things worse, with the entity feeding off the interest in its presence: 'these hauntings, they feed off of negative energy.' Micah quickly retorts with a bad joke: 'You shouldn't let your mother come over anymore.' Katie makes surreptitious gestures to Micah, asking him silently to stop mocking Dr Fredrichs. As the doctor is basically telling them that Micah's idea is bad, Micah must re-establish his 'macho' presence by mocking Dr Fredrichs's advice. The doctor gives Katie the name and telephone number of an expert in poltergeist activity. After the doctor leaves, Micah begs Katie to throw out the doctor's advice and call no one.

As in many toxic relationships, Katie reluctantly accepts, becoming complicit in a relationship that quickly degenerates. Indeed, the supernatural occurrences increase in aggressiveness, as Katie is pulled from the bed one night and drawn through the floor and stairs. Furthermore, there are signs that Katie is slowly being possessed by the supernatural presence, as she wakes up in the middle of the night and goes out of the house, sitting in the backyard for hours, without any recollection of doing so the next morning. Still, she complies with Micah, who rejects the idea of having the home invaded by a 'team of Jesus freaks'. Like in many toxic relationships, Katie is unable to search for help outside the home because Micah essentially cuts off all forms of healthy communication with the outside world.

Micah symbolises the brutal repressions involved in certain kinds of (hyper)masculinity, 'and the complicities in which this involves women'.[13] At one point, he asks Katie to make things 'happen' (meaning, triggering the supernatural activity rather than waiting for it to occur). She quickly retorts: 'I don't wanna make . . . them, it, whatever . . . I don't want it to happen at all. So I don't wanna force it to happen.' She is clearly stating that she wants nothing to happen, while Micah wants something to happen, even if it will traumatise his girlfriend. At this point, audiences should question Micah's motives: has he bought the camera to help Katie or just to have things recorded that may make him famous? Nevertheless, Katie begins to collaborate, even when the poltergeist activity increases night after night. As the camera is the only modification in their lives, Katie assumes that the recording is something that solidifies the supernatural intrusions. Micah continues recording and Katie allows him to do so. Micah even brings a Ouija board to their home to enhance the possibilities of contacting the supernatural entities haunting his girlfriend. She screams at him off-screen, while he smiles, oblivious to the fact that Katie is really upset. Faithful to the controlling ways of toxic masculinity, Micah tries to make her feel guilty about neglecting her responsibilities as a partner: 'I understand where you're coming from, just remember you didn't exactly warn me about this stuff before we moved in together.' Ashamed, Katie complies and Micah continues recording, even when the situation worsens; a possessed Katie kills Micah. Only through the intervention of a supernatural entity is Katie able to end the toxic relationship, only to fall into even worse hands, those of the demonic entity, a genderless being that further disempowers Katie after stripping her of any free will. She has finally become a puppet.

Micah's toxic masculinity is self-centred and destructively competitive, especially towards other men who can help Katie. He will be the model from which other toxic men in Blumhouse's films develop. Indeed, *Paranormal Activity 2* (2010) presents a new case of masculine toxicity. The film is a prequel to the original and begins two months before the events depicted in the first film. After experiencing what they think is a series of break-ins, a family sets up security cameras around their home, only to realise that the events unfolding before them are supernatural in nature. Like Micah in the previous film, the new 'man of the house', Daniel Rey, does not believe in the ghosts that his wife, Kristi, claims are plaguing the house. He finds a rational explanation to every weird occurrence, right up to the point of screaming to Kristi to stop bothering him with her fears. Soon, Kristi teams up with the other women of the house, her daughter Ali, her maid and her sister Katie. She finds alliance among people who are fairly disempowered; women bond together not just to battle supernatural manifestations, but also the man of house who keeps them trapped in a climate of supernatural horror. Much like Micah, Daniel's dismissal of anything non-rational is the real source of the horror, as the supernatural events increase in force without the family doing anything to stop them.

The insistence on the pre-eminence of reason and keeping women trapped within the home ends in doom for each family. In a similar vein to traditional Gothic villains, Micah and Daniel ask to be obeyed, their ada-mant rejection of women's arguments being the real source of the unfold-ing horrors. The stories are built around an unsettling pattern, in which the female protagonist is haunted by a cycle of dread from which they are unable to extricate themselves. The supernatural beings assaulting them may be sexless, but those summoning them are toxic men.

Only Micah and his 'solution' (the camera) are deemed rational, as recording the occurrences brings to mind documentary-like objective observation. Rationality is commonly associated with the mind, the sen-timental is associated with the body; thus, the women's reactions in the films are more visceral. In *Paranormal Activity*, Katie dislikes the camera and the Ouija board from the beginning, while in the sequel, Kristi is the first in the family (together with the family dog, arguably, both linked by the 'irrationality' deemed typical in 'less intelligent' beings) to link cer-tain occurrences with the supernatural. This 'irrationality', however, proves to be correct, while male 'rationality' is, basically, irrational. Micah and Daniel unwillingly and unwisely invite the supernatural to cast a strong-hold around their homes. This shift disturbs any essential linkage between women and irrationality and men and rationality. The swimming-pool cleaner mysteriously ending up outside the pool each day, for instance, is a sign of how the film is gendered. While Kristi starts to believe that something supernatural is pushing up the pool cleaner from the pool each day, Daniel finds many rational (but ultimately wrong) explanations. It is the poltergeist, the being that pushes the cleaner from the pool each day. Still, Daniel mocks his wife for being scared by a pool cleaner rather than take an active approach to end (or at least investigate) the supernatural.

Like Micah before him, Daniel is not responsible for ridding the family of the demons but is instead responsible for gaslighting the rational female protagonist. As in a traditional Gothic narrative, women must crawl out from the oppression of men and places – both equally toxic – for any manifestation of female agency. While the films remain neutral in their depiction of toxic masculinity – the real monsters being the supernatural entities – it should be noted that both Micah and Daniel are 'punished' with death at the end of the stories. This way, the films address – even if tangentially – the culpability of both men. The toxic masculinity delineated here is likely to bleed into other Blumhouse films, thereby becoming one of the company's most recognisable trademarks.

Toxic Parenthood

Toxic masculinity also frames institutions such as fatherhood, one of the pillars of patriarchy. Recently, however, the meaning of 'fatherhood' in Western society has shifted considerably beyond mere financial support to participation in actively raising children. Currently, there are two opposing trends in representations of fatherhood: 'the "good father", the new nurturing father who takes direct responsibility for child care, and the "bad father", an emotionally distant figure who is generally absent and spends little time getting to know his child.'[14] Of course, our notion of what a 'bad father' is today could have been considered a 'normal' conception of fatherhood in the past, since responsibility for the upbringing children was one of the 'essential' characteristics of womanhood in the division of labour.[15]

Economic crisis and its effects on fatherhood are tied to the idea of nurturing. Fathers, in the classical conception of fatherhood, maintain emotional distance from their children. Such distance could be explained because fathers were the only breadwinners of the household. Now, this responsibility is shared with the mother in many homes. Economic crisis, represented by the threat of globalised unemployment, destabilised the solid figure of the father as the one in charge of granting futures to their children. Since they cannot guarantee the futures of their offspring, this failure was supplanted by nurturing.[16]

On the other hand, Hannah Hamad argues that the 9/11 attacks have led to the fact that masculinity has had to rebuild itself into what could be called 'protective paternalism',[17] in which the (hyper)father must protect his family from external threats.[18] Framed by the anxieties provoked by the unstable context of a global world whose frontiers and boundaries are permeable to radical attacks (including neoliberal economic attacks), the father figure is obliged, at the threat of unemployment and nurturing, to 'man up' before the risk of feminisation, producing new manifestations of toxic masculinities. As such, both *The Purge* and *Sinister* present two father figures whose involvement in the neoliberal ethos produces toxic masculinity.

In the futuristic United States of *The Purge*, a wealthy family is held hostage for sheltering the target of a murderous mob during a 12-hour period in which any and all crime is legalised as a way to permit society to evacuate its brutal impulses in one night of violence. At this juncture, those who are most vulnerable are the homeless living on the streets and working-class families with common houses, while upper-class families are protected by elaborate security systems. In other words, the more technologised the house (i.e., upper class), the safer it is. This situation strongly resembles the United States after 9/11 when the increase in military budgets produced budgetary cuts in education and healthcare, leaving low-income families unprotected and in a dire situation.[19]

In *The Purge*, James Sandin gains his high income specifically by devising various technologies aimed at maintaining the safety of houses. He is a family man who has become rich by keeping families in his upper-class neighbourhood safe. By keeping the neighbourhood safe, James comes to represent the state, which within the film is called the 'New Founding Fathers of America' – a term that has always gendered the roots of the nation.[20] James is a man in charge of 'militarising' America against foreign threats. Similar to the *Paranormal Activity* films, male rationality comes with a careful, almost scientific-like surveillance. James's home is equipped with sophisticated cameras that clinically observe and record his entire neighbourhood while he sits safely inside. However, like the *Paranormal Activity* films, it is the 'man of the house' who turns the domestic space into a site of entrapment and horror.

James tries to marry his position as the ultimate neoliberal capitalist who only takes care of himself and his family, with the role of a modern father, thus uniting two images: the modern nurturing father with the hypermacho post-9/11 hero. The dinner scene is telling: James is dining with his family and asks for everyone to talk about their day to comply with the new role of communicative fatherhood. Even so, at the end, it is all about his capitalist success as the best salesman of security devices. His news of the day is that he 'did it' and he is 'on top' since his division sold the most upgraded security systems, more than any other company. There is no real communication between him and his children, and it is from this failed attribute that the horror begins. Both his son Charlie and his daughter Zoey allow strangers to access the house during the purge. Charlie lets in a stranger hunted by a horde of citizens while Zoey hides her boyfriend Henry, who wants to kill James, taking advantage of the purge period.

James has failed in communicating to his son a comprehensible reason behind the purge day. Thus, Charlie finds no fault in safeguarding a stranger during the purge. Meanwhile, he has neglected his daughter and her relationship with her boyfriend. When arriving home, James's wife Mary asks him to help his daughter, who has broken up with her boyfriend. He simply walks away, considering that his daughter's emotions are exaggerated, a woman's thing ('she'll get over it'). The failure in his highly calculated security system results from his status as a self-centred man rather than in technology. No one enters the house because the sophisticated system of alarms has failed: the access of strangers within the household is provoked by his inability to communicate with his own children. The sophisticated home is a marker of James's success as a businessman, but the house is a place of horror and entrapment for women and children.

The material-discursive production of toxic masculinity is intimately linked to the neoliberal ethos, as men are pushed to 'deliver' economically; failing to do so implies a 'feminisation' of their egos. Further, the capitalist, neoliberal framework of economic success turns the attention from 'leftist' ideas, such as gender equality and diversity, towards accumulation of capital, heavily associated with the marketplace. As argued by Gail Ukockis, 'the capitalist system can be as crushing as patriarchy',[21] undermining female experience as mere manual labour, while emphasising the male right to cut-throat success.

Sinister is another Blumhouse film in which conservative forms of fatherhood and neoliberal masculinity drown any possibility of being a non-toxic male. Ellison Oswalt is the father of a family who moves into a suburban house in which, years ago, a gruesome murder was committed. Ellison's goal is to investigate the crime and write a book about the case, a book that may help him to return to the top of the bestseller list, a place from which he fell a decade ago, since his later books never achieved the level of success of his first. It is his wife, Tracy, who economically supports the home, so that her husband can work on his new book.

Ellison resents that his wife is the home's breadwinner and wants desperately to reinstate his hegemonic masculinity through a reversal that places him once again as the financial supporter of the home, as the top of the household. So absorbed is he in this mission, that he completely neglects his wife and kids. His children, Trevor and Ashley, are slowly possessed by a supernatural presence haunting the house, while Ellison's wife is unable to reach him with her warnings about something going awry. Like Daniel, James and Micah in the other Blumhouse films, Ellison can think only of himself. Further, Ellison is falling into traditional forms of fatherhood that are distanced from nurturing. In one scene, Ashley takes a morning cup of coffee to her father who is working in his studio. The little girl knocks at the door and Ellison answers; he takes the coffee but closes the door without any further exchange of words with his daughter than a perfunctory 'thanks'. While Ashley clearly desires more time with her father, Ellison is too immersed in his race to success to care that he is neglecting his children. Furthermore, his son's sleep disorder and nocturnal terrors are making a return because, as the audience knows, there's an evil spectre in the house. It is Ellison who insists on keeping the family in the house, even when he knows that something horrid is happening. Indeed, Ellison spends the nights watching home videos that display whole families being slaughtered and a supernatural presence is present in all the recordings. He knows that his home may be the next target; yet he still insists on keeping his family trapped. Indeed, it seems that Ellison is willing to sacrifice his family if it means another bestseller. At this point, the film is critical of Ellison's position, as viewers are subjected to watch how his family disintegrates before his eyes while he – arguably the film's hero – can basically do nothing to prevent the invasion of supernatural forces. Worse still, his passivity deepens the horror.

It is much too late when Ellison discovers that his family is in serious danger and must leave the house. By this time, his daughter has been 'contaminated' by an evil supernatural being – the demon Bughuul – that reaches children through the use of images, and, much like what happened to the families depicted in the homemade films that Ellison watches, the Oswalts will be murdered by the younger child in the family.

It is the inability of both Ellison and James to communicate with the rest of the family that allows the horror to enter. On the surface, both men appear to be modern fathers who try to hold their family together with nurturing and care. However, they are in essence self-centred men, occupied by capitalist accumulation associated with old, passé forms of fatherhood. In brief, they are representations of toxicity because they do not work to escape the trappings of traditional patriarchy that infuse men with a sense of superiority. Even at their most 'nuanced', for these characters, 'macho' violence lurks at the borders of their personas.

Acts of Male Violence

The films analysed so far have engaged with toxic masculinities in the guise of 'modern' masculinity. All the men in these films act, apparently, for the welfare of their female partners and families. In *Paranormal Activity*, Micah insists on recording as the best way to help Katie; in *The Purge*, James has saved/trapped his family in his sophisticated home; and in *Sinister*, Ellison tries to return his family to a past economic bliss. These choices, however, rather than bring wellbeing, welcome horror, as the houses are signifiers of toxic masculinity.

Still, it is their toxic sense of masculinity that entitles them to disregard any female advice as hysteria or exaggeration. This is not to say that Blumhouse's films do not engage directly with issues of domestic violence or bullying. Intimate partner violence, sexual assault and bullying are some examples of the extreme consequences of toxic masculinity and Blumhouse Productions has not shied away from depicting explicit forms of male violence, such as in *The Boy Next Door* (2015) and *The Gift*.

The erotic psychological horror thriller *The Boy Next Door* is a rewriting of the themes dominating *Fatal Attraction* (1987), a film renowned for being deeply misogynistic[22] and with links to the Gothic.[23] Claire, a woman on the brink of divorce, has a love affair with her much younger next-door neighbour Noah Sandborn. The relationship is, for her, a one-night stand; however, Noah becomes increasingly erratic and violent as he obsesses over Claire. The film chronicles how Noah begins to tamper with Claire's life, stalking her, threatening her and turning Claire's son Kevin on his father. Noah exhibits all the elements associated with toxic masculinity – he is controlling and possessive. According to him, Claire's continuance of the romance is part of her 'confusion' and a 'mistake'. Soon, he is oppressing her, taking advantage of the fact that she wants to keep the relationship a secret. In Gothic fiction, 'property seems to loom larger than love'[24] and Claire becomes less-than-human, an object or property to be possessed by Noah, her will and subjectivity wholly dismissed as irrelevant.

Interestingly, the film begins by staging Claire's point of view. It is clear that she desires her new, handsome younger neighbour and the *mise-en-scène* complements her perspective. Noah is shown for the first time in the film in a very telling way: Claire is struggling with her garage door and Noah's strong biceps suddenly enter the frame to help her. Noah is deconstructed as muscles, body. In a later scene, Claire watches him through her window as Noah works on a car, his body glistening with sweat. She even watches him getting completely undressed at night in his bedroom.

While Jennifer Lopez remains fully clothed (at least up to this point), the film offers viewers many scenes of Ryan Guzman in different stages of undress. Laura Mulvey argues that classical cinema has fetishised the female image, turning it into an object to be looked at by the 'proper' (male) gaze.[25] *The Boy Next Door* reverses this logic – Claire is the bearer of the gaze, Guzman the object to be looked at. Even the film's poster depicts Lopez watching something from a window, emphasising her gaze. This queering of Noah's masculinity suffers a backlash, not coincidentally, after Lopez undresses for the first time in the story (one could argue that the film is putting things 'in the right place' with a patriarchal perspective) during her scene of lovemaking with her neighbour. From that point, Noah 'recuperates' his 'proper' manliness through possessive attitudes towards Claire.

Noah's stalking and killing – a femicide closer to the film's climax – mirrors the attitudes of many real men who produce a violent environment of domestic aggression (including verbal abuse, as Noah starts calling Claire a 'slut'). Still, the film displays another, more subtle form of poisonous masculinity. Claire is divorcing her husband Garret, who has cheated on her with a younger woman. While Claire is the film's heroine, Garret becomes her 'romantic interest' as the film narrates how he attempts to save the marriage. The story depicts Garret as a good man who has 'made a mistake'. The film, however, presents an ex-husband who is always trying to reconnect with his wife through intrusion into her new life. In one of the first scenes, Garret has planned an entire weekend with his son and Claire, without consulting his ex-wife first. She opts out of the family plan to give the men a chance to 'bond together', but she clearly does so to avoid the company of her cheating husband. As the film progresses, however, Garret is successful in accessing Claire's new house, where he tries to kiss her and, later, emphasises his presence spending the night – uninvited – in her home. It is only through the contrast with psychopath Noah that Garret is coded as a good man; however, he is a man who gives Claire no space in which to start a new life alone or make decisions regarding their marriage. Arguably, the film needs Garret to be at Claire's home to fuel Noah's jealousy. However, the narrative aligns itself with the toxic presence of an ex-husband who imposes his presence; indeed, Claire becomes romantically involved with Garret again, the two becoming the film's main couple. At the film's climax, and after Claire defeats Noah and saves Garret, the story abruptly ends. There is no final kiss shared between Claire and Garret that returns the story to its previous status quo, thus giving Claire some empowerment after defeating not one but two forms of damaging masculinity. The future of Claire and Garret as a couple remains elusive to viewers, making the film an ambiguous portrayal of toxic masculinity.

Noah (the 'psycho') and Garret (the husband/hero) from *The Boy Next Door* cohabit together in *The Gift*. The film positions two forms of masculinity in a Manichean scenario. At one end, there is Simon, the perfect, successful husband who loves and cares for his wife Robyn. At the other extreme, there is insecure, slightly unbalanced Gordo. Gordo is an old classmate of Simon, the latter barely recognising him. Yet, after a brief conversation, Simon invites him to dinner with Robyn. Gordo repeatedly makes kind, yet invasive gestures towards the couple, delivering wine or pets, and dropping by while Robyn is at home alone. While Robyn sees a sensitive man, Simon sees nothing but a creep who is invading his home.

The film plays masterfully with viewers' expectations. Gordo is the psychopath waiting to explode, while Simon (played by an actor famous for his comedic roles) is the man who will save his family at the climax. Eventually, however, buried secrets are brought to light: Gordo was bullied by Simon through his youth, to the point where Simon invented stories – revealing the homophobic streak in Simon's character – to damage Gordo's life. To end this new, uneasy relationship, Simon approaches Gordo to offer him an apology. For Simon, an apology for his behaviour as a child is a waste of time. He only does it to please the 'exaggerated' concerns of his wife. An alpha-male kid bullying a shy child is, for Simon, a natural stage of adolescence. When Gordo does not accept the apologies, Simon brutally beats him as a way to save his alpha masculinity, which has been slightly unbalanced in the act of seeking forgiveness – being sentimental is a negative form of 'feminisation'.

Simon's past as a bully is not a foreign side to the now successful businessman, but an integral part of his self. As revealed later in the film, Simon is climbing the social ladder in his job thanks to his abusive behaviour towards his peers, backstabbing and the fabrication of stories that harm those who cross his path. Even worse, Simon is unable to find fault in this behaviour, which he sees as integral to the neoliberal ethos of cutthroat competition.

It is Simon's disdain for Gordo's feelings that provokes the ire of his former classmate, who unleashes cruel vengeance on the family – maybe (or maybe not) raping Robyn. It is revealed that she is pregnant, perhaps expecting Gordo's child. Stealing paternity from Simon is the path chosen to damage his masculinity, turning the bully into a cuckold. If Simon at first epitomised control and power (two key characteristics of toxic masculinity), *The Gift* ends with his humiliation and disempowerment. As a cuckolded husband, he has failed to defend a value vital to the social order.

At the end of the film, Simon is depicted as the real villain, a man whose toxicity poisons all his relationships, bringing horror into the home – because he had bullied Gordo in the past, and because he invited him to dinner when they met as adults. Simon is the perfect embodiment of gendered Gothic. He is simultaneously the husband/hero and the narrative's main monster/villain. Arguably, Gordo is a real menace to Robyn; it is her husband, however, the man who better fits the politics of the Gothic and gothixity: his toxic masculinity invites horror into the home, thus damaging his wife and (unborn) children. Much like Micah, Daniel, James, Ellison and Garret in the other Blumhouse films discussed here, Simon sutures together the masculine hero-villain, blurring the distinctions between them, while keeping the female trapped in domestic horror. Actually, he is a 'good' husband (in the sense that he never mistreats his wife) who, due his toxic masculinity, brought vengeance that affected everyone around him, his wife trapped in a horror story in which she is completely innocent. Simon subverts cultural expectations regarding the neat separation between villain and hero, thus staging a return to the subversive nature of the traditional Gothic.

Blumhouse's linkage with forms of toxic masculinity reaches its apex with the studio's version of *Black Christmas*. The film met with negative reactions, mostly in relation to the portrayal of men as inherently toxic. Even men with good intentions, the film says, may be 'overruled by their true alpha nature'.[26] The film's plot revolves around a sorority house under attack by a serial killer that is revealed, at the film's climax, as a brotherhood of male killers angry at contemporary ideas of female empowerment. Three points of this film are crucial for my conclusions. First, the film, a remake of Bob Clark's *Black Christmas* (1974), is not an entirely new creature. Clark's film also engaged with toxic masculinity, even if marginally, as the film's male killer makes sexist calls to all the girls living at the sorority house. One character, Peter, is unable to hear and understand the opinions that his girlfriend Jess has regarding her unplanned pregnancy. Blumhouse's remake emphasises this marginal manifestation of toxic masculinity presented in Clark's film, bridging two eras framed by radical feminism. Indeed, Clark's *Black Christmas* opened in 1974, a decade – in terms of gender representation – dominated by the radical nature of second-wave feminism, a collective that viewed patriarchy as the primary form of oppression after which all other types of oppression have been modelled. The new iteration of *Black Christmas*, in turn, opens amidst a still nascent 'fourth wave' of feminism proposing a new awareness regarding gender issues. Second, the new *Black Christmas* presents a heroine, Riley, whose main romantic interest contrasts heavily with any form of toxicity. Certainly, Landon is a sensitive man whose shyness is the extreme opposite of the predatory nature of Riley's ex-boyfriend. Third, the new *Black Christmas* continues Blumhouse's interest in the portrayal of toxic forms of masculinity as analysed here.

Conclusions

As seen in many of Blumhouse's productions, the horror comes not only from the outside, but also from the intervention of men who want to have the last word, even when they are wrong. Their actions, inextricably linked to the neoliberal ethos of competition, macho attitudes and aggressiveness, open the door to the horrors out there. Like the villains of traditional Gothic literature, these men and their stories symbolise women's oppression while exposing the trappings of patriarchy.

Notes

1. Sarah Banet-Weiser, *Empowered: Popular Feminism and Popular Misogyny* (Durham NC: Duke University Press, 2018), p. 153.
2. S. Stewart, 'Elisabeth Moss gives it her all, but this *Invisible Man* isn't a must-see', *New York Post* (26 February 2020), *https://nypost.com/2020/02/26/elisabeth-moss-gives-it-her-all-but-this-invisible-man-isnt-a-must-see/* (accessed 30 June 2020).

3. Z. Wijaszka, 'Black Christmas: Smashes the Patriarchy with Strong Women', Film Inquiry (18 December 2019), www.filminquiry.com/black-christmas-2019-review/ (accessed 30 June 2020).

4. Ruth Bienstock Anolik, American Gothic Literature: A Thematic Study from Mary Rowlandson to Colson Whitehead (Jefferson NC: McFarland, 2018), p. 32.

5. Helene Meyers, Femicidal Fears: Narratives of the Female Gothic Experience (Albany NY: State University of New York Press, 2001).

6. T. A. Kupers, 'Toxic Masculinity as a Barrier to Mental Health Treatment in Prison', Journal of Clinical Psychology, 61/6 (2005), 713.

7. R. W. Connell, Masculinities (Cambridge: Polity Press, 2005), p. 77.

8. C. J. Pascoe and T. Bridges, 'Exploring Masculinities: History, Reproduction, Hegemony, and Dislocation', in C. J. Pascoe and T. Bridges (eds), Exploring Masculinities: Identity, Inequality, Continuity, and Change (New York: Oxford University Press, 2016), p. 18.

9. Pascoe and Bridges, 'Exploring Masculinities', p. 18.

10. Andrew Hock Soon Ng, Women and Domestic Space in Contemporary Gothic Narratives: The House as Subject (New York: Palgrave Macmillan, 2015), p. 1.

11. Diana Wallace, Female Gothic Stories: Gender, History and the Gothic (Cardiff: University of Wales Press, 2013), p. 125.

12. Donna Heiland, Gothic and Gender: An Introduction (Malden MA: Blackwell, 2004), p. 11.

13. Wallace, Female Gothic Stories, p. 114.

14. Jay Fagan and Glen Palm, Fathers and Early Childhood Programs (Clifton Park NY: Delmar Learning, 2004), p. 68.

15. Riki Wilchins, Queer Theory, Gender Theory: An Instant Primer (Los Angeles CA: Alyson Books, 2004), p. 128.

16. M. Donaldson, 'What is Hegemonic Masculinity?', Theory and Society, 22/5 (1993), 651.

17. Hannah Hamad, Postfeminism and Paternity in Contemporary U.S. Film: Framing Fatherhood (New York: Routledge, 2013), p. 52.

18. For more on this linkage, see F. G. P. Berns and C. A. R. Fontao, 'New Paternal Anxieties in Contemporary Horror Cinema: Protecting the Family against (Supernatural) External Attacks', L. Tropp (ed.), Deconstructing Dads: Changing Notions of Fatherhood in Popular Culture (Lanham MD: Rowman and Littlefield, 2016), pp. 165–79.

19. Kenneth Neubeck, When Welfare Disappears: The Case for Economic Human Rights (New York: Routledge, 2006), p. 154.

20. Andrew Schocket, *Fighting Over the Founders: How We Remember the American Revolution* (New York: New York University Press, 2015), p. 30.
21. Gail Ukockis, *Misogyny: The New Activism* (Oxford: Oxford University Press, 2019), p. 233.
22. Suzanne Leonard, *Fatal Attraction* (Malden MA: Blackwell, 2009), p. 70.
23. K. I. Michasiw, 'Some Stations of Suburban Gothic', in R. Martin and E. Savoy (eds), *American Gothic: New Interventions in a National Narrative* (Iowa City IA: University of Iowa Press, 1998), p. 241.
24. L. Fitzgerald, 'Female Gothic and the Institutionalisation of Gothic Studies', in D. Wallace and A. Smith (eds), *The Female Gothic: New Directions* (New York: Palgrave Macmillan, 2009), p. 15.
25. Laura Mulvey, *Visual and Other Pleasures* (New York: Palgrave Macmillan, 2009).
26. R. Hunter, '*Black Christmas* Review: Good Intentions, Questionable Execution', *Film School Rejects* (14 December 2019), *https://filmschoolrejects.com/black-christmas-2019-review/* (accessed 20 June 2020).

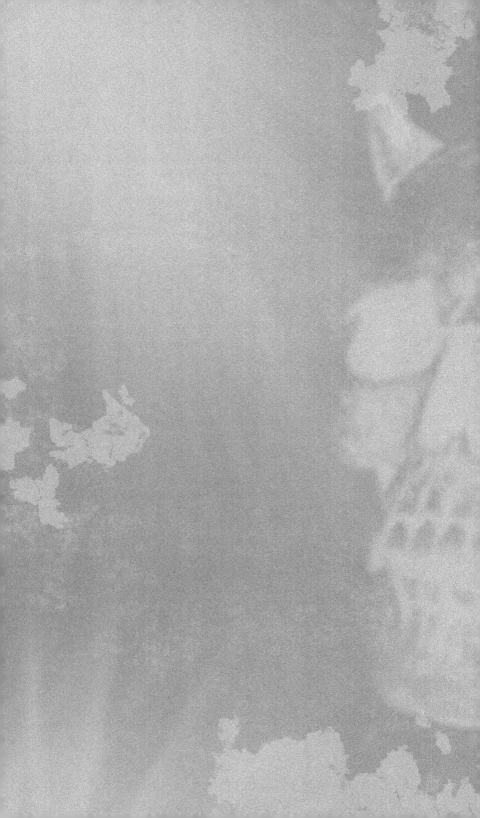

5

Space Invaders

Aliens and Recessionary Anxieties in *Dark Skies*

Craig Ian Mann

Hybrid Species

DARK SKIES (2013) is, in many ways, typical of Blumhouse's early horror output. As Bernice M. Murphy points out, the company's first forays into the genre – *Paranormal Activity* (2009), *Insidious* (2011) and *Sinister* (2012) – eschewed the narrative and aesthetic qualities of graphic 'torture porn' films such as *Saw* (2004) and *Hostel* (2005). Instead, as Murphy observes, they made 'a commercially savvy return to the kind of "Old School" scares found in the most prominent haunted-house movies of the 1970s and 1980s' and changed the landscape of mainstream American horror cinema in the process.[1] With the exception of *The Bay* (2012), all of Blumhouse's horror films up to and including *Dark Skies* are unified by a concern with relatively affluent couples or families finding themselves under attack by infernal forces within the confines of their own homes. And in most of them, the monster stalking middle-class Americans is demonic, something inherently evil from beyond the pale – most of them, that is, except for *Dark Skies*.

While it was written and directed by Scott Stewart (the filmmaker behind *Legion* (2010) and *Priest* (2011), two movies very much concerned with demonic creatures), *Dark Skies* is not a supernatural horror film. Rather, it is a hybrid of horror and science fiction and its monsters are extraterrestrials rather than demons. So, while it is largely representative of Blumhouse's early genre output, it also has a great deal in common with a number of earlier films about alien contact. Like *Dark Skies*, sci-fi-horror hybrids such as *The McPherson Tape* (1989), *Communion* (1989) and *Signs* (2002) largely take place in domestic settings and concentrate on families who are attacked by malevolent visitors from beyond the stars. In most of these films, the central characters experience close encounters in remote locations, miles from civilisation or even their closest neighbours – most of them, that is, except for *Dark Skies*.

Dark Skies is not set in one of those places we popularly associate with alien abductions – or, as Bridget Brown puts it, 'great rural expanses' such as farmland, forests, deserts or desolate highways.[2] Rather, it is set in a densely populated suburban street, and largely within the home of the middle-class Barrett family, including wife and mother Lacy, her husband Daniel and their two sons: thirteen-year-old Jesse and six-year-old Sam. The family is in financial trouble; Daniel is an unemployed architect, while Lacy is a real-estate agent who has not sold a house in some time. As they deal with those fiscal pressures, the Barretts begin to experience a number of odd occurrences. First, something enters their home in the small hours, setting off their security alarm, stealing from them and rearranging household items to create strange symbols; then each member of the family begins to exhibit odd behaviour under the influence of some otherworldly force. Having researched alien visitation, Lacy contacts a UFO expert, Edwin Pollard, who deduces that the Barretts have been targeted by an advanced extraterrestrial species (the 'Greys'). He warns Lacy and Daniel that the Greys want to abduct their children, and advises them to take every possible step to protect their family. Terrified, the Barretts fortify their home and prepare for attack.

So, *Dark Skies* borrows narrative elements from a certain kind of alien abduction or invasion film – in which extraterrestrial activity is focused largely on a single family in an isolated location – and inserts them into Blumhouse's lucrative 'haunted house' formula, which normally unleashes demonic forces on suburban middle-class households. Of course, there is a reason that the company's formula proved so successful before the release of *Dark Skies*. As Murphy argues, it was popular in large part because of its social, cultural and political relevance; these were films, she suggests, that met with box-office triumph because they '[tapped] into a rich seam of economic and class anxiety . . . afflicting the American middle classes' in the aftermath of the financial crisis of 2007–8 and the onset of the Great Recession.[3] By the end of 2012, Blumhouse had replicated it across no fewer than six films in the space of only five years (*Insidious*, *Sinister* and the first four instalments in the *Paranormal Activity* series), and there was no sense that audiences were growing tired of it; *Paranormal Activity 4* (2012) made $54 million at the domestic box office on a budget of only $5 million. But even if the formula remained profitable, Blumhouse nevertheless attempted to refresh it by marrying it with science fiction in *Dark Skies*.

Sadly, it was not a particularly successful attempt. *Dark Skies* made only $17.5 million in the United States when it was released by Dimension Films in February 2013 – a reasonable profit given that it was made for only $3.5 million, but a return that fell far short of the money taken by Blumhouse's more traditional haunted-house narratives. And unlike *Paranormal Activity*, *Insidious* or *Sinister*, *Dark Skies* did not launch a franchise. The film's failure to generate more than modest box-office receipts was perhaps due in part to its unusual genre hybridity and a confused marketing campaign. While its trailer boasts that it comes 'From the producers of *Paranormal Activity* and *Insidious*' and attempts to frame the film as a similarly suburban tale of demonic visitation, it also contains a great deal of science-fiction iconography, including alien figures, otherworldly symbols that resemble crop circles and blinding lights that recall *Close Encounters of the Third Kind* (1977) as they flood into the Barrett household. Given that it was sold on its association with Blumhouse's earlier genre output, its obvious departure from the supernatural was unlikely to be popular with audiences expecting narratives revolving around hauntings and demonic possession.[4]

Dark Skies is now one of Blumhouse's more obscure films, and it has been overlooked for the most part in discussions of the company's recessionary horror films (and, in fact, in academic work on economic horror more generally). Presumably due to the extraterrestrial nature of its antagonists, Murphy mentions that *Dark Skies* uses 'the same basic template' as her other case studies but does not discuss it any further.[5] Similarly, Barry Keith Grant briefly examines the film in relation to the 'economic pressures' of the Great Recession and compares it to *Paranormal Activity*, but affords the film only scant analysis.[6] That *Dark Skies* has not been analysed further seems odd given that even the film's critics recognised its cultural relevance, something that is rare for a mainstream horror film. *Variety* observed that the film juxtaposes 'idyllic suburban life' with 'many foreclosure signs';[7] the *Pittsburgh Post* noted that it is as much concerned with the horrors of 'long-term unemployment and a mortgage in arrears' as it is with alien abduction;[8] and the *Los Angeles Times* described it as a film about 'a family dealing with money troubles [and] mysterious entities looking to spirit them to parts unknown, perhaps even a less desirable ZIP code'.[9]

This chapter, then, will address this oversight by examining the place of *Dark Skies* among Blumhouse's recessionary horror movies. After outlining the broader context of modern economic horror and its rise following the financial crisis and the beginning of the Great Recession, it will discuss the film in relation to Blumhouse's 'haunted house' formula, revealing its thematic relevance during a period of American history defined by fiscal anxieties. Having established its commonalities with the *Paranormal Activity* series, *Insidious* and *Sinister*, it will then turn to the film's monsters and make the case for it as one of the company's most interesting recessionary narratives precisely because it makes metaphoric use of extraterrestrial antagonists (and 'Grey' aliens in particular). It will argue that – although they may have contributed to its middling box-office performance – the film's science-fiction elements significantly strengthen its social and political commentary and clearly set *Dark Skies* apart from the many Blumhouse movies in which middle-class protagonists are beset by supernatural evils.

Household Contact

While films that confront economic anxieties have long been a trend in American horror cinema, the threat of unemployment, property foreclosure, homelessness and destitution became a particularly acute theme in horror movies produced during the period following the financial crisis, the worst economic downturn since the Great Depression of the 1930s.[10] The financial crisis was caused by the bursting of the US housing bubble; as Robert J. Shiller notes, 'Home prices and homeownership had been booming since the late 1990s' in America, 'and investing in a house had seemed a sure route to financial security and even wealth'. He continues, 'home ownership rates rose over the period 1997–2005 for all regions, all age groups, and all income groups'.[11] This boom in the housing market was bolstered, as François Chesnais suggests, by the 'overbuilding of houses and over-capacity in the construction industry', which was in turn 'fuelled by debt-supported securitisation and unsustainable levels of leverage'.[12]

As Peter Hough recounts, the bubble burst 'when it became obvious that banks had been lending sums far in excess of what they owned' and, as a consequence, 'businesses lost confidence in them and the whole financial system was plunged into chaos'.[13]

The Great Recession had a global impact, but in the Western world it was especially ruinous for the United States. By February 2008, 'manufacturing activity was at a five-year low amid slowing demand and rising prices'.[14] Unemployment levels rose sharply and remained persistently high, with the national rate still standing at 9.5 per cent in 2010, up from 5 per cent in 2007.[15] The number of economic suicides recorded in America accelerated dramatically, leading to approximately 4,750 excess deaths between 2007 and 2010.[16] The effects of the Great Recession in the United States were most keenly felt in a housing crisis; as the nation's economy collapsed, mortgage lenders called in debts, putting a staggering number of people under severe financial strain. Many millions of Americans could not afford to pay their outstanding arrears, leading to an unprecedented number of repossessions. Foreclosures rose to record levels between 2009 and 2010 and ultimately seven million people lost their homes.[17]

This context produced a new wave of horror films focused on fiscal anxieties. As I have discussed elsewhere, a distinct cycle of independent horror films focused on the millennial experience of the Great Recession, as films such as *The House of the Devil* (2009), *The Innkeepers* (2011), *You're Next* (2011), *Cheap Thrills* (2013) and *Starry Eyes* (2014) weaved narratives around young, desperate men and women who 'put themselves in life threatening situations . . . or resort to horrific crimes' in order to find 'the stability they need to move forward with their static lives'.[18] Meanwhile, mainstream horror focused on middle-class protagonists and, unsurprisingly, figured their homes as the site of horrific events. One of the earliest films in this cycle is *Paranormal Activity*, in which an affluent couple's home is invaded by a demonic presence. In his work on the film and its first sequel, James D. Stone suggests:

> The first two *Paranormal Activity* films are tales of the recession, not only because they stress our blithe disregard for the steady, inevitable advance of a monster, but also because they track the gradual collapse of consumer capitalist dreams. The business of the demon is to lay waste to materialist splendor . . . Characters hold down prestigious, high-stakes occupations and fetishize a variety of consumer goods. And then, it all comes crashing down.[19]

While Stone's analysis of the two films is astute, it is not entirely accurate. Independently produced in 2006, Oren Peli's *Paranormal Activity* predates the financial crisis; it was not purposely designed to be a commentary on the Great Recession. However, the film was first seen on the festival circuit as the crisis was unfolding in October 2007. It was eventually released in a re-edited form two years later – after Peli had gained a producer in Jason Blum and then a distributor in Paramount Pictures – when the worst effects of the recession were being felt. It is, then, an example of a film that gained an unintended cultural relevance – and it set the template for several later Blumhouse films. *Insidious*, *Sinister* and a number of *Paranormal Activity* sequels followed, all of them following a familiar narrative formula with the backing of Hollywood distributors. As Murphy notes, these films depict 'the family home as an inherently insecure milieu ripe for invasion by sinister forces',[20] and are characterised by 'the manner in which they explicitly or implicitly reference the financial crisis' and its adverse effects on 'millions of ordinary Americans'.[21]

Although it has not been widely discussed as a recessionary horror narrative, *Dark Skies* references the financial crisis in a far more explicit way than any of its contemporaries. The film opens with a montage: the first shot follows a saloon car as it drives down a quaint residential street; the second lingers on a gardener using a leaf blower to clear the sidewalk; the third frames a teenager riding his bike on the road; the fourth shows a group of children having a water fight in a front yard. Several similar shots follow; the majority are further portraits of life in suburbia and several of them prominently feature American flags. But the meaning of this opening sequence – which would otherwise seem to be a celebration of middle-class existence, the so-called 'American Dream' – is shaped by its fifth shot, an image that jars with the others. Framed from a canted low angle, it shows a large, detached house and a carefully tended lawn. In front of it – in fact, looming over it – are two signs. The first reads 'For Sale', the second reads 'Bank Owned'. As Grant attests, this shot clearly recalls 'the images of foreclosed homes that were broadcast regularly on television news when the country was deep in the recession'.[22]

This montage is not a celebration of the 'American Dream', then, but rather a stark reminder of how quickly it can turn into a nightmare. That single image of a repossessed property recontextualises all the shots that surround it; the family that lived in this house met with financial ruin, suggesting that any of their neighbours – who are pictured obliviously going about their daily lives – could easily suffer the same fate (as could any middle-class citizen in the United States). To underline the notion that all Americans could become a victim of the Great Recession, *Dark Skies* never confirms exactly whereabouts in the nation it is set. The agent selling this foreclosed property professes to be offering 'Premiere Franklin County Real Estate', but this does not mean a great deal; it is no coincidence that there is a 'Franklin County' in twenty-four of the US states. In fact, 'Franklin' is the second most common place name in America. This is 'Anytown, USA'.

And it quickly transpires that the next residents of this quiet neighbourhood to face destitution are Lacy and Daniel Barrett, first pictured holding a barbecue for their neighbours in a scene that reveals their high social standing. In fact, the nation's economy is a topic of conversation, as one guest tells Daniel, 'The fed can prime the pump in DC all it wants', before lamenting that all a government stimulus package will do is 'raise the price of a cup of coffee in California'. Daniel feigns interest, but the following scene tells us that he is more concerned with his own fiscal problems than those faced by the nation at large. As he gets into bed with his wife and tries to distract her from a pile of paperwork littering the sheets, she resists his advances: 'I've got to prep these viewings. We need this'. Daniel disappointedly picks up a book from his bedside table, making clear that their financial troubles are having a detrimental effect on their marriage. We soon discover that the Barretts are struggling not just because Lacy is finding it difficult to sell houses in a recession; Daniel is one of many unemployed Americans, and the following day he attends a humiliating interview for an architectural position. The camera slowly tracks in on him as he sits in a grey, soulless boardroom – visualising his growing desperation – as the interviewer coldly questions him on why his previous contract was terminated. He does not get the job and he returns home to a reminder that his mortgage is in arrears.

Within the first ten minutes of *Dark Skies*, then, it is apparent that here the recession is not just a metaphorical concern. On the contrary, it is an integral part of the film's narrative; before they are attacked by an extraterrestrial force, Lacy and Daniel are already deeply afraid – of falling into debt, forfeiting their home and, importantly, losing the respect of their friends and neighbours. Murphy notes that in many of Blumhouse's early horror films, the central characters have just moved into their new homes, and 'the point when our protagonists achieve home ownership merely marks the onset of a series of horrific and seemingly inescapable supernatural complications'.[23] The Barretts, though, have been entrenched in their community for quite some time; they have spent many years building their suburban life, and Daniel is particularly keen to hang onto it. He is incensed when he discovers that Lacy has talked to their friends about their money troubles, appalled that he might be viewed as a bad husband and father. This is, then, an especially middle-class nightmare; Daniel is not just terrified that he will lose his wealth, but his long-held status. While Lacy is less concerned than Daniel with what the neighbours might think, she obviously shares his anxieties – she is deeply distressed when she learns that his interview did not go well – and their children, too, are struggling to cope; in an early scene, Sam asks his older brother if he thinks their father will leave them.

Much of the film thus plays out as what Stewart calls a 'suburban drama' rather than a horror or science-fiction film,[24] and it makes abundantly apparent the immense financial pressure bearing down on the Barretts. This means that when the film's genre elements come into play, it is clear that they are intended to be interpreted in a recessionary context. The family's actions, while under the control of the Greys, for example, seem more like extreme responses to their stressful circumstances than any extraterrestrial influence. Lacy experiences blackouts and finds that she is unable to remember stretches of time; Daniel begins sleepwalking and suffers intense nosebleeds; Jesse has violent seizures; and Sam enters catatonic states, wets himself in public and begins talking of a mysterious being that he believes is visiting him at night. Narratively, all these events are a consequence of the family's unwitting contact with the Greys; metaphorically, they are physical manifestations of their crippling anxieties. To reinforce this, Lacy and Daniel directly attribute Sam's odd behaviour to psychological stress and argue about whether they can afford to hire a therapist (a question that causes even further tension between them).

And when the Barrett household is invaded by otherworldly beings, the extraterrestrial activity that occurs inside the house is coloured by the family's financial troubles, metaphorically reflecting on their fear of losing everything. On the first night that the Greys enter the property, they raid the family's fridge and leave food strewn across their kitchen floor – a stark reminder that soon Lacy and Daniel may not be able to afford basic necessities. The next night, they rearrange furniture, food packaging and various household items to cast an alien symbol on the ceiling, a territorial marker suggesting that the family are losing ownership of their cherished possessions. And on the third night, all their family photographs are stolen, leaving only empty frames on the shelves: an indication that in the near future their home could belong to somebody else, those frames waiting to be filled with portraits of another family. With each invasion of this middle-class home, then, the Greys remind Lacy and Daniel that their material wealth is slowly diminishing. An assault on the house's exterior follows, when the alien presence inside the Barrett household causes several flocks of birds to fly directly into it. By the film's end, Lacy and Daniel have been forced to board up the doors and windows to protect themselves from the Greys, finally giving their home – as Grant suggests – the look of a repossessed property.[25]

While much of the film is set inside the Barrett residence, its second major location is a house that Lacy is attempting to sell throughout the narrative and which Jesse often uses as a place to meet his friends. In disrepair and adorned with 1970s décor, it is not the most desirable property and a significant downgrade from the Barrett's own stylish and modern home (to the point that Lacy tells potential buyers that they could 'do better'). As Mark Olsen notes in his *Los Angeles Times* review, this second location is a physical representation of Lacy and Daniel's anxieties, its 'once-groovy, now-tacky style a taunting reflection of their attempts to keep up'.[26] It is, in short, the kind of fixer-upper that they might be forced to move into if their home is repossessed and their aspirational lifestyle is destroyed. Its negative connotations are revealed early in the film when Lacy experiences her first blackout while conducting a viewing of the property – repeatedly smashing her face against a screen door – and reinforced in its final scenes, as Jesse falls under the Greys' influence and enters a hallucinatory trance. The walls of his childhood home melt away to reveal that other house, the frame filled with its outdated yellow wallpaper as he wanders into the kitchen. There he finds his mother lying dead, his father banging a shotgun against the bloodstained floor; Daniel utters 'I ruined everything' and shoots himself. This is the worst possible outcome of the film's 'suburban drama', in which financial ruin leads to a brutal murder-suicide. Even as he is in danger of being abducted by an extraterrestrial force, Jesse is still preoccupied with dark thoughts of what might happen if his parents lose everything.

And if Jesse's worries are realised in his nightmarish vision of how that 'suburban drama' might end, his parents' anxieties are reflected in the conclusion of the film's alien-contact narrative. As Murphy notes, Blumhouse's recessionary horror films are united by their tendency to put children in peril, a metaphor for the recession's potential to destroy the lives of middle-class families.[27] *Dark Skies* is no different; the aliens primarily focus their attention on Sam and Jesse. Their parents do everything they can to protect them – install surveillance cameras, adopt a guard dog, buy a gun and turn their home into a fortress – but it is not enough. The film ends with Jesse's abduction, an event that literalises the Barretts' deepest fear: of failing their children. While they might be afraid of losing their friends, their material possessions and even their home, they are most frightened by the prospect of being unable to provide for their sons, here represented by their inability to save Jesse from the Greys. In a 'feel-bad' climax typical of Blumhouse's early horror movies,[28] Lacy and Daniel can only scream as their eldest child is awoken from his dream state to find himself surrounded by otherworldly beings. And in a flash of blinding light, he is gone.

Superior Beings

So *Dark Skies* is largely characteristic of Blumhouse's recessionary horror films, ostensibly unusual only in its particularly explicit references to the financial crisis. But there is something atypical about the film: its monsters. As Murphy suggests, most of the company's early horror movies revolve around demonic entities that possess three shared characteristics. First, they target children. Second, they are not bound to the house in which the initial supernatural activity takes place, but will follow their victims 'like a bad credit history'.[29] This is also true of the Greys in *Dark Skies*; when Lacy and Daniel meet with alien expert Edwin Pollard, Daniel suggests that the Barretts will simply move. Pollard replies: 'These beings almost certainly came millions of light years to get here. Do you really think moving to the next town or checking into a hotel will stop them from finding you?' The third characteristic shared by the demons present in the *Paranormal Activity* series, *Insidious* and *Sinister* is that they have a single motivation: to inflict, in Murphy's words, 'pain and suffering'. In this, they embody the anguish caused by financial strife and are designed to 'represent evil of the very broadest, most unambiguous variety'.[30]

This, then, is where the Greys depart from their demonic counterparts. For there is no sense in *Dark Skies* that the aliens toying with the Barrett family are motivated by a desire to cause suffering (even if that is a clear side effect of their actions); in fact, the film provides no real explanation of their motives at all, beyond a vague suggestion from Pollard that they might be 'studying' humankind. As Grant suggests, they are 'experimenting with humans for reasons unknown, analogous to the way the youngest of the two Barrett boys, Sam, keeps a tailless lizard in a box for his amusement'.[31] They are not simply 'evil', and thus it is limiting to consider *Dark Skies* a film in which 'demons have been replaced by . . . extraterrestrials'.[32] After all, aliens carry their own thematic connotations – and this is particularly true of the 'Grey' alien.

While cinematic extraterrestrials have come to Earth in all shapes and sizes, from humanoid in *The Man from Planet X* (1951) to distinctly inhuman in *Arrival* (2016), the most prolific depiction of extraterrestrial life across all media is the Grey. Normally characterised as a grey-skinned 'humanoid . . . with large, black, almond shaped eyes',[33] the Grey alien has featured prominently in North American abduction accounts since at least 1961.[34] According to John Edward Campbell, they were 'introduced to the general public' by Whitley Strieber's *Communion* (1987) – the horror writer's allegedly non-fiction account of his own abduction experiences – and its 1989 film adaptation of the same name before being further entrenched in popular culture by T*he X-Files* (1993–2018).[35] In truth, *Close Encounters of the Third Kind* popularised Greys ten years before the publication of *Communion*, but in a far more benevolent form; since the late 1980s, they have more often been depicted in film and television as a malevolent species. In addition to *Dark Skies*, they appear in several other modern genre films and are particularly common in found-footage movies; *Extraterrestrial* (2014) is another more traditional sci-fi-horror narrative to feature a Grey.

Dark Skies draws directly from the mythology surrounding Greys. While they are still sometimes depicted as peaceful, they have long been associated with experimentation on human subjects, their activities in science-fiction media more often mirroring abductees' claims that Greys subjected them to 'intense interrogation and invasive medical exams, usually accompanied by bright, blinding lights'.[36] Also common are reports that the beings had 'placed implants, usually through the nose or ear, inside their bodies'.[37] Importantly, it is rare – both in science fiction and in reports of supposed abductions – for any purpose or motive to be ascribed to these behaviours. As Eden Lee Lackner suggests, Greys are most often portrayed as 'technologically advanced and intelligent beyond human understanding', which has given them a cultural status as 'dangerous, unknowable others'.[38] In other words, it is precisely the ambiguity that surrounds the Greys' rationale for their actions – their utter alienness – that makes them so terrifying. Lackner is supported by Brown, who suggests that due to their 'superior intellect', Greys are often depicted as 'godlike in their omniscience and omnipotence', and thus have come to 'represent . . . the gamut of powers that are perceived to control and/or oppress us'.[39]

There is no better monster to represent the capitalist establishment. As Murphy suggests, there is 'a sense of sheer *unfairness*' in Blumhouse's early horror films, a feeling that:

> the arrogance, incompetence, and sheer unbridled greed of major financial institutions across the world seems, to ordinary citizens, to have gone almost entirely unpunished, while the consequences of their reckless decisions disproportionately impact on those least equipped to cope.[40]

But this notion is far more evident in *Dark Skies* than any of Blumhouse's tales of demonic visitation. The Greys are not 'evil' but, as highly evolved beings with vast knowledge and resources, they are cold and uncaring. As Pollard tells the Barretts, the Greys have no more regard for their test subjects than a scientist has for a lab rat. They simply do not recognise the pain of those they torture – and whatever their purpose is, they consider it far more important than human suffering. They are a superior species who can and will do as they please, and the film illustrates time and again that humans have no way to combat or repel them. As Brown asserts, alien abductions are often imagined as a 'power struggle' in which abductees are forced to play 'the role of hapless, resourceless victims'.[41] This is exactly what occurs in *Dark Skies*, a narrative that serves as a particularly potent metaphor for the power imbalance between the greedy and hubristic elite class that caused the financial crisis and the ordinary Americans who suffered its effects.

In fact, an acute sense of powerlessness is palpable throughout the film. As Lackner attests, it is common for those who claim to have been victims of alien abduction to express a particular 'anxiety around the loss of their autonomy'.[42] This is all too apparent in the Barrett's experiences with the Greys. Borrowing directly from abduction accounts, the film has its aliens place implants behind their ears that are used, in Pollard's words, to 'control you – make you do things you can't remember, make you see things that aren't there'. While the plethora of demons that appear in the *Paranormal Activity* series, *Insidious* and *Sinister* are seen to possess individuals, these implants allow the Greys to exert their influence over the entire Barrett family; at some point in the narrative, every single one of them has their body and mind hijacked by the aliens. This is not singular *possession* but plural *control*.

In his audio commentary on *Dark Skies*, Stewart shares a sentiment that clearly links this total loss of autonomy with the everyday experience of capitalist modernity. In describing the themes of the film, he states: 'There's this feeling of being thrown around on these tidal forces, that your life is out of control . . . You didn't cause the banking crisis, you didn't make your house suddenly lose a lot of value.'[43] The Greys, then, embody forces – financial institutions, the stock exchange, the housing market – that are far beyond the influence of working people. When they fall under the aliens' sway, the Barretts become puppets manipulated by an external force and retain no control over their actions, allegorising not just the psychological stress of their fiscal situation but the debilitating feeling of powerlessness that comes with living in a capitalist society. And while the possessions that occur in Blumhouse's other early horror films might serve a similar metaphorical purpose, this theme is all the more potent here because it afflicts every member of the family rather than just one unfortunate individual.

Furthermore, *Dark Skies* makes explicitly clear that the Barretts are not exceptional. Unlike the protagonists in Blumhouse's other recessionary films, they have not been singled out by some infernal creature; the Grey's activities are widespread. As Lacy seeks answers from Pollard, she asks him: 'What makes us so special?' The expert replies, simply: 'Nothing. There's nothing special about you.' As Pollard tells them, in a statement that could speak to their fiscal troubles as much as their extraterrestrial encounters, 'Others have experienced what you're going through and have struggled the way you're struggling now'. In fact, Pollard himself is also a victim of the Greys and reveals that he once lived in the suburbs before moving to his current residence, a cramped apartment filled with aging furniture – linking his own experience of alien visitation with financial ruin. He claims to have interviewed thousands of other people who have recounted identical experiences and, at the end of the film, a brief scene shows him cutting out a newspaper article detailing Jesse's disappearance before taping it to a wall next to hundreds of similar reports. All of this reinforces the relevance of the film's themes to its contemporary audience; *Dark Skies* works hard to emphasise that the Barretts are far from the only people to have been targeted by the Greys – a reminder that they are also not unique in their suffering under capitalism and even, perhaps, a suggestion that they are far more privileged than many. And the film tells us that the Greys are not just ubiquitous but well-established, their activities having escalated over a long period without society at large becoming aware of their presence.

As Pollard explains: 'People think of aliens as these beings invading our planet in some great cataclysm . . . But it's not like that at all. The invasion already happened. No one knows exactly when, but they're here. They've been here.' Similarly, the financial crisis was not a random and unpredictable event; it was the result of American economic policy stretching back to at least the 1980s, when the Ronald Reagan administration ushered in the age of neoliberalism.

A staunch believer in the free market, Reagan deregulated the American financial sector as a matter of urgency, creating what Thomas Palley calls a 'financial boom' that 'provided consumers and firms with collateral to support debt-financed spending'.[44] As Palley notes, it was the over-extension of this unsustainable system that eventually resulted in the bursting of the US housing bubble.[45]

And while the Great Recession might have inspired a great deal of anti-capitalist sentiment,[46] 'the most perverse legacy of the global crisis has been a further entrenchment of neoliberal rationalities and disciplines'.[47] The Grey's longstanding and yet concealed occupation of Earth thus acts as a metaphor for the way in which the Western world has slowly – and for those not fortunate enough to be a member of the financial elite, unwittingly – fallen under corporate control. As Pollard states (in a comment that implicitly links a covert alien invasion with the insidious march of late capitalism), 'The presence of the Greys is now a fact of life. Like death and taxes'.

Like capitalism, the alien invaders of *Dark Skies* are a seemingly unstoppable force. They have spent many years tormenting humankind and have a relentless nature that echoes the wider cultural depiction of 'Grey' aliens. The cinematic adaptation of *Communion*, for example, ends with Whitley Strieber's fictional analogue coming to accept their encroachments on his life. While the Barretts certainly do not accept the presence of the Greys, it is revealed that their encounter has lasted for much longer than they had previously realised. Once Jesse has been taken, Lacy discovers a series of drawings inside a box containing his possessions – clearly sketched when he was a young child – that depict himself and other members of his family surrounded by alien figures. Lacy then recalls that Jesse was often ill in childhood, the apparent result of his early contact with the Greys. Furthermore, it becomes clear in the film's last moments that the aliens are still watching the family; Sam hears his brother's voice through an old walkie-talkie, suggesting that they might soon return for him. This future threat is even clearer in the film's original ending, where the final shot is of Sam convulsing while suffering a heavy nosebleed.[48] Variously attributed to Fredric Jameson and Slavoj Žižek,[49] a famous quote suggests that 'it is easier to imagine the end of the world than it is to imagine the end of capitalism'. This idea – that escape from capitalist conditions is impossible – is echoed in the ending of *Dark Skies*, as the Barretts' tormentors promise to continue visiting them for years to come. As a tagline used repeatedly in the film's marketing material states, 'Once you've been chosen, you belong to them'.

Out of Space

While *Dark Skies* is fairly typical and representative of Blumhouse's recessionary horror narratives, there are ways in which it significantly differs from the *Paranormal Activity* series, *Insidious* and *Sinister*. First, it has a far more obvious concern with the financial crisis and its effects. While recessionary anxieties are largely subtextual in the company's supernatural horror films, *Dark Skies* is plainly concerned with the recession on a textual level from its very beginning until its end. It opens, of course, with that image of a foreclosed property – which foreshadows its final scene. Lacy discovers Jesse's drawings because she is packing his things, along with the rest of the family's possessions, into boxes; the Barretts have, apparently, finally lost their house. It is not explicitly confirmed that their home has been repossessed in the film's theatrical ending, but it is made clear in the sequence that was originally intended to close the film. In the alternate epilogue, Daniel stares dejectedly at his neighbours going about their lives – perhaps wondering which of them will be next to lose everything – before he and Lacy walk past the signpost that has been erected in their front yard. In a mirror image of that shot in the opening montage, two signs are attached to the post: the first reads 'Bank Owned'. The second reads 'For Sale'.

The film's major departure from the Blumhouse formula as described by Murphy is its rejection of demonic monsters in favour of extraterrestrial antagonists. While the various demons in the company's other early horror movies pile 'inescapable supernatural complications' on their victims and broadly function as embodiments of the 'pain and suffering' that comes with financial strife,[50] the Greys are a more complicated metaphor.

Drawing on the cultural connotations of the 'Grey' alien, so often depicted as an emotionless being with unfathomable intelligence, the film uses its otherworldly invaders as a representation of the capitalist establishment: the wealthy, powerful and seemingly untouchable elite whose actions and decisions decide the health of the economy. In this, *Dark Skies* utilises Greys in much the same way as those people who believe they have experienced abductions, using a tale of alien contact to give physical form to 'the disabling impact of otherwise abstract social forces'.[51] And, of course, *Dark Skies* would not be the first science fiction film to use an advanced extraterrestrial species as a metaphor for modern capitalism. In *They Live* (1988), released at the end of the Reagan era, America has been covertly invaded by aliens who control humanity via subliminal consumerist messaging in a glaring 'critique of class divisions and capitalist power'.[52]

Perhaps the most striking quality of *Dark Skies*, then, is its unusual deployment of text and subtext; it tackles the horror of the recession both literally and allegorically. In this sense, it has much in common with another Blumhouse film released only a few months later, *The Purge* (2013) – which, as Stacey Abbott has noted, casts explicit concerns about populist politics, systemic racism and social inequality in the contemporary United States into a dystopian future.[53] As Stewart states, *Dark Skies* is in large part a 'suburban drama',[54] quite literally the story of one American family who struggle to survive amidst economic turmoil. It is also, though, a cleverly metaphoric sci-fi-horror film that uses an alien abduction narrative to allegorise the day-to-day experience of living in a capitalist society, where the fortunes of the masses are at the mercy of the elite. These two plotlines play out concurrently – gradually interweaving to create one of Blumhouse's more unique, interesting and impactful recessionary nightmares.

Notes

1. B. M. Murphy, '"It's Not the House That's Haunted": Demons, Debt, and the Family in Peril Formula in Recent Horror Cinema', in M. Leeder (ed.), *Cinematic Ghosts: Haunting and Spectrality from Silent Cinema to the Digital Era* (New York: Bloomsbury, 2015), pp. 235–6.

2. Bridget Brown, *They Know Us Better than We Know Ourselves: The History and Politics of Alien Abduction* (New York: New York University Press, 2007), p. 12.

3. Murphy, 'It's Not the House That's Haunted', p. 236.

4. It is worth noting that Blumhouse's first attempt to make a horror film featuring aliens, *Area 51* (2015), was a far worse commercial failure. Greenlit in 2009, it was delayed by script rewrites, reshoots and a lengthy post-production process. Paramount Pictures eventually released the film in 2015 via video-on-demand platforms alongside a very brief theatrical run in Alamo Drafthouse cinemas, grossing only $7,556.

5. Murphy, 'It's Not the House That's Haunted', p. 237.

6. Barry Keith Grant, *Monster Cinema* (New Brunswick NJ: Rutgers University Press, 2018), pp. 112–13.

7. D. Harvey, '*Dark Skies*', *Variety* (4 March 2013), 18.

8. R. Moore, '*Dark Skies* is Light on Originality', *Pittsburgh Post* (25 February 2013), C8.

9. M. Olsen, '*Dark Skies* Above Suburbia', *Los Angeles Times* (23 February 2013), D8.

10. Peter Hough, *Understanding Global Security* (third edition) (New York: Routledge, 2013), p. 192.

11. Robert J. Shiller, *The Subprime Solution: How Today's Global Financial Crisis Happened, and What to Do About It* (Princeton NJ: Princeton University Press, 2008), p. 12.

12. François Chesnais, *Finance Capital Today: Corporations and Banks in the Lasting Global Slump* (Leiden: Brill, 2016), p. 29.

13. Hough, *Understanding Global Security*, p. 106.

14. Jerry M. Rosenberg, *The Concise Encyclopedia of the Great Recession 2007–2010* (second edition) (Lanham MD: Scarecrow Press, 2012), p. 403.

15. Sarah Bohn and Eric Schiff, *The Great Recession and Distribution of Income in California* (San Francisco CA: Public Policy Institute of California, 2011), p. 8.

16. A. Reeves, M. McKnee and D. Stuckler, 'Economic Suicides in the Great Recession in Europe and North America', *British Journal of Psychiatry*, 205/3 (2014), 246.

17. Atif Milan and Amir Sufi, *House of Debt: How They (and You) Caused the Great Recession and How We Can Prevent It from Happening Again* (Chicago IL: University of Chicago Press, 2015), p. 27.

18. C. I. Mann, 'Death and Dead-End Jobs: Independent Horror and the Great Recession', in P. Bennett and J. McDougall (eds), *Popular Culture and the Austerity Myth: Hard Times Today* (New York: Routledge, 2017), pp. 179.

19. J. D. Stone, 'Horror at the Homestead: The (Re)Possession of American Property in *Paranormal Activity* and *Paranormal Activity II*', in K. Boyle and D. Mrozowski (eds), *The Great Recession in Film, Fiction, and Television:*

Twenty-First Century Bust Culture (Lanham MD: Lexington Books, 2013), pp. 51–2.

20. Murphy, 'It's Not the House That's Haunted', p. 241.
21. Murphy, 'It's Not the House That's Haunted', p. 243.
22. Grant, *Monster Cinema*, p. 113.
23. Murphy, 'It's Not the House That's Haunted', p. 251.
24. S. Stewart, 'Commentary with Writer/Director Scott Stewart, Producer Jason Blum, Executive Producer Brian Kavanaugh-Jones and Editor Peter Gvozdan', *Dark Skies*, Blu-ray (Toronto: eOne, 2013).
25. Grant, *Monster Cinema*, p. 113.
26. Olsen, '*Dark Skies* Above Suburbia', D8.
27. Murphy, 'It's Not the House That's Haunted', p. 237.
28. Murphy, 'It's Not the House That's Haunted', p. 248.
29. Murphy, 'It's Not the House That's Haunted', pp. 241–2.
30. Murphy, 'It's Not the House That's Haunted', p. 250.
31. Grant, *Monster Cinema*, p. 112.
32. Murphy, 'It's Not the House That's Haunted', p. 227.
33. D. R. Burleson, 'The Alien', in S. T. Joshi (ed.), *Icons of Horror and the Supernatural: An Encyclopedia of Our Worst Nightmares* (Westport CO: Greenwood Press, 2007), p. 2.
34. E. L. Lackner, 'Grays', in M. M. Levy and F. Mendlesohn (eds), *Aliens in Popular Culture* (Santa Barbara CA: ABC-CLIO, 2019), p. 136.
35. J. E. Campbell, 'Alien(ating) Ideology and the American Media: Apprehending the Alien Image in Television through *The X-Files*', *International Journal of Cultural Studies*, 4/3 (2001), 331.
36. Lackner, 'Grays', p. 135.
37. Jerome Clark, *Extraordinary Encounters: An Encyclopedia of Extraterrestrials and Otherworldly Beings* (Santa Barbara CA: ABC-CLIO, 2000), p. 3.
38. Lackner, 'Grays', p. 135.
39. Brown, *They Know Us Better than We Know Ourselves*, p. 14.
40. Murphy, 'It's Not the House That's Haunted', p. 251.
41. Brown, *They Know Us Better than We Know Ourselves*, p. 14.
42. Lackner, 'Grays', p. 137.
43. Stewart, 'Commentary with Writer/Director Scott Stewart'.
44. T. Palley, 'America's Flawed Paradigm: Macroeconomic Causes of the Financial Crisis and Great Recession', *Empirica*, 38/1 (2011), 5.
45. Palley, 'America's Flawed Paradigm', 4–5.
46. A. H. Yagci, 'The Great Recession, Inequality and Occupy Protests around the World', *Government Opposition*, 52/4 (2017), 640–70.

47. J. Peck, N. Theodore and N. Brenner, 'Neoliberalism Resurgent? Market Rule after the Great Recession', *South Atlantic Quarterly*, 111/2 (2012), 265.

48. This alternate ending was filmed and is included as a special feature on the film's DVD and Blu-ray releases. According to Stewart, a new epilogue was shot to avoid confusing audiences, as the original sequence features a Grey taking Sam's form – something that the aliens are not seen to do at any other point in the film.

49. Mark Fisher, *Capitalist Realism: Is There No Alternative?* (Winchester: Zero Books, 2009), p. 2.

50. Murphy, 'It's Not the House That's Haunted', pp. 250–1.

51. Brown, *They Know Us Better Than We Know Ourselves*, p. 14

52. D. Harlan Wilson, *They Live* (New York: Wallflower Press, 2015), p. 10.

53. S. Abbott, 'When the Subtext Becomes Text: *The Purge* Takes on the American Nightmare' (paper presented at Fear 2000: Horror Media Now, Sheffield Hallam University, Sheffield, 6 April 2018).

54. Stewart, 'Commentary with Writer/Director Scott Stewart'.

6

The (Blum)House that Found-Footage Horror Built

Shellie McMurdo

WHILE THEY HAVE BEEN, perhaps unfairly, referred to as producing 'a ramshackle assortment of found footage thrill rides and creepy doll origin stories',[1] Blumhouse Productions have become a central player in contemporary horror cinema. This legacy has been cemented by their release of critically acclaimed horror films such as *Get Out* (2017) and *The Invisible Man* (2020) and their position at the helm of the long-running and extremely popular *Insidious* and *The Purge* franchises. Blumhouse's synonymy with some of the most intriguing developments in post-millennium horror cinema, as well as a string of genre hits, have led journalists to assert that the company has 'reshaped the landscape of horror'.[2] With other commercial and critical successes such as *Sinister* (2012), *The Gift* (2015) and *Split* (2017) bearing the Blumhouse ident, the production house has become one of the most visible and recognisable producers of horror cinema in recent years.

An understudied element of Blumhouse Productions' rise to prominence, however, is the strong and enduring connection between the company and the found-footage horror subgenre. This is a curious oversight given that the initial growth of the production house can be seen as stemming from the enormous success of a film belonging to that subgenre,

Paranormal Activity (2009) and its sequels. This chapter will examine the clear and continual return to the found-footage format in Blumhouse's production history, highlighting commonalities in criticisms of both the production house and the subgenre before investigating how both are seemingly preoccupied by their cultural context, positioning this as a possible explanation for their close relationship. I will then track formal shifts both subtle and seismic within selected Blumhouse produced found-footage horror entries and demonstrate their connection to broader cultural shifts such as the rise in surveillance technology post-millennium, and the exponential growth of internet-based communication. In order to examine the relationship between Blumhouse Productions and the found-footage horror format, however, it is first necessary to accurately position both within the topography of modern horror cinema, underlining their respective centrality to this field and charting their initial entanglement.

When Blumhouse Found Footage

Although the found-footage horror subgenre has historical antecedents in *The Legend of Boggy Creek* (1972) and *Cannibal Holocaust* (1980), it was with the release of *The Blair Witch Project* (1999) that this distinctive format first gained widespread attention. Despite critical acclaim, an increase in found-footage horror production did not immediately follow the film's release, with it being noted that imitations of *The Blair Witch Project*'s format were conspicuous only by their absence.[3] Found-footage horror did not disappear entirely in the first decade of the new millennium following *The Blair Witch Project*, with key films such as *Cloverfield* (2008) finding critical and financial success, but it did retreat from the mainstream considerably. It would not be until the release of Blumhouse's *Paranormal Activity* that the subgenre would again find itself in the spotlight, this time followed by a widespread emulation of the found-footage aesthetic and a significant increase in production for the format.

Paranormal Activity was charged with 'instantly changing horror films for the decade',[4] with its impact reverberating through the genre in the following years. Just as *The Blair Witch Project* was positioned as a minimalist salve to the dominant horror trends of the late 1990s, contrasting with the glossy production values and 'smart alecky, tongue in cheek attitude'[5] of the neo-slashers, the low-fi quality of *Paranormal Activity* was similarly noted to be an alternative to the visual excesses of torture porn.[6] As Adam

Charles Hart notes, the film was something of 'a genuinely strange cultural phenomenon for its rejection of so many of the things the industry thought audiences wanted from horror in 2009'.[7] There was a discernible and undeniable rise in the number of found-footage horror films produced in North America following *Paranormal Activity*. This is especially apparent if we are to compare the number of films adhering to the format in the four years previous to its release, of which there are eleven in total, to the four years following its release, where forty-one found-footage horror films emerged.[8] The success of *Paranormal Activity* gave an enormous financial boost to Blumhouse Productions, with the film being created on a meagre budget of $15,000 and going on to gross more than $193 million worldwide.[9] It is also a significant film within the company's production history, in that it marks the point at which Blumhouse Productions turned almost primarily to the horror genre.

The presence of found-footage horror within Blumhouse's horror filmography is essential. Of their catalogue, sixteen are what I will term as 'pure found-footage horror', meaning that the film adheres to the found-footage conceit for most of its run time. Further to these sixteen pure found-footage horror films, there are also a number of films produced by Blumhouse that I term 'found-footage horror adjacent', meaning that the aesthetics and conventions of the format are used as a key narrative device during the film. An example of this would be *Sinister*, in which the story revolves around a box of found VHS tapes and, as Bernice Murphy rightly points out, in which 'important sequences . . . are shot as though being recorded on authentically grainy 8mm . . . film'.[10] Within *Sinister*, it is fair to say some of the most atmospheric and genuinely tense moments within the film originate from this 'found footage' and its role within the narrative is crucial. If we are to isolate the pure found-footage horror films and combine them with the found-footage adjacent films, such films comprise nearly half of Blumhouse's overall horror production history.

It is evident that there is a clear and continual return throughout Blumhouse's production history to the found-footage horror subgenre that has yet to be examined. It could be argued, that Blumhouse's repeated return to the format may be down to myriad of reasons, including the worth of found-footage horror, as a subgenre that can be produced on very little money, to a company that sets quite strict budgetary limitations.[11] This chapter will demonstrate, however, that the links between the subgenre and the production house run deeper than financial prudence.

Blumhouse Productions and the found-footage horror subgenre have a commonality in terms of recurrent criticisms that have been aimed in their direction. Although Blumhouse has been positioned as the production house poised to 'save' the horror genre,[12] it would be false to claim that the company has escaped unfavourable analysis. A recurrent theme in journalistic appraisal of Blumhouse Productions is the suggestion that there is an overarching focus for the company on the quantity of their filmic output rather than the quality. This can be seen in multiple references to how they are 'cranking out' or 'churn out' films,[13] functioning as an 'assembly line'[14] for the 'best and *worst* of modern horror'.[15] There is a proposition in many of these accounts that Blumhouse is not so much preternaturally skilled at spotting the next possible horror hit, but that its chances of producing one are 'elevated by sheer volume alone'.[16] Moreover, it has been argued that Blumhouse's prolific rate of production has resulted in 'a glut of lower-tier films, some of which are so lazy and uninspired ... that they threaten to give horror a bad name'.[17] There is also a suggestion here that the output of the company is limited by its (self-imposed) budgetary constraints, resulting in a persistent usage of the word 'cheap'[18] or the phrase 'cheap looking'[19] to describe the films produced by Blumhouse, even in otherwise complimentary accounts.

Found-footage horror cinema has similarly been described as 'cheap',[20] in addition to being 'a grabby, artless gimmick'[21] or 'an ingenious way to excuse crap production values'.[22] Because the found-footage horror aesthetic is easy to reproduce on incredibly limited budgets, the subgenre is prolific and – as I will explore – the saturation of the format within the horror genre is perhaps one of the reasons that it draws critical ire. The stylistic limitations of found-footage horror have also featured in both journalistic accounts[23] and scholarship surrounding the subgenre and are positioned as hindrances to be overcome in order for the format to survive.[24] However, as the remainder of this chapter will argue, it is precisely the limitations of Blumhouse Productions' budgets and found-footage horror's style and form that enable their symbiotic relationship.

Cheap/Woke: Blumhouse, Found-Footage Horror and Cultural Commentary

Perhaps due to its production of recent films that deal with socially relevant themes such as *Get Out, The Invisible Man* and *The Hunt* (2020), Blumhouse has been repeatedly framed as a production house that is acutely conversant with its contemporary cultural climate. Indeed, this awareness of the production contexts of its films has led to criticism that the company is perhaps trying too hard to produce 'woke' horror,[25] with films such as *Black Christmas* (2019) characterised as 'less of a horror film and more of a thinkpiece, a hodgepodge of buzzwords and ideas, aiming high but crashing into the snow'.[26] The sociopolitical resonance of the films that it produces appears to be a growing matter of importance to Blumhouse, as is its amplification of previously marginalised voices within the horror genre. Blumhouse Productions has, for instance, recently focused on increasing the number of films that it produces by Black and ethnic minority creators, spearheaded by the aforementioned *Get Out*, and including *Thriller* (2018), *Us* (2019) and *Sweetheart* (2019). This is in addition to films that focus on groups or individuals that have previously been somewhat absent from, or caricatured by, the horror genre – for example, the overarchingly Latino cast of *Paranormal Activity: The Marked Ones* (2014), the disabled final girl of *Hush* (2016) and the African-American family at the centre of *Don't Let Go* (2019). Blumhouse founder and CEO Jason Blum has been directly criticised for a lack of diversity in terms of the gender of directors that helm Blumhouse films,[27] but this would appear to be an imbalance that is beginning to be actively addressed, with the announcement and release of four female-directed horror films.[28] Of course, Blumhouse, in its function as a production company, cannot be given sole credit for the ways in which many of these films broach culturally relevant themes, but the ongoing political underpinnings of recent Blumhouse-funded films is underlined by Jason Blum's inclination towards commenting on a variety of pertinent social issues in various interviews. In an interview with *Variety* magazine, Blum noted that his impetus for producing culturally resonant horror was due to his desire to highlight relevant issues: 'I'm deeply personally upset with what's happening in the world, and I look for any possible way I can try and change it. The tool at my disposal is we make TV shows and movies.'[29] Blum is also known for being politically engaged, having been removed from the stage at the Israel Film Festival in 2018 for speaking out against President Trump.[30]

The found-footage horror subgenre is similarly preoccupied with its cultural context at both a narrative and formal level. As I have discussed elsewhere,[31] the subgenre's fixation with the context that it is created in manifests in its presentation of narratives as occurring in the audience's reality rather than adjacent to it, with this being achieved by an adoption of ever-evolving representations of reality. The subgenre's adaptability and keen emulation of new reality 'looks' enables it to maintain an association with the audience member in their current cultural moment, an element that is key to its appeal. The found-footage horror subgenre therefore includes many different 'looks' under its subgeneric banner, from the handheld style of *The Blair Witch Project*, through to the emulation of reality television in *Grave Encounters* (2011), mimicking of a VICE documentary in *The Sacrament* (2013) and the social media aesthetic of *Unfriended* (2015). This adaptability of found-footage horror cinema has allowed the subgenre to engage with a variety of cultural anxieties, as well as confronting and even revisiting US national traumas such as 9/11 and the Jonestown Massacre, in a much more direct way than other subgenres. Found-footage horror stands as perhaps one of the most socially aware subgenres in cinematic horror history, perhaps necessitated by its keen interest in adopting ever-evolving technologies and reality aesthetics. At the heart of many found-footage horror narratives is the character's drive towards capturing evidence of the unique or unprecedented, whether this be an event, an act or an entity. As Cecilia Sayad argues, 'the found footage cycle is considered a symptom of its time, and a topical one, for the act of filming one's life is widespread'.[32] In a society ever more affected by and attentive to visual evidence of events around the world, the found-footage horror film is a format that has a particular resonance.

It would seem then, that Blumhouse Productions, as a company that leans towards social relevance, and found-footage horror, as a subgenre that lends itself well to cultural commentary and is fixated on its production context, are particularly well matched. In addition to being a subgenre that can be produced comfortably within Blumhouse's budgetary limitations, the ability of the format to adapt and respond quickly to broader shifts – both cultural and technological – resonate within a production house that seeks to be at the forefront of thematic and aesthetic shifts within the horror genre. Although found-footage horror cinema has been termed 'visually simplistic'[33] or, more pejoratively 'tired and lazy',[34] these criticisms discount several evolutionary shifts, both thematic and aesthetic, that have occurred within the subgenre since its inception. The found-footage horror films produced by Blumhouse in particular have moved the subgenre in often startling directions. Beginning with an overview of the *Paranormal Activity* franchise and culminating with an analysis of *Unfriended*, the next section of this chapter will chart some of the transformations that have taken place within Blumhouse-produced found-footage horror, and how these have connected to broader cultural and technological changes.

'Whatever Happened to the Little Handheld?': Subtle and Seismic
Shifts in Blumhouse's Found Footage

Despite the fact that the *Paranormal Activity* franchise has been described
as a 'crassly commercial venture' in which each instalment 'follows the
same predictable pattern',[35] and that it has been dismissed as a series that
'offers the same ghostly clap trap over and over',[36] it is within these films
that we can begin to discern formal innovations that act as subtle shifts
within the subgenre's format. The reception to *Paranormal Activity* was
overarchingly positive, with it being hailed as a 'new claustrophobic classic'[37] that was 'brutally committed to simplicity'.[38] Although much was
made of *The Blair Witch Project*'s minimalist aesthetic, *Paranormal Activity*
managed to pull the found-footage horror subgenre into even more aus-
tere territory, using only one HDV camera utilised in a handheld capacity
during the day by the character of Micah and placed on a tripod facing
Micah and his girlfriend Katie's bed at night. The sparse aesthetic of *Paranormal Activity* led to it being framed as 'formally postmodern',[39] and as
a text that presented an 'interrogation of [the] properties of cinema'.[40] It
is the static frames of the overnight footage within *Paranormal Activity*
that mark the film as a significant departure from previous found-footage
horror aesthetics.

While static camera shots have been used previously in the subgenre,
it is the long duration of these sequences within *Paranormal Activity*, as
noted by Cecilia Sayad,[41] that act as a departure from previous found-footage horror aesthetics. The seemingly inactive frames in the franchise,
particularly in *Paranormal Activity 1*, *2* and *3*, compel the viewer to 'sit
through long sequences in which *literally nothing happens*'.[42] This encourages the viewer to scan the screen actively for information or movement,
and can lull them into a sense of false complacency when nothing appears
to be occurring. The effect of this is twofold; first, the inaction on screen
coupled with the viewer's close attention as they try to discern anything
significant intensifies the effect – and indeed the affect – of any sudden
movement or noise. Second, the viewer is rewarded for their close attention when they are provided with privileged visual information, such as
when one of the overnight shots of Katie and Micah's bed allows the viewer
to witness Katie, in a sleepwalking state, stand over Micah's sleeping form
for several hours. This is an event that the characters within the film are
unaware of until the following day when they review the footage. This is
a notable departure from other found-footage horror films up until this

point, where the viewer was placed more often than not in the same distinctly unprivileged position as the character operating the camera, with information revealed to both at the same time. Despite accusations that *Paranormal Activity 2* (2010) replicated 'the exact formula of the original' film,[43] this innovative push towards more static and surveillance-based aesthetics in *Paranormal Activity* was more fully realised in the sequel. Within *Paranormal Activity 2*, security cameras are placed in various locations both inside and outside of the house of Kristi, Katie's sister, after an apparent burglary. It is from these six security cameras that the majority of the 'found footage' within the film originates, with sporadic use made of a handheld camera at various points. Both *Paranormal Activity* and to a greater extent *Paranormal Activity 2*, largely eschew the embodied viewer experience that had characterised the subgenre up until this point – where the camera adopted the very human movements of its operator – and give preference to a more impassive and inhuman gaze.

I propose that although the found-footage horror subgenre as a whole grew in popularity explosively during a time of increased access to consumer-grade cameras and user-generated content websites such as YouTube, the *Paranormal Activity* franchise seems to speak in particular to the abundance of CCTV footage that has become common to mainstream news broadcasts. Furthermore, this emphasis on more dispassionate and disembodied cameras can be productively connected to the ubiquity of surveillance technologies post-millennium. In particular, the massive investments in various forms of security monitoring in a post-9/11 world, and the position of the franchise within an ever more mediated culture and society. As David Lyon notes, after the events of 11 September 2001, 'Already existing surveillance was reinforced at crucial points, with the promise of more to come'.[44] It is important to note that found-footage horror was not the only subgenre to respond to this cultural shift, with it being proposed that torture porn also adopted surveillance aesthetics in earnest.[45] *Paranormal Activity 2* in particular constructs much of its tension and horror around this style. The six security cameras within the film are situated in high corners of rooms or doors, with their lenses looking down on the characters and positioned in places where no human operator could logically be. This space is 'a place of impossible subjectivity'.[46] Given that found-footage horror is a subgenre that had been characterised by the distinctly human movements of its camera operators at this point, this new aesthetic gives a particular sense of unease. In making this move towards a focus on operatorless surveillance cameras, *Paranormal Activity 2* marks more of a full realisation of the departure from the traditional handheld found-footage style typified by *The Blair Witch Project* that *Paranormal Activity* instigated. The unfeeling, immovable gaze of its cameras allows the viewer to mediate on empty spaces and rooms, scanning them for significance without the directional input or commentary of a diegetic cameraperson.

Further instalments within the series continue the innovation shown in the first two entries, with each new film adhering to what became the franchise's model of formal innovation. For example, the introduction in *Paranormal Activity 3* (2011) of the 'fan cam', a camera attached to the base of an oscillating fan. Whereas the static cameras of the series thus far had presented the viewer with a more or less unobstructed view of the room they were placed in, the fan cam of *Paranormal Activity 3* obscured as much as it revealed. With the camera in constant motion, the audience is not provided with uninterrupted access to a stable view as the camera lens sweeps from side to side, showing only part of the room at any given time. This footage capitalised on a sense of unease around the off-screen space, and as Steven Shaviro rightly notes, for the audience 'the sense of lurking danger is enhanced as much by our fear about seeing things as by our anxiety about what we do not see'.[47] This tension is amplified by the fan cam in several key scenes, as the viewer's vision is restricted to where the camera lens is pointing at that moment. These subtle shifts and experiments in form are continued to a certain extent in both *Paranormal Activity: The Marked Ones* and *Paranormal Activity: The Ghost Dimension* (2015), the fifth and sixth instalments of the franchise. It is with *Paranormal Activity 4* (2012), however, that this drive towards innovative form began to branch into the adoption of internet-based communicative technology, with the inclusion of laptop webcams playing a significant role in the film's aesthetic.

In its release of the *Paranormal Activity* films, Blumhouse Productions positioned itself at the forefront of the burgeoning found-footage horror movement, which had rapidly become the 'subgenre *du jour*'[48] of the contemporary horror landscape. It was around the time of the release of *Paranormal Activity 4*, however, that criticism of found-footage horror began to dominate critical engagement with the format. References were made repeatedly to the limitations of the subgenre that its films seemed, at times, unable to transcend.[49] Furthermore, films such as *Chronicle* (2012) – a non-horror found-footage film – were reported to have been 'hamstrung and ultimately strangled' by the 'claustrophobic cage' of the conceit.[50] Perhaps due to the large amount of found-footage horror films that followed in the wake of *Paranormal Activity*, the format was deemed a 'stylistic fad',[51] the widespread adoption of which had led the horror genre to become oversaturated with the 'tiresome' subgenre.[52] The limitations of found-footage horror, such as its often-shaky presentation, obscured shots and the limits of its frame – all aspects that are central to the construction of fear in the subgenre and essential to its claims of authenticity – were now considered too 'rigid'.[53] The *Paranormal Activity* franchise in particular was often reduced to being positioned as 'cheaply made mass-marketed movies that have lined the pockets of producers who chanced upon the holy grail of license-to-print-money filmmaking'.[54] Moreover, it was noted that the Paranormal Activity series had 'turned the concept of "found footage" from a legitimate stylistic choice to a groan-inducing mistake',[55] leaving the format without 'anywhere new to go'.[56] I have so far argued that the *Paranormal Activity* films are the site of several formal innovations within the found-footage horror format, and that these were connected to concurrent shifts in broader culture towards surveillance and an increasingly mediated society. It was with the release of *Unfriended* in 2015, however, that the potential of the internet as a site of horror, hinted at in *Paranormal Activity 4* and *5*, would be fully realised, and it is this film that stands as a seismic shift in Blumhouse Production's found-footage horror production history.

Whereas the formal experimentation found in the *Paranormal Activity* series was often subtle, the aesthetics of *Unfriended* moved the found-footage horror subgenre into new territory entirely. Although films such as *The Den* (2013) and *Open Windows* (2014) had previously used internet-based aesthetics, both are distinct from *Unfriended* due to their use of proxy versions of software and applications within their diegesis. For example, in *The Den*, the character of Elizabeth is carrying out research on a social media website that teams the user with a random online partner for a video chat. Rather than featuring Chatroulette – a real life website that has this exact function – the film uses a stand in called 'The Den'. Similarly, in *Open Windows*, the film's aesthetics are primarily formed of software and applications that either do not exist or would not be available to the average audience member. Furthermore, *Open Windows* is presented through a high-tech, computer-based imagery aesthetic, rather than as an actual computer screen. *Unfriended* is constructed visually in a way that sets it apart from these films, traditional filmmaking as a whole and previous films in the found-footage subgenre.

The narrative of *Unfriended*, which centres on the suicide of teenager Laura Barns, is contained within the rigid limits of a laptop screen. The story unfolds primarily through a Skype video chat between a group of Laura's friends, Blaire, Adam, Mitch, Val, Jess and Ken, on the anniversary of her death. In its use of real-life software and web applications such as Google, Chatroulette, Facebook, YouTube, LiveLeak, Facebook Messenger, Skype and Spotify, *Unfriended* attempts to marry its fictional narrative with the audience's real-life experience of internet interaction. *Unfriended* clearly recognises the rise in streaming services and the ways in which audiences utilise various mediums to view films. It marks a profound shift in the found-footage horror format in the way that it deliberately plays with the audience's perception of the media that it is presented as being recorded on or broadcast through. In *Unfriended*, the viewer is bombarded with several software applications or windows of information being open at the same time. These visuals, along with common computer alert tones and the sound of fingers tapping on a keyboard, encourages an immersive experience for the audience, particularly if they are watching the film on a laptop themselves. As the director of the sequel film, *Unfriended: Dark Web* (2018), Stephen Susco, notes in relation to his own viewing of *Unfriended*, he found himself:

> Watching the mouse move across the screen and feeling my fingers moving and realising I was trying to move the mouse. That was so profound about what this new movie did . . . it tapped into the fact that we all use computers, some of us for 10, 11, 12 hours a day.[57]

The uploadable aesthetics of user-generated content websites are continually evoked within the film, not only though the Skype call, but through elements such as a video that was uploaded to YouTube by Laura before her suicide. The video, in which Laura holds up flash cards instead of speaking, is aesthetically remarkably similar to the pre-suicide video of Amanda Todd, a girl who committed suicide in real life after she was subjected to an extended online bullying campaign. In addition to the use of flashcards, both girls wear black vest tops, both have long dark hair and both of the videos are in black and white. The similarities are striking and deliberate. This use of internet-based aesthetics also extended beyond the film itself. Another video, showing the suicide of Laura Barns, and which both opens and features within the film, was hosted until relatively recently on real life shock website Liveleak.com, where it could be accessed alongside real videos of graphic injuries and suicide. In addition, various Facebook accounts were created for the characters within the film.

Unfriended is a narrative that clearly engages with its contemporary context, as Laura's suicide is framed within the film as a result of an internet-shaming campaign against her, which, it becomes apparent, was led by her supposed friends. 'Shaming' in this context, is when an individual is targeted for humiliation through use of social media, or through videos/photographs shared in online spaces. Internet shaming often plays a significant part in cyberbullying, with several cases leading to suicide. For example, the death of Izzy Laxamana, a thirteen-year-old girl who took her life after her father uploaded a video showing he had cut off her hair as a punishment.[58] Other cases, such as Tyler Clementi, Audrie Pott and Amanda Todd – mentioned above – have resulted in teenagers killing themselves due to extended cyberbullying campaigns. *Unfriended*, in its inclusion of this theme and its adherence to the aesthetics of online interaction and social media, provides a filmic space for investigating these emergent cultural anxieties around social media, cyberbullying and the threat of digital anonymity. These references to internet culture are, however, presented as less of a critique of social media or of a generation that has been said to be 'addicted to the internet',[59] but more to build a sense of realism through incorporating visual aspects that viewers may be familiar with and as a response to our increasing enmeshment with the internet in everyday life. In an age where our experience of the world is mediated often through social media and bystander footage, *Unfriended* marked the next logical step for both a subgenre that strives to connect with the cultural moment, and a production house that endeavours to move forward in its engagement with sociopolitically relevant themes.

The films that this chapter has engaged with are all centred on the supernatural. This is perhaps no surprise, due to the growing dominance of supernatural narratives within the post-millennium horror genre. Todd Platts and Mathias Clasen have suggested that this kind of horror narrative found popularity in this period 'because of a cultural and psychological climate particularly hospitable to such films'. As they go on to highlight, however, the growth of this thematic strand cannot be explained by cultural relevance alone, and they note that a key reason for this rise also stems from the fact that supernatural horror films cost considerably less money to produce than other types of horror film. This may be due to their tendency to suggest at monstrous forms rather than present them directly through the use of expensive visual effects, making this type of horror film 'particularly attractive to emerging low budget production companies such as Blumhouse Productions'.[60]

This cost effectiveness makes supernatural narratives particularly well suited to both Blumhouse Productions *and* the found-footage horror subgenre – which similarly emphasises suggestion rather than overt depictions of horror – but I would argue that it is perhaps the cultural resonance of these films that is key to their appeal to audiences. As Annette Hill proposes, popular representations of the supernatural 'tend to be located in moments of political and social change', and that these changes can be related to 'War, religious and political unrest, violence and mass trauma, new scientific developments [and] challenges to orthodoxies'.[61] In addition, Adam Charles Hart takes his cue from Jeffrey Sconce's concept of 'haunted media',[62] in arguing that 'Our anxieties about media inspire our horror stories, and our ghosts take on the forms and qualities of our media'.[63] This would suggest that there is more at play within these films than the need to appropriate new media and technology in order to maintain a relationship with audiences purely for positive financial return.

Conclusion

It is not my intention to propose that formal and thematic innovation in the found-footage horror subgenre can be found only in films produced by Blumhouse. Recent examples of the ever-evolving nature of the format can be seen in its movement across different mediums – for example, in the emergence of what could be described as 'found audio' podcasts such as *The Stroma Sessions* (2016) and *Video Palace* (2018), and the use of found-footage aesthetics within video games such as *Outlast* (2013), *The Final Take* (2016) and the augmented reality mobile-phone game *Night Terrors: Bloody Mary* (2018). From the subtle innovations present in the *Paranormal Activity* franchise to the revolutionary shift within the subgenre seen in *Unfriended*, found-footage horror has deftly adapted to emergent technologies and reality looks. This has not only enabled a connection with its audience to be maintained, but it has also allowed engagement with emerging cultural anxieties. This chapter has repeatedly placed the self-reflexive subgenre as an apt vehicle for Blumhouse Productions, as not only can found-footage horror be created on a limited budget, but it has a distinct leaning towards sociopolitical commentary.

In closing, I note that despite a drop in Blumhouse's found-footage horror production since 2015, *Paranormal Activity: Next of Kin* was released in 2021. The ever-evolving found footage format will return again to the house of Blum.

Notes

1. B. Webb, 'Horror Specialist Blumhouse has Quietly become 2020's Most Exciting Film Studio', *NME* (14 May 2020), *www.nme.com/features/horror-specialist-blumhouse-has-quietly-become-2020s-most-profitable-film-studio-2668647* (accessed 21 May 2020).

2. R. Fletcher, 'How Jason Blum Changed Horror Movies', *Den of Geek* (3 March 2020), *www.denofgeek.com/movies/how-jason-blum-changed-horror-movies/* (accessed 4 May 2020).

3. R. Gilbey, 'Commission Us: "Found footage" – the Discovery that Disappeared Again', *Guardian* (14 October 2010), *www.theguardian.com/film/film-blog/2010/oct/14/found-footage-blair-witch-project* (accessed 25 June 2020).

4. S. Bowen, 'How Jason Blum Makes Horror Movies with a Message', *Nylon* (20 September 2019), *www.nylon.com/jason-blum-interview* (accessed 6 May 2020).

5. Thomas M. Sipos, *Horror Film Aesthetics: Creating the Visual Language of Fear* (Jefferson NC: McFarland, 2010), p. 23.

6. A. C. Hart, 'Millennial Fears: Abject Horror in a Transnational Context', in H. M. Benshoff (ed.), *A Companion to the Horror Film* (London: Wiley-Blackwell, 2014), pp. 329–45.

7. Adam Charles Hart, *Monstrous Forms: Moving Image Horror Across Media* (New York: Oxford University Press, 2020), p. 19.

8. This number continued to grow between 2014 and 2018, where forty-four found-footage horror films were created in North America.

9. D. Pomerantz, 'The Triumph of *Paranormal Activity*', *Forbes* (18 October 2012), *www.forbes.com/sites/dorothypomerantz/2012/10/18/the-triumph-of-paranormal-activity/#5ebb1bc37b68* (accessed 25 June 2020).

10. B. M. Murphy, '"It's Not the House That's Haunted": Demons, Debt, and the Family in Peril in Recent Horror Cinema', in M. Leeder (ed.), *Cinematic Ghosts: Haunting and Spectrality from Silent Cinema to the Digital Era* (New York: Bloomsbury, 2015), p. 238.

11. For more details on this model and its successes, see Todd K. Platts's chapter, Blumhouse at the Box Office, 2009–2018.

12. See, for example, M. Peikert, 'Why Jason Blum Loves Making Horror', *Backstage* (22 October 2015), *www.backstage.com/magazine/article/jason-blum-loves-making-horror-9432/* (accessed 21 June 2020); J. Humphreys, 'The Haunted House that Blum Built – How an Indie Producer Saved Horror and Changed Hollywood', *Cineramble* (20 October 2018), *http://cineramble.com/2018/10/the-haunted-house-that-blum-built-how-an-indie-producer-saved-horror-and-changed-hollywood/* (accessed 21 June 2020).

13. See L. Bradley, 'This Was the Decade Horror Got "Elevated"', *Vanity Fair* (17 December 2019), *www.vanityfair.com/hollywood/2019/12/rise-of-elevated-horror-decade-2010s* (accessed 6 May 2020); Trace Thurman, 'The 10 Best Blumhouse-Produced Horror Films!', *Bloody Disgusting* (17 September 2015), *https://bloody-disgusting.com/editorials/3361660/best-blumhouse-horror-films/* (accessed 25 June 2020).

14. M. Guthrie and T. Siegel, 'From *American Horror Story* to *Walking Dead*, How Horror Took Over Hollywood', *Hollywood Reporter* (9 October 2013), *www.hollywoodreporter.com/news/american-horror-story-walking-dead-645007* (accessed 4 May 2020).

15. B. Parsons, 'The Blumhouse Model: Factory Filmmaking or Artist's Dream?', *The Boar* (20 September 2020), *https://theboar.org/2020/04/the-blumhouse-model-factory-filmmaking-or-artists-dream/* (accessed 6 May 2020), emphasis added.

16. Parsons, 'The Blumhouse Model'.

17. B. Hertz, 'Producer Jason Blum is Revolutionizing Horror Movies – for Better or Worse', *Globe and Mail* (5 June 2017), *www.theglobeandmail.com/arts/film/producer-jason-blum-is-revolutionizing-horror-movies-for-better-or-worse/article25400806/* (accessed 7 May 2020).

18. Humphreys, 'The Haunted House That Blum Built'.

19. B. Lee, '*Black Christmas* Review – Woke Slasher Remake is an Unholy, Unscary Mess', *Guardian* (13 December 2019), *www.theguardian.com/film/2019/dec/12/black-christmas-review-remake-unscary-mess* (accessed 8 May 2020).

20. J. Arbues, 'Found-footage Horror Movies that are Actually Good', *Looper* (16 October 2019), *www.looper.com/170479/found-footage-horror-movies-that-are-actually-good/* (accessed 6 May 2020).

21. O. Gleiberman, 'As *Blair Witch* Flops, is the Found-Footage Horror Film Over?', *Variety* (18 September 2016), *https://variety.com/2016/film/columns/blair-witch-is-the-found-footage-horror-film-over-1201864069/* (accessed 10 April 2019).

22. M. Warren, 'How to Fix Found Footage in Three Easy Steps', *Film Independent* (20 October 2016), *www.filmindependent.org/blog/fix-found-footage-three-easy-steps/* (accessed 13 May 2020).

23. S. Schaeffer, '*Blair Witch* and the Evolution of the Found-Footage Genre', *Screen Rant* (17 September 2016), *https://screenrant.com/blair-witch-found-footage-discussion/* (accessed 21 June 2020).

24. X. Aldana Reyes, 'The *[Rec]* Films: Affective Possibilities and Stylistic Limitations of Found Footage Horror', in X. Aldana Reyes and L. Blake (eds), *Digital Horror: Haunted Technologies: Network Panic and the Found Footage Phenomenon* (New York: I. B. Tauris, 2016), p. 157.

25. 'Woke' meaning acutely aware of social injustices.

26. Lee, '*Black Christmas* Review'.

27. M. Patches, 'Blumhouse has Never Produced a Theatrically Released Horror Movie Directed by a Woman – but Hopes to', *Polygon* (18 October 2018), *www.polygon.com/2018/10/17/17984162/halloween-blumhouse-female-director* (accessed 21 June 2020).

28. *The Lie* (2018), *Run Sweetheart Run* (2020), *Nocturne* (2020), and *The Craft: Legacy* (2020) were directed by Veena Sud, Shana Feste, Zu Quirke and Zoe Lister-Jones respectively.

29. *Variety*, 'Jason Blum: Variety Cover Shoot', *YouTube* (12 June 2018), *https://youtu.be/a2wTuT3WL-8a* (accessed 27 June 2020).

30. E. Nyren, 'Jason Blum Booed, Removed at L.A.'s Israel Film Festival after Anti-Trump Comments', *Variety* (6 November 2018), *https://variety.com/2018/film/news/jason-blum-booed-israel-film-festival-anti-trump-comments-1203021778/* (accessed 17 June 2020).

31. Shellie McMurdo, *Blood on the Lens: Trauma and Anxiety in American Found Footage Horror* (Edinburgh: Edinburgh University Press, forthcoming).

32. C. Sayad, 'Found-Footage Horror and the Frame's Undoing', *Cinema Journal*, 55/2 (2016), 49.

33. A. Swanson, 'Audience Reaction Movie Trailers and the *Paranormal Activity* Franchise', *Transformative Works and Cultures*, 18 (2015), 2.

34. S. O'Malley, '*Paranormal Activity: The Marked Ones*', Roger Ebert (4 January 2014), *www.rogerebert.com/reviews/paranormal-activity-the-marked-ones-2014* (accessed 21 June 2020).

35. S. Shaviro, 'The Glitch Dimension: Paranormal Activity and the Technologies of Vision', in M. Beugnet, A. Cameron and A. Fetveit (eds), *Indefinite Visions: Cinema and the Attractions of Uncertainty* (Edinburgh: Edinburgh University Press, 2017), p. 317.

36. P. Sobczynski, '*Paranormal Activity: The Ghost Dimension*', Roger Ebert (23 October 2015), *www.rogerebert.com/reviews/paranormal-activity-the-ghost-dimension-2015* (accessed 21 June 2020).

37. P. Bradshaw, '*Paranormal Activity*', *Guardian* (25 November 2009), *www.theguardian.com/film/2009/nov/25/paranormal-activity-review* (accessed 21 June 2020).

38. S. Crook, '*Paranormal Activity* Review', *Empire* (22 October 2009), *www.empireonline.com/movies/reviews/paranormal-activity-review/* (accessed 21 June 2020).

39. D. Stevens, '*Paranormal Activity*', *Slate* (30 October 2009), *https://slate.com/culture/2009/10/paranormal-activity-reviewed.html* (accessed 21 June 2020).

40. S. Everhart, 'Framework of Fear: The Postmodern Aesthetic of *Paranormal Activity 2*', *Cinethesia*, 1/1 (2012), 8.

41. Sayad, 'Found-Footage Horror'.

42. Shaviro, 'The Glitch Dimension', p. 317, emphasis in original.

43. F. Scheck, '*Paranormal Activity 2*: Film Review', *The Hollywood Reporter* (22 October 2010), *www.hollywoodreporter.com/review/paranormal-activity-2-film-review-32162* (accessed 21 June 2020).

44. D. Lyon, 'Surveillance Studies: Understanding Visibility, Mobility and the Phonetic Fix', *Surveillance and Society*, 1/1 (2002), 1.

45. See C. Zimmer, 'Caught on Tape? The Politics of Video in the New Torture Film', in A. Briefel and S. J. Miller (eds), *Horror After 9/11: World of Fear, Cinema of Terror* (Austin TX: University of Texas Press, 2012), pp. 83–106; Steve Jones, *Torture Porn: Popular Horror After Saw* (New York: Palgrave Macmillan, 2015).

46. Slavoj Žižek, *Enjoy Your Symptom!: Jacques Lacan in Hollywood and Out* (third edition) (New York: Routledge, 2008), p. 231.

47. Shaviro, 'The Glitch Dimension', p. 55.

48. Alexandra Heller Nicholas, *Found Footage Horror Films: Fear and the Appearance of Reality* (Jefferson NC: McFarland, 2014), p. 3, emphasis in original.

49. I. Buckwalter, 'Shorter is Scarier: Why Horror Anthologies Need to Make a Comeback', *The Atlantic* (8 October 2012), *www.theatlantic.com/entertainment/archive/2012/10/shorter-is-scarier-why-horror-anthologies-need-to-make-a-comeback/263312/* (accessed 25 June 2020).

50. Ben Childs, '*Chronicle*'s Found-Footage Fetish Weakens Its Superhero Powers', *Guardian* (27 January 2012), *www.theguardian.com/film/filmblog/2012/jan/27/chronicle-found-footage-superhero-powers* (accessed 21 May 2020).

51. S. Meslow, '12 Years After *Blair Witch*, When Will the Found-Footage Horror Fad End?', *Atlantic* (6 January 2012), *www.theatlantic.com/entertainment/archive/2012/01/12-years-after-blair-witch-when-will-the-found-footage-horror-fad-end/250950/* (accessed 20 April 2020).

52. C. Orr, '*V/H/S*: Is There Life Left in Found-Footage Horror', *The Atlantic* (5 October 2012), *https://www.theatlantic.com/entertainment/archive/2012/10/v-h-s-is-there-life-left-in-found-footage-horror/263272/* (accessed 21 May 2020).

53. S. Tobias, '*Paranormal Activity 4*', *The A. V. Club* (19 September 2012), *https://film.avclub.com/paranormal-activity-4-1798174682* (accessed 21 June 2020).

54. L. Buckmaster, '*Paranormal Activity 4* Movie Review: Milking the Digicam Cash Cow', *Crikey Inq* (29 October 2012), *https://blogs.crikey.com.au/cinetology/2012/10/29/paranormal-activity-4-movie-review-milking-the-digicam-cash-cow/* (accessed 22 June 2020).

55. J. Berardinelli, '*Paranormal Activity 4*', *Reelviews* (19 October 2012), *www.reelviews.net/reelviews/paranormal-activity-4* (accessed 21 June 2020).

56. C. Bumbray, 'Review: *Paranormal Activity 4*', *Jo Blo* (19 October 2012), *www.joblo.com/movie-news/review-paranormal-activity-4* (accessed 21 June 2020).

57. Quoted in J. Yamato, 'With *Searching*, *Unfriended* and beyond, Timur Bekmambetov Seeks a New Cinematic Language that Mirrors Our Digital Lives', *Los Angeles Times* (17 August 2018), *www.latimes.com/entertainment/movies/la-ca-mn-timur-bekmambetov-searching-unfriended-dark-web-screenlife-20180817-story.html* (accessed 25 June 2020).

58. A. Hess, 'The Shaming of Izzy Laxamana', *Slate* (12 June 2015), *https://slate.com/technology/2015/06/izabel-laxamana-a-tragic-case-in-the-growing-genre-of-parents-publicly-shaming-their-children.html* (accessed 27 June 2020).

59. S. Cassidy, 'The Online Generation: Four in 10 Children are Addicted to the Internet', *Independent* (9 May 2014), *www.independent.co.uk/life-style/gadgets-and-tech/news/the-online-generation-four-in-10-children-are-addicted-to-the-internet-9341159.html* (accessed 25 June 2020).

60. T. K. Platts and M. Clasen, 'Scary Business: Horror at the North American Box Office, 2006–2016', *Frames Cinema Journal*, 11 (2017), *https://framescinemajournal.com/article/scary-business-horror-at-the-north-american-box-office-2006-2016/* (accessed 30 June 2020).

61. Annette Hill, *Paranormal Media: Audiences, Spirits and Magic in Popular Culture* (New York: Routledge, 2010), p. 2.

62. See Jeffrey Sconce, *Haunted Media: Electronic Presence from Telegraphy to Television* (Durham NC: Duke University Press, 2000).

63. Hart, *Monstrous Forms*, p. 3.

7

Insidious Patterns

An Integrative Analysis of Blumhouse's Most Important Franchise

Todd K. Platts, Victoria McCollum
and Mathias Clasen

STANDING AT FOUR FILMS and counting, and raking in a cumulative $555.1 million at the global box office against combined budgets of $26.5 million, the *Insidious* franchise (2011–present) stands not only as one of Blumhouse's most significant properties, but also as one of the most high-profile horror franchises of the 2010s. Unsurprisingly then, scholars have examined the series for its implicit and explicit encoding of contemporary social issues. In brief, researchers have argued that the franchise offers insights into the crisis of post-recessionary family life[1] and of family drama more generally,[2] but have done so at the expense of other analytical perspectives such as the economic motivations underwriting the production of each film and the psychological intrigue offered in them. Accordingly, this chapter adds to standing research on *Insidious* by combining it with industrial and (evolutionary) psychological academic traditions, thereby painting a fuller picture of one of modern horror cinema's touchstone franchises. Specifically, this chapter will draw on a framework of film analysis developed by two of the chapter's authors in a study of slasher cinema.[3] In brief, the framework highlights the extant sociopolitical and cultural forces captured in cinematic texts, takes stock of the industrial climate at the time of production, and inventories the transhistorical deep-seated fears elicited in films or sets of films. In sum, subjecting the *Insidious* franchise to the framework shows how the series captures familial drama of relevance to young families, how the Blumhouse model has influenced the production process and how the franchise is situated within the business landscape of contemporary Hollywood, and how, through a close examination of the first film, the franchise taps into evolved psychological dispositions by depicting characters in conflict with dangerous forces of evil in order to achieve the genre-defining aim of horrifying the audience. The chapter proceeds by first offering brief summaries of each film to situate the reader, followed by an articulation of the framework employed, and ends with an application of the framework across the *Insidious* films.

The *Insidious* Franchise

As of writing, the *Insidious* franchise comprises the following films: *Insidious* (2011), *Insidious: Chapter 2* (2013), *Insidious: Chapter 3* (2015) and *Insidious: The Last Key* (2018); a fifth instalment is in the works. The first two films revolve around the Lambert family and psychic Elise Rainier's attempts to rescue them from the grips of 'The Further', a place where tormented souls go to linger and suffer and where the Lambert's eldest son, Dalton, and later patriarch, Josh, are held captive. The first film focuses on Dalton's travails in The Further and uncovering Josh's repressed memories of the realm. Early on, Dalton lapses into a coma after falling from a ladder. After medical doctors cannot explain the persistence of Dalton's coma, Josh's mother Lorraine calls psychic Elise Rainier and her duo of paranormal investigators Specs and Tucker. Elise discovers that Dalton's comatose state is not related to his fall. Instead, he is stuck in The Further where the 'Lipstick-Face Demon' has imprisoned him to use his body as a portal for other malevolent spirits and demons to enter this world. As it turns out, Elise helped young Josh to ward off another demon from The Further and then to suppress his ability to project between realms and his memories of doing so. Josh must now re-enter The Further to save his son years later. In The Further, Josh helps Dalton to escape from the Lipstick-Face Demon while also confronting the old woman demon from his childhood. When exiting, however, Josh's demon manages to possess his body, causing him to choke Elise to death.

Insidious: Chapter 2 provides more details on Josh's backstory with the film opening on his childhood sessions with Elise. Much of the narrative oscillates between the past and the film's present (2010) in the quest to exorcise Josh's demon. It is revealed that what appears to be an old woman possessing Josh is actually a man, Parker Crane, whose mother forced him to act like a female. The spirits of Elise and Josh, with the help of Elise's former associate Carl, vanquish the spectre of Parker's mother, which allows Carl and Josh to escape The Further with the help of Dalton. With the family reunited, Josh and Dalton have their memories repressed by Carl.

The third and fourth films focus more on Elise and her coming to terms with her psychic powers. *Chapter 3* chronicles the genesis of Elise's association with Specs and Tucker. At the start of the film, Elise is shown to no longer pursue cases involving The Further due to the negative impact that it is having on her. She declines to work with the Brenner family whose matriarch, Lily, recently passed away. With daughter Quinn experiencing increasingly violent paranormal episodes, father Sean decides to enlist the help of Specs and Tucker who are soon exposed as incompetent and possibly fraudulent. In the meantime, Carl encourages Elise to pursue the Brenner case. Elise decides to recruit the help of Specs and Tucker as she ventures back into The Further to help Quinn combat her demon, known as 'The Man Who Can't Breathe'. Quinn overcomes the demon with the help of Lily and family order is restored.

The Last Key occurs just before the events of *Chapter 2* and vacillates between Elise's childhood in 1953 and 1960 and the film's present (2010). Elise's flashbacks are triggered by working on a case in her childhood home. During the film, Elise reconciles her estranged relationship with her brother Christian, and helps her niece Imogen harness her psychic powers to save Elise's other niece Melissa. With the help of her mother's spirit, Elise overcomes the demon known as KeyFace and rescues Melissa from The Further. As suggested by the ending of *Chapter 2*, which is the last of the films in chronological order, Elise is no longer haunted by The Further, but exists peacefully in the spirit world. At the time of writing, details concerning the next *Insidious* instalment are being kept under wraps. What is known is that the film will focus on the Lamberts once again and Patrick Wilson, who played Josh, will direct.

Despite following a fairly formulaic narrative, *Insidious* is known for building three-dimensional characters with depth, personality and clear motivations, leaning into the central theme of the haunted-house story as a metaphor for generational trauma and psychic scarring – while not losing sight of the fun that audiences derive from scenes of dread and horror.

The Integrated Framework

The framework employed in this chapter takes as its point of departure the notion that films reveal something about the time in which they were released, they bear the watermarks of their production milieu, and films that resonate with large audiences do so because they depict and evoke adaptive concerns that have evolved over millions of years, such as concerns over survival (in horror movies), mating (in romantic movies) and social conflict (in drama). What follows is a necessarily truncated explication of the framework.

According to scholars advocating for the sociohistorical perspective, horror films absorb diffuse social and cultural forces, sometimes intentionally, sometimes unintentionally, such as political upheavals, armed conflicts, economic turmoil and general social angst, and reflect them back to audiences, thereby serving as indices to a period's dread and misgivings.[4] As a genre designed 'to scare and/or disturb its audience',[5] horror has developed various subtypes that achieve either or both goals in different ways. For instance, the *Insidious* franchise combines both the ghost/haunted-house and possession subtypes. The former tends to dramatise issues of middle-class patriarchal authority, while the latter encodes changes in sexual norms and family structure.[6] In general, then, sociohistorical analysis situates films in the context of their release.

While individual films might provide prescient insight into a particular society, culture or time, that is not their primary purpose. At their core, horror films, like all other films, are produced to make money in an incredibly competitive market. What types of film are made, how many examples of a type are made, and for how long that type remains viable are all determined by the profit imperative. Although horror films are not the most lucrative genre, they have proven to be shrewd investments when produced on modest or low budgets, something that Blumhouse has refined to a near-science with a spate of releases that boast a very impressive return on investment, as shown in Platts' chapter (this volume) on Blumhouse at the box office. In other words, horror filmmaking makes good business sense.[7] Blumhouse's early reliance on ghost and haunted-house films can, in part, be explained by the fact that they carried cheaper budgets than other horror subtypes and return similar profits.[8] Moreover, Blumhouse also operates in an environment where it performs a role similar to the major studios' semi-autonomous subsidiaries, insofar as it operates under a first-look deal with Universal that allows it to bankroll low-budget genre pictures.[9] Such observations are all part of industrial analyses, which locate films in their economic and business surroundings.

Humans are fearful creatures. Like other organisms, we have evolved defensive physiological and behavioural systems that serve to protect us from the dangers posed by predators, aggressors, disease and environmental hazards.[10] Thus, humans – like many other animals – are equipped with a psychological 'fear module', and the human fear module is stimulated by horror texts.[11] The fear module evolved largely in a world that is long gone, which is why common phobias do not always match actual dangers. They target ancestral threats rather than current ones. People are more likely to fear sharks than coconuts, despite the empirical fact that more people are killed by falling coconuts than by bloodthirsty sharks globally every year.[12] Thus, evolutionarily relevant, ancestral dangers preferentially trigger the fear module. Sharks, spiders, snakes, murderers and cues of disease reliably frighten us, much more so than saturated fats and cigarettes, despite the over-representation of the latter in present-day mortality statistics. Horror texts take advantage of the construction of the fear module by presenting us with depictions that reflect ancestral dangers. The monsters and frightening situations in horror narratives are constrained by the parameters of our evolved psychology, but are modulated by salient social and cultural concerns.[13] When horror stories are effective, they provide a mental playground wherein we can vicariously and safely play out dangerous scenarios that may prepare us to handle similar situations in real life.[14] The evolutionary perspective thus gets at the root of the appeal of the transhistorical aspects of horror films as well as at the underlying structure of the genre and its monsters.

Applied

The sections below locate the textual properties of the *Insidious* franchise within a specific historical moment in the United States and within perennial family issues, allowing for a deeper appreciation of how the films resonate with audiences; spotlight the business practices that brought the films to the screen, affording insight into franchise management; and inventory the deeply entrenched topics addressed in the franchise, permitting an augmented understanding of the films' transhistorical and transcultural appeals.

Sociohistorical

Upon its release, *Insidious* joined a growing cycle of haunted-house horror films that included *Mulberry Street* (2006), *The Haunting in Connecticut* (2009) and, of course, *Paranormal Activity*. That these films, and others that followed them, rose to prominence in the wake of the 2008–9 recession has been seen as no coincidence. Scholars have argued that films in the cycle foreground issues of foreclosure, home repossession and economic struggle at a time when job quality and job stability declined,[15] all of which significantly strained familial relations and constancy.[16] *Insidious* and *Insidious: Chapter 2* play into these anxieties by showing a family living beyond their financial means, a common situation during the recession, Kimberly Jackson argues.[17] Despite earning a teacher's salary, Josh is somehow able to support his family living in a large house. The family even seems to inexplicably have enough finances to move into another spacious house to get away from the demonic ghosts, something not afforded in other recessionary haunted-house films. *Chapter 3* and *The Last Key* have, at best, subtle allusions to economic fears, with *Chapter 3* focusing on a single father caring for his family in an apartment and *The Last Key* showing Elise's working-class background and alcoholic father. Hence, the franchise tangentially belongs to the cycle of financial horror films, in which the instability of homeownership is horrifyingly palpable. Indeed, it is no coincidence that *Insidious* was released, and subsequently became popularised, hot on the heels of the collapse of the US housing bubble, which led to mortgage delinquencies, foreclosures and the devaluation of housing-related securities across the globe.

Claire Cronin argues the *Insidious* films belong to another cycle of horror films, what she calls the 'family melodrama', or films that use hauntings as catalysts for family healing, a process she calls 'transcendental repair'.[18] Along these lines, the common thread linking each *Insidious* film is a family in peril. Specifically, the first three films offer father-in-peril plotlines. *Insidious* and *Insidious: Chapter 2* dramatise the struggles of Josh Lambert to control his family. In the first half of the original film, Renai, the family's matriarch, must battle with the consequences of Dalton's coma and the progressively hostile presence of malevolent spirits from The Further without the assistance of her husband. Josh routinely brushes off her concerns and becomes increasingly absent from the family. Ultimately, Josh must save his family by coming to terms with his childhood and acknowledging the spiritual, including the reality of demons and otherworldly dimensions. *Chapter 3* offers a similar plotline. Sean Brenner is grieving the loss of his wife Lily. Their daughter, Quinn, also crestfallen over the death, begins to exhibit more and more aggressive behaviour from demon possession. Like Josh, Sean must also come to accept the spiritual domain in order to help save his family.

In this sense, the first three films encode a coming to terms with what Ralph LaRossa has termed the 'new culture of fatherhood', a model of fathering brought to fruition through the decline of the breadwinner ideal and that sees fathers taking on more nurturing duties for their children.[19] In these films, sensitive fathers, filling a vacuum left by emotionally listless relationships, typically take on a blended form of masculinity. This uneasiness towards (traditional) patriarchy's decline results in the patriarchy simultaneously being terrified and terrorising: infuriated by a paradoxical desire for its own annihilation. The transition to the new culture of fatherhood has fostered conflict in heterosexual relationships as men and women negotiate the interpersonal aspects of new gender norms. Berns and Fontao argue that this blended position has emerged against a backdrop where economic changes have destabilised the provider role of fathers, something that the first three *Insidious* give haunting voice.[20] Josh and Sean start the films emotionally distant from their families, unwilling and unable to accept anything beyond rational explanations for the paranormal disturbances. Such strict adherence to secular views is often coded as masculine in horror films. By contrast, sensitivity and willingness to pursue spiritual answers are often coded as feminine. As each film progresses, Josh and Sean transition from staunch rationalists to full believers in metaphysical reality. That is, they move from a fully coded masculine position to a blended position – one where the men adopt a nurturing position in their families.

In *The Last Key*, the family in peril is Elise's. She is estranged from her younger brother Christian, who resents Elise running away from the family when she was sixteen. As with the other *Insidious* films, the family is eventually bonded through their shared experience with ghosts and demons. Elise comes to realise her abusive father was possessed by the demon KeyFace. With the help of her niece Imogen, Elise forgives her father before KeyFace stabs him in The Further. With the help of Elise's mother's spirit, Imogen and Elise defeat KeyFace to save Melissa. This, in turn, helps to reunite Elise and Christian.

Although Cronin reads *Insidious* as an instance where ghostly hauntings further damage a family and *Chapter 2* as offering 'false, ironic closure', taken together, the films show families in crisis brought together through their shared experiences with the paranormal.[21] In such horror films, the family serves as the symbol for the nation itself, as both perpetrator and prey, as the site where the roots of deterioration can be discovered and where the damage wrought by it can be assessed.[22] While reading the sociocultural baggage brought to the fore can help us understand why so many people continue to buy tickets to see new instalments of the franchise, it is important to not conflate this with the economic logic underwriting the production of each film. We next situate the franchise in its milieu of production.

Industrial

From a purely business standpoint, it can be argued that *Insidious* is Blumhouse's most important franchise. Where *Paranormal Activity* helped put Blumhouse on the map as a significant producer of horror films, *Insidious* can be credited for moving the company 'beyond found-footage movies' and putting its films on par with the production aesthetics of mainstream Hollywood films.[23] By way of contrast, *Paranormal Activity* utilised a barebones setup, which relied heavily on the director's own home, naturalistic camera work, low-key lighting and unscripted performances by unknown actors. *Insidious* boasted listed historical buildings, complex cinematography set-ups, high-contrast lighting, practical and digital effects, and an ensemble of stars – yet still achieved on a micro-budget, $1.5 million. *Insidious* helped to demonstrate that Blum had the ability to produce high-quality, modestly budgeted horror. Indeed, *Insidious* was identified as a critical part of Blumhouse securing a first-look deal with Universal in 2011.[24] Put succinctly, Blumhouse entered *Insidious* as the little company behind *Paranormal Activity* and came out of the franchise a *bona fide* brand in horror. By shining light on *Insidious*'s production history, greater insight can be gained on the industrial conditions animating the films as well as Blumhouse's establishment as an industry leader in horror.

Blumhouse came to prominence amid shifting industry conditions that saw a gradual incline in horror budgets, stagnant ticket sales of those films, the near-collapse of the DVD market (which had helped sustain the horror market) and the jettisoning of speciality units tasked with making genre fare,[25] all of which were exacerbated by the 2008–9 recession.[26] This environment eventually, if momentarily, closed opportunities for big-budget horror films akin to *I am Legend* (2007) and *R.I.P.D.* (2013) with few exceptions. Studios, however, were still willing to release horror films because the genre had historically sold tickets on modest budgets. Blumhouse helped to fill the demand for horror at a time when fewer films in the genre were reaching the silver screen. Importantly, in response to industry hesitancy to invest in bigger-budgeted horror films, Blumhouse innovated an unusual micro-budget model of $5 million or less for original films and $10 million or less for sequels, the viability of which was confirmed by the *Insidious* franchise after *Paranormal Activity* served as a successful test case.

Insidious not only helped to establish the contemporaneous appeal of haunted-house films, it also offered an opportunity for Blumhouse to refine its financing and aesthetic model. Just prior to the film's release, cinematic horror was awash with torture porn and zombie films – subtypes notable for their use of over-the-top gore to disgust rather than inspire fear and dread in audiences. As these subtypes encountered dips in ticket sales, *Paranormal Activity* exploded onto the scene, demonstrating the potential profitability of such films to keen-eyed filmmakers and producers. Referencing audiences' sense of fatigue with horror of the mid-2000s, in his review of *Paranormal Activity*, Jon Hamblin of *SFX Magazine* advocates for the film: 'If you've spent any amount of time bemoaning the current state of horror films, slagging off Platinum Dunes remakes and mocking the CGI-and-tits tosh that passes for cineplex terror these days, you owe it to yourself to go and see this film.'[28] Similarly, film critic Adam Woodward praised the film: 'this is still postmodern horror, but if nothing else *Paranormal Activity* proves that you don't need buckets of gore and a tacked on twist to send chills racing down audience spines.' However, though *Paranormal Activity* might have been the surprise hit of 2009, single hits do not necessarily generate cycles, as cycles require the presence of confirmatory hits, as Richard Nowell points out.[30]

Enter director James Wan and writing partner Leigh Whannell, whose *Saw* (2004) helped spark the torture-porn cycle, and who were looking to rebound from the commercial disappointments of *Dead Silence* (2007) and *Death Sentence* (2007), the latter of which only involved Whannell as an actor, by showing critics that they could make a film that did not rely on gross-out effects and set-piece torture spectacles.[31] According to Wan, he made *Insidious* 'to remind people that [he] could make an old-school movie that harkened back to suspenseful storytelling'.[32] Wan was given a small budget, around $1 million initially, Wan's 'lowest-budget film yet', and creative control, which he recalls as helping make his 'vision an actuality'.[33] Critics recognised Wan's efforts with Matt Armitage seeing it as a throwback to 1970s horror films for its use of 'fine-tuned atmosphere, tension, direction, and perfectly timed jump scares to grab the audience by the delicate parts and make them genuinely nervous as to what is going to happen next'.[34]

At the time of *Insidious*'s production, however, Blumhouse was a relative unknown in the industry. Blum was barely able to get the film screened at the Toronto International Film Festival, where nearly all distributors passed on optioning the film except Sony,[35] who requested extensive reshoots through its subsidiary FilmDistrict.[36] Despite minimal advertising, *Insidious* raked in nearly $100 million at the domestic box office,[37] leading to almost immediate negotiations for a sequel,[38] and cementing the saleability of haunted-house films in the cinematic horror market. According to Scott Mendelson, it 'kickstarted the post-*Saw* wave in mainstream horror, substituting real-world violence and grindhouse gore for supernatural spirits and (where applicable) religious fights'.[39] Though Blum credits *Paranormal Activity* for teaching him to 'do more with less',[40] *Insidious* was the company's first successful film to rely on standard production aesthetics on its characteristically low budgets. Consequently, most Blumhouse films greenlit in its wake followed its aesthetic lead, including *Sinister* (2012), *Dark Skies* (2013) and *The Purge* (2013), while fewer films pursued the look of *Paranormal Activity*.

With a hit on its hands, Blumhouse had a licence to produce at least one *Insidious* sequel, something Sony hoped for.[41] For sequels, Blum insists on retaining key creative personnel for new franchise instalments. In the case of *Insidious*, this includes director James Wan and writer Leigh Whannell. David D'Alessandro explains the unusualness of the practice: 'typically, when it comes to horror sequels, studios will shoehorn in a new director, because it's cheaper and too expensive to carry the original creator or stars from sequel to sequel.'[42] True to Blumhouse's doctrine, each new *Insidious* instalment has involved James Wan and Leigh Whannell with Wan transitioning to a hands-off producer and Whannell to writer, producer and director of *Chapter 3*, then to writer and producer for *The Last Key* and the forthcoming sequel. Since then, many of Blumhouse's films have followed a similar formula – a small upfront budget exchanged for creative control of the film's content. As explored below, the *Insidious* films combined two subtypes of horror – the haunted house and the bodily possession narrative. It is significant that the two subtypes are some of the most economical horrors from the perspective of producing for profit.[43] The *Insidious* franchise has retained its profitability even as haunted-house films have been on the wane, suggesting that the series is imbued with timeless qualities.

Evolution

From an evolutionary psychology perspective, the *Insidious* franchise became an audience hit because it effectively engaged evolved psychological mechanisms in audiences. It did so by depicting threat scenarios that resonated with audiences' evolved fears and mobilised powerful emotions. More specifically, the films effectively tap into evolved intuitions about supernatural forces (disembodied agents) at work in the world. Such intuitions are in conflict with the tenets of materialistic science, but seem to be a part of humans' natural way of thinking. Because we are keenly social creatures, we evolved the ability to put ourselves into the minds of others (to infer other people's intentions from their behaviour, for instance). A by-product of this mentalising or 'mind-reading' ability is an intuitive metaphysical dualism. Humans intuitively assume that other people consist both of a material dimension – the body – and a spiritual essence – the soul or spirit or self.[44] Belief in ghosts and spirits arises from the intuition that a person's immaterial essence may survive the death of the flesh. Thus, by depicting fiction worlds in which immaterial agents are afoot, the *Insidious* franchise taps into and exploits such intuitions, and by focusing on malicious agents with an ability to possess innocents, the films manage to frighten audiences.

Consider the first and, by many accounts, scariest film in the franchise.[45] In attempting to fulfil his ambition of creating a horror movie that relied more on dreadful atmosphere than gory shock, Wan carefully establishes an aura of anticipatory dread in the beginning of the film. Early on, audiences are given hints that uncanny agents are present in the Lambert home. This strategy of merely suggesting the presence of dangerous agents taps into an evolved response to situations characterised by ambiguity of threat.[46] When we are faced with a situation or individual that may or may not pose a threat to us (e.g., an abandoned, dilapidated house), our adaptive response is one of anxious vigilance, which prompts use to seek additional information.[47] We scan the surroundings for signs of danger. Thus, by carefully presenting the audience with subtle cues of vaguely defined danger in the beginning of the film (e.g., shadowy figures occurring briefly in the background of the frame or a home security system going off for no apparent reason), Wan prompts his viewers to pay careful and anxious attention to the story and suggests that preternatural agents are loose and are a threat to characters for whom Wan has been careful to establish sympathy. By encouraging his viewers to form empathetic bonds with the main characters (e.g., through depictions of their struggles and interactions with family members), Wan ramps up emotional investment and compounds the dread of the uncanny threats with sympathy for imperilled characters. The film eventually confirms the reality of supernatural forces of evil within its own diegesis. Not only are the ghosts and demons real, but they can hurt people (as the audience sees in several scenes) and they look frightening.

Indeed, special effects were used to create apparitions with traits that reliably trigger an aversive response. In one of the most famous jump-scare scenes of modern horror history (from the first film in the franchise), Josh's mother is recounting an eerie dream involving a demonic intruder. The scene ends with a close-up of Josh's incredulous face, from behind which a demonic visage suddenly appears. This demonic character has peculiar colouration on its face, strangely coloured eyes with tiny irises, and a mouth brimming with sharp teeth. Research has found that people tend to be disturbed by distortions of natural forms,[48] and distortions of the face seem to be particularly effective, presumably because the face carries a wealth of socially relevant information (e.g., about intentions). People tend to pay particular attention to the eyes and mouth because these areas carry especially rich information about the attention and the mood of other individuals. It is therefore no accident that the demonic character in this scene is fitted with contact lenses and prosthetic teeth to disturb viewers, who are shocked by the vision of a human-like creature with strange colouration, distorted eyes and a mouthful of predatory teeth.

The supernatural agents of evil in the *Insidious* franchise are dangerous to the human characters, and are particularly disturbing because they do not follow the laws of biological organisms. Characters must learn the rules that govern the behaviour of the supernatural agents to find out how to neutralise or even kill them; simply shooting the ghosts and demons will not work. The fact that the supernatural agents do not obey natural law makes them unpredictable – it allows them to exploit a deep-seated and adaptive fear of the unknown[49] and so makes them particularly disturbing. Moreover, the supernatural agents have the capacity to possess human characters. The saliency of the possession motif in horror fiction also grows out of an evolved psychological tendency to view the world (and humans) in dualistic terms – that is, to intuitively assume that a spiritual essence can be divorced from the body, and so take up abode in another body. This evolved substrate of possession belief explains the trope's universality.[50] The prospect of being possessed by another consciousness is terrifying to most people – especially so when that alien consciousness is evil. This is why the horror genre has proven hospitable to this particular trope, and the films in the *Insidious* franchise use it to great effect, especially when the characters possessed are vulnerable (like young Dalton) and/or sympathetic (like Quinn).

The *Insidious* franchise resonated with topical fears about homeownership and fragile family relations, it found a receptive industrial milieu, and it managed to elicit powerful emotions in audiences by exploiting evolved psychological mechanisms. Humans, through millions of years of biological evolution, evolved to be on the lookout for danger, and not just in the physical realm. We are natural-born metaphysical dualists, prone to belief in spiritual dimensions and supernatural agents. The *Insidious* films exploit these aspects of human nature quite effectively by offering the audience vivid depictions of such dimensions and agents. The films play on a range of emotional buttons, from diffuse dread produced through the subtle suggestion of vaguely defined malicious forces to acute fright produced by well-constructed jump-scares, thus offering horror fans a rich palette of emotional stimulation.

Conclusion

This chapter has argued that the runaway success of the *Insidious* franchise can be attributed to its alignment of prescient social concerns, the economic conditions of low-budget filmmaking in the 2010s and evolved human dispositions. Specifically, it was argued that the *Insidious* films arose in a period when many families were in flux due to the after-effects of the financial crisis and ever-changing gender arrangements. The franchise reached a tremendous level of financial success, in part, due to its effective dramatisation of these issues. While not foregrounded to the extent of other haunted-house horror films from the period, the *Insidious* franchise routinely depicted economically precariat families: the first two films portraying a family living way beyond their reasonable means; *Chapter 3* showing a family struggling under the confines of financial insecurity in a claustrophobic apartment complex; and *The Last Key* presenting a family divided by the vagaries of working-class frailties set in the often-nostalgic 1950s. Moreover, the first three films feature father-in-peril narratives, wherein Josh and Sean must eschew traditional masculinity and adopt a blended gender model to restore their families from the clutches of The Further. *The Last Key* shows the reconciliation of two estranged siblings through shared struggle with malevolent spirits.

In terms of business dynamics, the *Insidious* franchise occurred at an important crossroads for cinematic horror. The gory films associated with torture porn, zombie films and the resurgence of slasher remakes were starting to bring in less return on investment. At the same time, *Paranormal Activity* and, later, *Insidious* established the bankability of haunted-house films, which could be produced for less money at a time when studio executives were turning away from sanguinary pictures.[51] Shortly after *Insidious* scared up surprising profits, Blumhouse signed a first-look deal with Universal as a cheap way for the studio to get back into horror production.[52] In the intervening years Blumhouse has supplied Universal with box-office draw after box-office draw, with Blumhouse making only slight adjustments to their production model.

Psychologically the films touched deep nerves related to humans' sentiment towards supernatural forces. The subtle build that malicious spiritual forces are present in the families of *Insidious* causes the evocation of ambiguity threat, wherein audiences are anticipating visual manifestations of those forces but do not know where and when they will happen. These feelings are fraught even further through emotional attachments to characters under paranormal siege. When the supernatural forces make themselves visible, they are visually scary through their exaggerated bodily features (e.g., skin, teeth, eyes). Since the demons are not beholden to natural laws, their movement and actions disrupt humans' ability to anticipate behaviour, while their existence evokes fear of the unknown. The use of possession plays with the belief that the human body has spiritual and corporeal components with the former, constituting the essence of humanity. That this can be hijacked by ill-intended spirits only adds another layer to the films' scariness. The franchise shows no signs of concluding at the time of writing this chapter.

Notes

1. See, for example, T. Snelson, 'The (Re)possession of the American Home: Negative Equity, Gender Inequality, and the Housing Crisis Horror Story', in D. Negra and Y. Tasker (eds), *Gendering the Recession: Media and Culture in an Age of Austerity* (Durham NC: Duke University Press, 2014), pp. 161–80; B. M. Murphy, '"It's Not the House That's Haunted": Demons, Debt, and the Family in Peril Formula in Recent Horror Cinema', in M. Leeder (ed.), *Cinematic Ghosts: Haunting and Spectrality from Silent Cinema to the Digital Era* (New York: Bloomsbury, 2015), pp. 235–51.

2. See, for example, C. Cronin, 'Transcendental Repair: The Ghost Film as Family Melodrama', *Horror Studies*, 10/1 (2019), 27–43; Kimberly Jackson, *Gender and the Nuclear Family in Twenty-First-Century Horror* (New York: Palgrave Macmillan, 2016), pp. 81–99; C. J. Miller, 'Coming Home to Horror in *Insidious: The Last Key*', in C. J. Miller and A. B. Van Riper (eds), *Horror Comes Home: Essays on Hauntings, Possessions and Other Domestic Terrors in Cinema* (Jefferson NC: McFarland, 2020), pp. 206–18.

3. M. Clasen and T. K. Platts, 'Evolution and Slasher Films', in D. Vanderbeke and B. Cooke (eds), *Evolution and Popular Narrative* (Boston MA: Brill, 2019), pp. 23–42.

4. T. K. Platts, 'A Comparative Analysis of the Factors Driving Film Cycles: Italian and American Zombie Film Production, 1978–82', *Journal of Italian Cinema and Media Studies*, 5/2 (2017), 195.

5. Mathias Clasen, *Why Horror Seduces* (New York: Oxford University Press, 2017), p. 3.

6. T. K. Platts, 'The New Horror Movie', in B. Cogan and T. Gencarelli (eds), *Baby Boomers and Popular Culture: An Inquiry into America's Most Powerful Generation* (Denver CO: Praeger, 2015), pp. 150–1, 154.

7. Suzanne Lyons, *Indie Film Producing: The Craft of Low Budget Filmmaking* (Burlington: Focal Press, 2012), p. 66.

8. T. K. Platts and M. Clasen, 'Scary Business: Horror at the North American Box Office, 2006–2016', *Frames Cinema Journal*, 11 (2017), https://framescinemajournal.com/article/scary-business-horror-at-the-north-american-box-office-2006-2016/ (accessed 30 June 2020).

9. T. Platts, 'Cut-Price Creeps: The Blumhouse Model of Horror Franchise Management', in M. McKenna and W. Proctor (eds), *Horror Franchise Cinema* (New York: Routledge, 2021), pp. 114–15.

10. A. Öhman and S. Mineka, 'Fears, Phobias, and Preparedness: Toward an Evolved Module of Fear and Fear Learning', *Psychological Review*, 108/3 (2001), 483–522.

11. M. Clasen, 'Monster Evolve: A Biocultural Approach to Horror Stories', *Review of General Psychology*, 16/2 (2012), 223.
12. Daniel T. Blumstein, *The Nature of Fear: Survival Lessons from the Wild* (Cambridge MA: Harvard University Press, 2020), p. 9.
13. Clasen, 'Monsters Evolve', 224–6.
14. Platts and Clasen, 'Evolution and Slasher Films', p. 31. See also, C. Scrivner, J. A. Johnson, J. Kjeldgaard-Christiansen and M. Clasen, 'Pandemic Practice: Horror Fans and Morbidly Curious Individuals are More Psychologically Resilient during the COVID-19 Pandemic', *Personality and Individual Differences*, 168/1 (2021).
15. M. Cooper and A. J. Pugh, 'Families Across the Income Spectrum: A Decade in Review', *Journal of Marriage and Family*, 82/1 (2020), 277–9.
16. S. E. Cavanaugh and P. Fomby, 'Family Instability in the Lives of American Children', *Annual Review of Sociology*, 45 (2019), 495–7.
17. Jackson, *Gender and the Nuclear Family*, p. 82.
18. Cronin, 'Transcendental Repair', 29.
19. Ralph LaRossa, *The Modernization of Fatherhood: A Social and Political History* (Chicago IL: University of Chicago Press, 1997), p. 11.
20. F. G. P. Berns and C. A. R. Fontao, 'New Paternal Anxieties in Contemporary Horror Cinema: Protecting the Family against (Supernatural) External Attacks', in L. Tropp (ed.), *Deconstructing Dads: Changing Notions of Fatherhood in Popular Culture* (Lanham MD: Rowman and Littlefield, 2016), pp. 166.
21. Cronin, 'Transcendental Repair', 40.
22. Natasha Zaretsky, *No Direction Home: The American Family and the Fear of National Decline, 1968–1980* (Chapel Hill NC: University of North Carolina Press, 2007).
23. M. Fleming Jr, 'How Jason Blum Honed His Micro-Budget Blockbuster Formula – *Deadline* Disruptors', *Deadline* (16 May 2017), *https://deadline.com/2017/05/jason-blum-blumhouse-jordan-peele-disruptors-interview-news-1202094624/* (accessed 1 January 2021).
24. M. Fleming Jr, 'Universal Makes First-Look Deal with Jason Blum of *Paranormal Activity* and *Insidious*', *Deadline* (29 June 2011), *https://deadline.com/2011/06/universal-in-first-look-deal-with-paranormal-activity-and-insidious-producer-jason-blum-144401/* (accessed 30 January 2021).
25. Platts, 'Cut-Price Creeps', 112–13
26. J. Fleury, B. H. Hartzheim and S. Mamber, 'Introduction: The Franchise Era', in J. Fleury, B.H. Hartzheim, S. Mamber (eds), *The Franchise Era: Managing Media in the Digital Economy* (Edinburgh: Edinburgh University Press, 2019), p. 1–28.

27. T. K. Platts, 'Unmade Undead: A Post-Mortem of the Post-9/11 Zombie Cycle', in J. Fenwick, K. Foster and D. Eldridge (eds), *Shadow Cinema: The Historical and Production Contexts of Unmade Films* (New York: Bloomsbury, 2020), pp. 257–8.

28. J. Hamblin, '*Paranormal Activity* Reviews', *Rotten Tomatoes*, www.rottentomatoes.com/m/Paranormal_Activity/reviews (accessed 15 January 2021).

29. A. Woodward, '*Paranormal Activity* Reviews', *Rotten Tomatoes*, www.rottentomatoes.com/m/Paranormal_Activity/reviews (accessed 15 January 2021).

30. Richard Nowell, *Blood Money: A History of the First Teen Slasher Film Cycle* (New York: Bloomsbury, 2011), pp. 41–54.

31. Platts, 'Cut-Price Creeps', 118–19.

32. Quoted in John Horn, 'Shifting Gears', *Los Angeles Times* (12 September 2013), D6.

33. Quoted in L. Spiderbaby, 'Wan on Wan,' *Fangoria* (April 2011), 39.

34. M. Armitage, 'Horror in the 2010s – Part 1: The House that Blum Built?' *25 Years Later* (12 September 2017), https://25yearslatersite.com/2020/07/03/horror-in-the-2010s-part-1-the-house-that-blum-built/ (accessed 1 January 2021).

35. Horn, 'Shifting Gears', D6.

36. A. Stewart, 'Sony Scores in Pickup Game', *Daily Variety* (7 December 2010), 16.

37. P. McClintock, '*Insidious* is the Most Profitable Film of 2011', *Hollywood Reporter* (26 April 2011), www.hollywoodreporter.com/news/insidious-is-profitable-film-2011-182335/ (accessed 1 January 2021).

38. P. Nemiroff, '*Insidious Chapter 2* Producer Talks Micro-Budget Horror & *Amityville: Lost Tapes*', *Screen Rant* (9 September 2013), https://screenrant.com/insidious-2-interview-jason-blum-amityville-lost-tapes/ (accessed 1 January 2021).

39. S. Mendelson, 'Box Office: Why *Insidious* is Hollywood's Most Underrated Horror Franchise', *Forbes* (29 October 2020), www.forbes.com/sites/scottmendelson/2020/10/29/patrick-wilson-will-direct-insidious-5-for-blumhouse/?sh=4a18fe695942 (accessed 16 January 2021).

40. P. McClintock, 'Trio's New Alliance', *Daily Variety* (5 February 2010), 12.

41. Stewart, 'Sony Scores in Pickup Game', 16.

42. D. D'Alessandro, 'How Miramax & Blumhouse Brought *Halloween* Back from the Dead', *Deadline* (22 October 2018), https://deadline.com/2018/10/halloween-jamie-lee-curtis-john-carpenter-box-office-reboot-blumhouse-miramax-1202486748/ (accessed 1 January 2021).

43. Platts and Clasen, 'Scary Business'.

44. Paul Bloom, *Descartes' Baby: How the Science of Child Development Explains What Makes Us Human* (New York: Basic Books, 2004).

45. See, for example, M. Kennedy, 'Every *Insidious* Movie Ranked, Worst to Best', *Screen Rant* (12 January 2020), *https://screenrant.com/insidious-movies-ranked-best-worst/* (accessed 31 January 2021); D. Rester, 'Ranked *Insidious* Films,' *We Live Entertainment* (13 October 2020), *https://weliveentertainment.com/welivefilm/ranked-insidious-films-halloween-horror-month/* (accessed 31 January 2021). In a very limited sample of horror films, *Insidious* was named the 'scariest horror film of all time', see, S. Thompson, '*Insidious* has been Named the Scariest Horror Film of All Time', *Pop Buzz* (29 September 2020), *www.popbuzz.com/tv-film/news/insidious-scariest-movies-all-time-ranking/* (accessed 30 January 2021).

46. F. T. McAndrew and S. S. Koehnke, 'On the Nature of Creepiness', *New Ideas in Psychology*, 43 (2016), 14.

47. F. T. McAndrew, 'The Psychology, Geography, and Architecture of Horror: How Places Creep Us Out', *Evolutionary Studies in Imaginative Culture*, 4/2 (2020), 47–62.

48. J. Cantor, 'Fright Reactions to Mass Media', in J. Bryant and D. Zillmann (eds), *Media Effects: Advances in Theory and Research* (second edition) (Mahwah NJ: Lawrence Erlbaum Associates, Publishers, 2002), p. 292.

49. R. N. Carleton, 'Fear of the Unknown: One Fear to Rule them All?', *Journal of Anxiety Disorders*, 41 (2016), 5–21.

50. B. B. Boutwell, M. Clasen and J. Kjeldgaard-Christiansen, '"We Are Legion": Possession Myth as a Lens for Understanding Cultural and Psychological Evolution', *Evolutionary Behavioral Sciences*, 15/1 (2021), 1–2.

51. M. Graser, 'Hollowood Rethinks Its Scare Flair . . .', *Variety* (30 July–5 August 2007), 1.

52. B. Barnes, 'Spinning Horror into Gold', *New York Times* (21 October 2013), *www.nytimes.com/2013/10/21/business/media/turning-low-budget-horror-into-gold.html/* (accessed 3 February 2021).

8

The Purge

Violence and Religion – A Toxic Cocktail

Amanda Rutherford and Sarah Baker

THE PURGE (2013) is the first film in the *Purge* series of dystopian action horror films that centre on an annual human expulsion and how groups of people manage the violent night. This annual event was set up after the New Founding Fathers of America (NFFA) took political power, creating the human eradication event in a bid to reduce rates of unemployment, crime and social unrest. Purge night is also referred to in the films as a holiday, a celebration of the 'cleansing' of America, but the antics of the NFFA could be argued to represent a thinly veiled corollary of right-wing extremist policies in the present-day United States. Megan Armstrong suggests that these films succeed through their presentation of vast class differences, and the heightened sense of racial and ethnic marginalisation and exclusion.[1] However, as much as *The Purge* franchise is about class and race and the power of the elite, with an emphasis placed on the vigorous exertion of a right-wing political agenda, there is much in these films about 'divinely sanctioned violence'. This form of structural violence is based on a more conservative biblical understanding of passages where biblical laws are used to scaffold and sustain inequalities and violent practices against others. The *Purge* films are, as such, framed with religious imagery and slogans that play on these tropes, alluding to how these actions are somehow sanctioned or validated by religious teachings or context. The connection between the religious imagery and politics enforced with violence is a potent example of contemporary America. For a twelve-hour period, all crime becomes legal, including murder, which sees the elite and wealthy, who have the financial means to invest in expensive security and barriers, hiding behind their elaborate and impenetrable homes, while the less fortunate are left to fend for themselves. The sound of flickering static, high-pitched beeps and distorted interference acts as the 'noise' of the right-wing media that ushers in the purge night, with an emergency broadcast message and warning siren that appears across every television. The rule voiced to the United States is that all crime is permissible, except any attempt on high-ranking government officials – the warning concludes with a blessing for the leadership and a prayer that God might be with all. Horror provides a space for the infusion of extremist political and religious commentary and this chapter examines and contrasts the ideas and references from these films to present-day America, showing how injustice and atrocity are being masked by tropes of religious and moral fortitude. *The Purge* films use religious quotes and themes as a reprehensible excuse for the 'sanctioned' violent political attacks against others, masking the reality of the event. This portrayal and symbolism acts as a mirroring of a United States of both the past and present under the ruling of the forty-fifth President, Donald Trump.

Blumhouse productions has pioneered a new model of studio film-making, with high-quality, micro-budget films. In addition, the horror genre is more likely than other genres to produce successful 'sequels, reboots/remakes, and derivative retreads'.[2] This combination has seen *The Purge* series become 'one of Hollywood's most surprising success stories'.[3] Debuting in 2013, *The Purge* franchise – which helped to build Blumhouse into a company synonymous with horror – has, before the release of *The Forever Purge* (2021), a combined worldwide box office of $458.4 million against combined budgets of $35 million.[4]

Jason Blum believes that films do not need the large budgets that many filmmakers have used in the past. The horror genre itself also has a tradition of 'transforming bargain-basement shockers into hits with enviable profit multipliers'[5] as several chapters in the volume suggest of *Paranormal Activity*. Brigid Cherry states that throughout the twentieth century and into the twenty-first century, horror films have continued to proliferate, evolve and diversify in so many ways[6] – we argue that *The*

Purge films have become a part of the new contemporary horror scene. Blumhouse Productions has a 'knack for making movies with slim budgets into profitable successes' and the *Insidious, Sinister* and *Purge* franchises are 'conspicuously well-made movies that often splice social commentary into their scenes.[7]

Initially, *The Purge* was categorised as a classic home-invasion plot,[8] 'where a wealthy patriarch attempts to protect his family and home from a group of Purgers', but the second instalment 'takes the audience out onto the urban streets',[9] redefining the plot to examine the sociopolitical implications of if and why this could happen, and serving as a critique to what is currently unfolding in the United States. Stacey Abbott posits that Blumhouse's franchises 'highlight a conscious marketing of horror toward large mainstream, multigenerational audiences, producing the films independently and then distributing them via larger studios such as Universal'.[10] By infusing the horror genre with contemporary social commentary, these films offer both the United States and the world, a politically based enhanced exploration of past and present atrocities within US history, providing visual fodder for the heightened anxieties surrounding the Trump presidency and his far-right compatriots who actively promote his white supremist viewpoints.

The New Founding Fathers

The controlling party of the United States throughout the collection of *Purge* narratives is the NFFA. Originally coming to power in 2014, their name – the New Founding Fathers of America – closely associates itself to the 'birth' or independence of America from Great Britain in 1776, when the Founding Fathers of America signed the Declaration of Independence. The Founding Fathers of America consisted of a group of wealthy businessmen and plantation owners who fought for the freedom and prosperity of their country, with members such as George Washington, John Adams, Thomas Jefferson and James Madison becoming the first presidents. George Washington was a soldier and successful planter (farmer) who owned many slaves. Although in time his viewpoint softened towards slavery, he was known to refer to the slaves as his 'property', individuals owned by him who were without any civil rights.[11] Washington had also been known for his social injustices and violent acts against non-compliant Native Americans.[12] By comparing the Founding Fathers of America to the NFFA of *The Purge* franchise, the NFFA leader, Caleb Warrens, carries similar opinions and prejudices as were held by George Washington in the eighteenth century. There is an inherent shared belief that not all people are equal, and therefore there are some individuals without 'value', unworthy of compassion, because they are perceived as a drain on the society at large. Judith Butler refers to this as the 'differential distribution of precarity' where individuals are perceived to be less 'grievable', and therefore made to 'bear the burden of starvation, underemployment, legal disenfranchisement, and differential exposure to violence and death'.[13] Another similarity is that both political leaders are white, wealthy, conservative and educated individuals. Their political parties share a common goal – to rid the United States of the 'unsavouries' – the unemployed, homeless and poor people within society. The majority within these categories are African Americans and Hispanic in ethnicity, an economic burden on the white elite class that must be addressed. Essentially, like the views of their Founding Fathers of America forefathers, these individuals are 'disposable' or 'ungrievable', which results in the planned 'culling' event to bring much needed 'relief' from their drain on society. Dr May Updale creates this platform in the form of an annual purge, resonating the present United States where President Trump referred to 'draining the swamp' to exterminate all those who stand in his way, rather than the original reference to removing those who had used their money and influence to get their own way.

Establishing the NFFA as the mirror reflection of 1776 American politics creates the expectation for a film franchise filled with the horrors of social injustice, cruelty and an elitist ideology. The films highlight issues such as 'white supremacy, systemic racism, [and] the abuse of the lower classes'[14] that also existed in early US history. An additional link is found on comparison of these leaders to the forty-fifth President of the United States, Donald Trump, who secured his victory 'with the help of racism, xenophobia, and exclusionary white supremacist tactics'[15] in the 2016 US elections, and continued to hold a high level of support in 2020, albeit not enough to secure a second term in office. Therefore, *The Purge* franchise serves not only as a replication of past American atrocities, but also to present a current state of US political affairs and acts as a platform to express anxieties of modern United States and the world. In the *Purge* films, the NFFA facilitates government-approved and funded legal murder on one night per year, initially limited to the poor area of Staten Island, and rolling out across the country thereafter. There are no criminal charges brought to those who commit crimes during this period in a bid to inspire participation, and citizens are encouraged to hold or store their violent thoughts and acts until this twelve hour no-questions-asked period. The false promise is made that by supporting this evening and, more so, partaking in the killing, the United States will be returned to 'greatness'. Through examination of the dystopian horror within these films, the United States is visualised as a country where class, poverty and race are presented as markers of not just discrimination but as ways that people are exterminated. Horror films that tap into present-day anxieties around security and safety are 'perceived as particularly relevant and effective by audiences looking for an emotionally rousing movie experience'.[16] *The Purge* series addresses these fears surrounding US politics and leadership and posits terror as the backbone of the 'fantasy' of the films. Producer, Jason Blum, commented that when they began working on the idea for *The Purge*, he thought the concept was both fantastic and bizarre, however, 'because we have a wacko for a President, it seems a lot less outlandish now'.[17]

This film is a United States of the past, but arguably a representation of the future to come for a divided US nation under the forty-fifth president. Trump continues to push for the reversal of many laws and practices that were designed to create equality for all citizens. He supports capital punishment and is opposed to gun control; he often opposes gay rights and is appealing for *Roe v. Wade* (1973) to be overturned; he proposed building a wall along Mexico, which would be militaristically patrolled; and he implemented several temporary travel bans based on race and ethnicity including a 'Muslim ban'. Present-day United States is thus ripe for scrutiny and has become the base of many Hollywood horror films. According to Chauncey K. Robinson:

> Horror movies frighten by playing on our fears of what could be lurking in the dark corners of our rooms or the unlit space under our beds . . . but [they are terrifying] because they hold up a mirror to the atrocities of our reality and paint a picture of future terror that's not necessarily as fictional as we might hope.[18]

The Purge films attach their narrative to political themes, encompassing clear critiques of the elite 1 per cent and racial inequity. The NFFA is a secretly fascist group that is an allegory for the current Republican party in the United States. In an interview, director James DeMonaco said that he had heard from people that *The Purge* series was 'too anti-American',[19] as the series was set in a near-future dystopia in which a dominant ultra-conservative party set up the purge to solve society's ills. The elite and wealthy are largely unaffected, while the rest of the population become easy prey during the purge night. In *The Purge* series, 'the Haves can prey upon the Have Nots with impunity',[20] much like the early leaders in US history, and the Trump administration from 2016 to 2020. While the first film was 'an attack on the nuclear family and upper-middle-class privilege, the second is an expose of the hardships facing the socially and economically disenfranchised'.[21] The series thus represents the genre as a specific examination of horror created by people; turning to the uncertainties and instability of modern American life and its impact on citizens and the rest of the world. 'Horror films have traditionally sunk their teeth into straitened times, reflecting, expressing and validating the spirit of the epoch, and capitalizing on the political and cultural climate in which they are made',[22] and these horror films suggest that the real horrors lie within the leadership of society, highlighting how people treat each other, and reflecting on historical and present horrors of the United States, where prosperity is measured solely through financial gain, where the wealthy increase their worth while promoting racist and xenophobic ideology.

Religion and Politics Connect

The popularity of the horror genre remains high due to its 'unique ability to let us meaningfully engage with our deepest fears'.[23] *The Purge* franchise has risen to success through a use of horror that resonates closely with the heightened present-day US fears around political leadership and a threatened democracy. The United States is not only a country currently filled with increased violence, hatred and unrest; but it is also a place that has historically seen religious ideology and sacred biblical text selectively intertwined within the words of political candidates and leaders. This franchise mimics these religio-political moves through the inclusion of constant referencing to Christian phrases and iconography, issuing a warning of how damaging this form of rallying can become, and raising fears surrounding the close and potent 'real' view threat of the Trump leadership.[24] The deliberate attempts to link faith and God to current US politics can be seen, for example, in how Trump uses religious items as cultural props. In June 2020, at the St John's Episcopal Church in Washington DC, Trump posed for his Bible-holding photo-opportunity. The Bible and churches hold sacred value for Christians; therefore, the intention of Trump was to gain their support and voter share by presenting himself as a 'faithful' follower of the Lord, 'one of them' in order to give religious authority to his political ideologies and policies. These ideologies include use of force against those people deemed troublesome to his agenda, shown by forcefully clearing the path to this church by sending armed forces to fire tear-gas canisters and flash grenades at the peaceful protesters who had gathered in Lafayette Square, implying that his actions are sanctioned, because they are done in the name of something sacred.

In the 1960s, American Liberalism flourished with the rise of Black Power, the growing militancy of the anti-war movement and the rise of gay and lesbian rights. All these movements in turn experienced a growing backlash, as anxieties and fears rose within conservative communities resulting in a political shift towards the right. The emerging trends of conservatism started in the 1950s and continued beyond, bringing together different yet connected factions.[25] Anti-communism, advocates of a free market and believers in traditional morality capitalised on the era's discomfort with changes to sexual norms and racial hierarchy resulting in more religio-political alliances being made with conservative Christian groups. Therefore, within the rise of the right there has been more attention paid to the role of religion in the development of conservatism, and the evident importance of conservative churches and the growth in the ideologies associated with it. Interestingly, the research by Kim Phillips-Fein shows 'Christian conservatives as upper-middle-class people who saw belief in business principles and market ideas as natural extension of their religious faith'.[26] It is these elements that the franchise shows is the underpinning of the shift in US society reflected in the films. There are several examples of 'religious' sacrificing, prayer and blessings given to those who engage in purging, but the films also illuminate the dangers in trying to mix politics and religion.

Much has been written about the class and race aspects of *The Purge*;[27] however, it is the overtones of religious infusion in the purge that drives the ritual and holiday and makes what happens terrifying. These films examine current societal issues and re-present them in the form of horror. 'Blessed be America, a nation reborn' is a commonly used phrase throughout the film and part of the opening announcement at the commencement of each annual event, serving to connect this politically motivated action against the poor and minority groups to a higher God-fulfilling and therefore acceptable purpose. People must show their support for the carnage by placing blue Baptisia flowers by their door-ways. 'Baptisia' originates from the Greek word meaning 'to immerse', therefore the flowers aptly signify that while those displaying them on purge night may not be personally involved in the murder of others, they are immersed in the process of the purge as engaged supporters. Ironi-cally, these flowers are toxic, but they serve to remind purgers of their occupants' support and to leave the occupants alone, to pass them by. The placing of the flowers is also connected with sacred text in the story of the Passover, where the Israelites were told by God to sacrifice lambs in his honour and place the blood of these animals over the doorways of their homes. Those who heeded God's instruction were 'saved', while God poured his wrath upon the unmarked homes. Therefore, by placing the blue Baptisia flowers in the doorways in 'support' of those to be sac-rificed in the purge, they too will be 'saved' by God.[28]

The First Purge examines the origins of the annual event and is the fourth film in the franchise. The purge is held in 2017 in the isolated and poor area of Staten Island, at a time that sees the country facing substan-tial debt. The NFFA offers to pay any resident the sum of $5,000 if they will remain within the city boundaries, and additional payments to those who participate in the actual purging experience. These residents are poor, mostly unemployed individuals, now tempted and actively promoted to rape, maim, kill, loot and destroy people and property over the course of the night of 21 March 2017 – and the film shows large queues of residents signing up. Most residents have decided to stay within the city limits solely because the funds received will bring much relief to their present living conditions, framing the film as a move by the mostly white, privileged elite class to coax poorer individuals into turning on and killing each other for financial gain. In so doing, the government will reduce the financial burden on the economy through manipulation of the lowest-ranking indi-viduals in society 'into destroying themselves'.[29]

The action of purging, however, has both historical and biblical ori-gins. Political leaders such as Adolf Hitler, Joseph Stalin, Saddam Hussein and Pol Pot, for example, used purging as a means of showing authority, power and control by committing horrific atrocities against their perceived enemies that resulted in the death of millions through acts of violence and genocide. This dark history has influenced horror narratives for decades by tapping into these unthinkable and despicable acts. The ability of horror films to encapsulate the anxieties and threats perceived across the screen serves to enable audiences to explore these fears from a point of physical, if not psychological safety. There is a strong tie in these films to both religion and political conservatism, creating a platform of terror using misguided ideologies, rites and rituals in the physical act of purging. Although this may not have been the intended vision of the first film, the series has begun to look more prophetic with each new addition, or perhaps it can be said to have been used to guide certain political leaders in achieving their necessary outcomes, such as the use of the phrase 'Keep America Great'. *The Purge* franchise is possibly a cultural marker of where contemporary America was going in the original *Purge* film, and in later iterations explaining how current America has mirrored key aspects of the films.

In holy texts there are several examples of God's wrath being unleashed over people on Earth, such as the Flood in the time of Noah, the story of Sodom and Gomorrah or the angel of God killing every first-born son during Jewish 'Pesach' or Passover. These purging events present the case of an omnipotent or supernatural power that can strike at will, but also show that those who follow his instruction will be granted peace and safety. Furthermore, God also tells His people to purge – 'all things are cleansed with blood, and without shedding of blood there is no forgiveness' (Hebrews 9: 22) – and although misinterpretation has occurred, these ideas create a terrifying platform ripe for exploration by the horror genre. We argue that the very foundation of *The Purge* franchise is based on the re-telling and re-adaptation of biblical purging, combined into a US politicised drama with all its horrors, where the act of purging has become almost a sacred duty to appease God. These films play on the conceptualisation of a purging event as a form of cleansing, spiritual ritual to be embraced by all citizens, who excitedly prepare for the annual event to expunge their anger in an acceptable offering to their country and God. The NFFA has thus successfully connected the act of killing to that of a religious form of sacrifice and purification that will 'save their souls' from damnation.

The Purge and Trump Politics Converge

By permitting crime once a year, relative peace prevails for the remaining 364 days a year, and the government knowingly and wilfully places the less privileged in society at huge risk of becoming the target of such actions because they are unable to effectively protect themselves – they thus become 'sacrificial lambs'. The NFFA believes, much like the Founding Fathers of America in early US history, that these people are, at their core, nothing short of animals, meaning that it can therefore situate its argument as one of biblical animal sacrifice. These actions effectively serve a dual purpose – honouring God, while decreasing the number of 'dependants', tying neoliberal economic reality and religion together. The horror of *The Purge* franchise projects a combination of violent dehumanising acts in which the United States permits great suffering and injustices in its pursuit of a utopian dream. The United States depicted here has no compassion for the poor or non-white members of the society, providing full entitlement and right to this terror and death. The films address depictions of modern-day anger and discontent that face-off with religious imagery through use of intense violence that seemingly drives the madness. Their model plays on distorted use of 'patriotism, Christianity, and socio-economic Darwinism to justify and inspire a war against the poor, minorities, and other vulnerable groups'.[30] *The First Purge* shows how revenge, racism and elitism are 'the making of a nightmare',[31] becoming a catalyst for chaos in *The Purge* films. While *The Purge* was made before Trump was elected, the tropes in this film include isolation, segregation and elitism, which Trump leaned heavily on during his presidency, to the extent that these tactics have now become known as specifically 'Trumpian': neoliberalism, fear, nationalism, racism and inequality.[32] For example, Trump 'isolated' by giving the executive order to build the Mexican wall and pulling out of various trade agreements; he segregated through the immediate travel ban of seven Muslim countries; and he increased the divide between the 'haves' and the 'have nots' through the reversal of the Obamacare, effectively removing free care to underprivileged and minority groups.

By the time that *The Purge: Election Year* was released, President Bracken clearly shows the party's intentions. He delivers a speech to his cabinet saying they need to 'do what it fucking takes' to get rid of their opposition. 'I've had it with all these idealistic pigs. They want the impossible, everyone to have. Some cannot have. Not enough to go around'. Bracken reinforces the need to purge the uneconomically viable members of society, and that by killing those who oppose these ideals the United States will remain profitable. He says 'it's time to do something about all these cocksuckers like that rat Bishop and the Senator trying to dismantle everything we've built. We're going to use this year's purge to do some spring-cleaning gentlemen'.

The purgers in these films dress up and accessorise for the occasion. Initially, the first film used one main mask, known as the 'Polite Stranger'. The use of masks has grown to more than twenty masks, with new inclusions in every film.[33] The masks have become highly synonymous with terror due to their increasing use as a prop in popular culture, and often are seen with religious or political connotation. The 'God' mask for example, is simplistic but chilling with its black and red smudging and the word 'God' scrawled across the forehead. It portrays the word of peace, love and kindness; however, its wearer is a cold-blooded violent killer who derives great pleasure from the pain and suffering that he inflicts. There are red, white and blue costumes to depict allegiance and patriotism, some clearly depicting neo-Nazi symbolism, but also masks, torches and iron crosses presented as strong symbolism of the Ku Klux Klan (KKK) and other extreme right groups. In addition, Blumhouse launched an extensive merchandising and marketing campaign attached to *The Purge* franchise, in partnership with Universal Studios, which has resulted in the *Purge* themes, props and costumes becoming popular for events such as Halloween.[34] Universal Studios now hosts a 'patriotic' purge theme as part of its annual 'Halloween Horror Nights', with patrons having to 'survive' the explosions, fire and anarchy, while weapon-wielding purgers roam the park terrorising guests in the streets.

Many of the themes and costumes in the films resonate with the American people and are being used in their political issues and protests today. While some of the films were produced prior to Trump's presidency, *The First Purge* was conceptualised after Trump was elected to power in 2016, and thus, while the earlier films served as a visual warning of the systemic racial, ethnic and cultural prejudices growing within the United States, *The First Purge* acts as a reflection or mirror of an America under Trump control with people divided and enraged. For example, the anti-lockdown protests that were witnessed during the global COVID-19 pandemic: 'thousands of angry Americans are taking to the streets . . . which are being likened to "zombie hoards" . . . wearing Guy Fawkes masks, Make America Great Again hats, and Stars and Stripes shirts.'[35] These protests were largely organised by conservative Trump allies within Democratic states who wanted restrictions of movement lifted despite widespread condemnation. Trump's criticism of these Democratic governors 'for going too far with economic restrictions, and his recent tweets calling for those states to be "liberated" was seen as an endorsement of their actions'.[36] These words of disdain from Trump towards his opposition resemble the words of President Bracken, encouraging his followers to do whatever necessary to secure economic stability, even if the cost of life is high. Their deaths in the face of COVID-19 are the sacrifice offered for financial gain. Mark

Bray argues that there was an increase in development and incidents from the alternative right and far-right organisations once Trump became President in 2016, stating that:

> In just the first thirty-four days after his election more than 1,094 'bias incidents' were reported according to the Southern Poverty Law Center. Hate crimes increased by 94 percent in New York City over the first two months of 2017 compared to the same period in 2016.[37]

These incidents, together with previous displays of racism like that of the Charleston church shootings in 2015 we argue, have provided vast amounts of 'material' for *The Purge* films, and *The Forever Purge* that is set for release in 2021.

Additional parallels can be made between the film and current US events such as the protests lead by activist group Black Lives Matter following the murder of George Floyd by policemen in May 2020, where some of the peaceful protests turned ugly. It is believed that extremist groups used the opportunity to cause damage to property. Trump openly blamed Antifa and other left-wing extremists for the damage and chaos, although there was never any evidence and the Federal arrests did not find this to be the case.[38] We argue that there was some evidence found indicating right-wing extremists' involvement[39] and thus the situation became a prime opportunity to cast doubt on the protests and the Antifa group so that Trump could declare them a terrorist organisation. This narrative runs close to that of *The First Purge* film where the experiment was proving unsuccessful as the people were not participating to the extent that the government had hoped. To achieve the required reduction in the poor, uneducated, non-white 'dependants', the government sent in its own mercenaries to kill, so that the purging night is deemed a success.

A week before the end of his term in office in 2021, Trump was impeached for a second time for 'incitement of insurrection'. He called his supporters to action, encouraging them to fight 'like hell' because he believed (without evidence) that the election had been stolen from him. These extremist followers stormed the Capitol on 6 January and several donned *Purge* masks and attire. Therefore, *The Purge* mirrors Trump both in his leadership style and the blind faith afforded to him. He aids in the 'construction of societal taboos against racism, sexism, homophobia, and other forms of oppression that constitute the bedrocks of fascism'[40] using any means possible to gain support, including but not limited to the use of religion. For example, in *The Purge: Election Year*, the inference to being faithful and pleasing God while committing murder with words such as 'Purge, my son. Purge. It's your right as an American . . . you're a son of God. God wants you to Purge' borders exceptionalism ideology.

The Purge was the first dystopian horror film in the series, and the second in chronological order. It is set in 2022, when unemployment is stated to be at an all-time low of 1 per cent, and crime is almost completely non-existent. The United States is presented as being pulled back from the point of complete financial collapse. The reason for the economic upswing is said to be a direct result of the introduction of the NFFA, which rose to power eight years earlier in 2014. The NFFA leaders adopted a new doctrine where religion, conservatism and politics have been purposefully intertwined to manipulate the American people into the belief that the NFFA is some sort of saviour or messiah figure. By promoting its agenda as something almost holy through the use of prayer, religious artefacts and sacred ritual, the purge is now seen by the citizens as a sacrificial and pleasing way to concentrate crime, rage and general societal disorder into one night, with the NFFA even naming it a holiday. In this respect, there is no longer a requirement for the government to financially assist those who are disadvantaged as the need has been eliminated. The wealthy remain wealthy and are further advantaged as they have the ability to purchase weapons and security. When they are inspired to partake in purging, they hire individuals to seek out and capture victims on their behalf, to ensure their own safety remains intact, and then perform horrific acts of violence on their captives – acts that are arguably more vicious than the actions taken by the rest of society on purge night.

The Purge depicts the fifth annual event of the purge. It centres around the Sandin family, who are like the other advantaged, mid to upper-class families. James Sandin has provided his anti-home invasion equipment to most of his neighbours at a high price, resulting in some neighbourhood tension. As the purge night commences, an injured Black man begs to be let in and disappears to hide within the house. While searching for him some university nihilists arrive, demanding the Black man for their purge and citing their right to cleanse themselves and make sacrifice. They threaten to purge the entire family if they are ignored, accusing them of being unpatriotic. Their inability to locate the stranger in their house results in chaos that sees their home breached, the youngsters entering the house, and many brutally killed in the hunt. The family is captured by the young leader who thanks them for their sacrifice before the daughter reigns bullets into him to save her family. The neighbours arrive only to continue the madness as their intention is to purge the Sandins due to their substantial financial gains at their expense.

Although this film was made well before the inauguration of Donald Trump in 2016, the narrative resonates like prophetic pieces of a modern, divided United States in a global COVID-19 pandemic that has recently seen a wave of protests driven by 'Black Lives Matter'. 'The franchise is less about the fear of invasion or an otherwise external threat, rather focusing on internal crises and the potential dangers of reactionary political responses'[41] and the horror that it engenders. The purge event has become an accepted holiday, with much US infrastructure rebuilt to account for it: insurance and security. Many of the aspects of the purge have now become accepted traditions: parties and get togethers are common among passive participants, but the class divide has become clear. Perhaps the true horror is that neoliberalism has reached this new watershed moment. These films indicate 'a political edge that is increasingly prevalent across numerous other twenty-first-century horror films' and 'demonstrate that rather than seeing sequels and franchises as representing an emptying of meaning, thought provoking and politicised readings are equally possible'.[42]

Armstrong makes the connection between horror and politics, arguing that there is value in the dystopian horror as they challenge narratives about the state and that *The Purge* franchise presents and conceptualises a future United States, 'challenging the intersections of structural economic inequality and racism in the neoliberal state'. Further she suggests that 'since 2013, cinema audiences have been offered a frightening possibility for the near future of the United States [where for 12 hours] there is no law'.[43] Therefore, the Blumhouse creation 'demonstrates the complexity of the mainstream horror market and counters the perception that sequels and franchises represent the dumbing down of horror'.[44]

Conclusion

Blumhouse Productions has created these films to explore the suffering and exploitation found throughout the United States of the past. But also to provide a commentary through a form of horror that is politically engaged in a sociopolitical climate characterised by the angst of civil conflict, terrorism and war; the manipulation and deception of alternative facts and religion; and fears surrounding catastrophe under the threat of nuclear or biological conflict. Meredith Clarke states:

> *The Purge* films are low-budget movies for a mass audience that accidentally became the perfect political commentary for our garbage-fire age: Kind of stupid, desperate to survive and constantly stumbling upon some new horror dreamed up by the men in charge . . . None of the movies in the series are masterpieces, but their ability to anticipate and respond to cultural anxieties has deepened as James DeMonaco, the producer, writer, and director of the first three instalments, added to the world and cranked them out to match the national mood.[45]

Within this context the *Purge* franchise emphasises the more cerebral aspects of horror and places the story and plot at the centre, with strong connection to religious imagery on purging under the guise of 'sacrifice', as a means of justification for merciless killing. The films contain a 'deeper sense of the cultural concerns of the audience' and the 'anxieties of the times they live in, rather than pandering to what is often seen as instant sensations and quick monetary returns'.[46] *The Purge*, franchise as much as it centres around religious and political connections, reflects the clear move to political chaos that the Trump era contained – an era of dangerous slogans generating violence and political instability in the United States. The films address the issues surrounding vast class indifferences, race prejudices and the effects of conservative patriarchal ideology of the elite within an America of past and present, and acts as a warning of an unchecked future for the United States.

Notes

1. M. A. Armstrong, '"A Nation Reborn": Right to Law and Life in *The Purge* Franchise', *Journal of Intervention and Statebuilding*, 13/3 (2019), 388–90.
2. T. K. Platts and M. Clasen, 'Scary Business: Horror at the North American Box Office, 2006–2016', *Frames Cinema Journal*, 11 (2017), *https://framescinemajournal.com/article/scary-business-horror-at-the-north-american-box-office-2006-2016/* (accessed 30 June 2020).
3. J. Kim, 'How the *Purge* Horror Franchise became a Successful, Unlikely Political Allegory', *Medium* (29 June 2018), *https://medium.com/rethink-reviews/how-the-purge-horror-franchise-became-a-successful-unlikely-political-allegory-5cb2100f8247/* (accessed 20 January 2021).
4. S. Kelley, 'An Oral History of *The Purge* Franchise: From Micro-Horror Breakout to Trump-Era Cautionary Tale', *Los Angeles Times* (4 July 2018),

www.latimes.com/entertainment/movies/la-et-mn-the-purge-series-oral-history-20180704-story.html/ (accessed 20 January 2021).

5. G. Virtue, 'Why Smart Horror is Putting the Fear into Sequel-Addicted Hollywood', *Guardian* (12 April 2018), *www.theguardian.com/film/2018/apr/12/horror-quiet-place-get-out-hollywood/* (accessed 20 January 2021).

6. Brigid Cherry, *Horror* (New York: Routledge, 2009).

7. Virtue, 'Why Smart Horror is Putting the Fear into Sequel-Addicted Hollywood'.

8. A. Leadbeater, '*The Purge* Timeline Explained: 2014–2040, *Screen Rant* (6 July 2018), *https://screenrant.com/purge-movie-timeline-explained/* (accessed 20 January 2021).

9. Stacey Abbott, 'James DeMonaco's *The Purge Anarchy* (2014) – Post-Millennial Horror', in Simon Bacon (ed.), *Horror: A Companion* (New York: Peter Lang, 2019), p. 121.

10. Abbott, 'James DeMonaco's *The Purge Anarchy* (2014) – Post-Millennial Horror', p. 121.

11. Joseph J. Ellis, *His Excellency: George Washington* (New York: Vintage Books, 2005).

12. K. Morgan, 'George Washington and the Problem of Slavery', *Journal of American Studies*, 34/2 (2000), 279–301.

13. Judith Butler, *Frames of War: When is Life Grievable?* (London, Verso, 2009), p. 25.

14. S. Szabo, 'Small Details You Missed in *The First Purge*', *Looper* (9 July 2018), *www.looper.com/128083/small-details-you-missed-in-the-first-purge/* (accessed 20 January 2021).

15. J. Williams, 'Donald Trump and Race', *Social Justice* (11 January 2017), *www.socialjusticejournal.org/donald-trump-and-race/* (accessed 20 January 2021).

16. Platts and Clasen, 'Scary Business'.

17. A. Gordon, 'Making America Gory Again: How the *Purge* Films Troll Trumpism', *Guardian* (4 July 2018), *www.theguardian.com/film/2018/jul/04/how-the-purge-trolls-trumps-america-jason-blum-first-purge/* (accessed 20 January 2021).

18. C. K. Robinson, '*The First Purge*: A Horror Movie Terrifyingly Close to Reality', *People's World* (3 July 2018), *www.peoplesworld.org/article/the-first-purge-a-horror-movie-terrifyingly-close-to-reality/* (accessed 20 January 2021).

19. Kelley, 'An Oral History of *The Purge* Franchise'.

20. J. Crucchiola, 'Let's Recap the Twisted Mythology of *The Purge*', *Vulture* (2 July 2018), *www.vulture.com/2018/07/lets-recap-the-twisted-mythology-of-the-purge.html/* (accessed 20 January 2021).

21. Abbott, 'James DeMonaco's *The Purge Anarchy* (2014) – Post-Millennial Horror', p. 122.
22. V. McCollum, 'Introduction', in Victoria McCollum (ed.), *Make America Hate Again: Trump-Era Horror and the Politics of Fear* (New York: Routledge, 2019), p. 6.
23. Platts and Clasen, 'Scary Business'.
24. D. Fear, 'What Do *The Purge* Movies Say About Us?', *Rolling Stone* (2 July 2018), *www.rollingstone.com/movies/movie-features/what-do-the-purge-movies-say-about-us-666940/* (accessed 20 January 2021).
25. Lisa McGirr, *Suburban Warriors: The Origins of the New American Right* (Princeton NJ: Princeton University Press, 2001).
26. K. Phillips-Fein, 'Conservatism: A State of the Field', *Journal of American History*, 98/3 (2011), 733.
27. See, for example, Leadbeater, '*The Purge* Timeline Explained'; Szabo, 'Small Details You Missed in *The First Purge*'; Abbott, 'James DeMonaco's *The Purge Anarchy* (2014) – Post-Millennial Horror', pp. 119–26.
28. Leadbeater, '*The Purge* Timeline Explained'.
29. Leadbeater, '*The Purge* Timeline Explained'.
30. Kim, 'How the *Purge* Horror Franchise became a Successful, Unlikely Political Allegory'.
31. Robinson, '*The First Purge*'.
32. Leadbeater, '*The Purge* Timeline Explained'.
33. J. Oleksinski, 'How the *Purge* Team Created Its Terrifying Masks', *New York Post* (5 July 2018), *https://nypost.com/2018/07/05/how-the-purge-team-created-its-terrifying-masks/* (accessed 20 January 2021).
34. Kim, 'How the *Purge* Horror Franchise became a Successful, Unlikely Political Allegory'.
35. C. Sutton, 'Covid 19 Coronavirus Backlash: US Citizens Protest Lockdown in "Zombie Hordes"', *New Zealand Herald* (17 April 2020), *www.nzherald.co.nz/world/covid-19-coronavirus-backlash-us-citizens-protest-lockdown-in-zombie-hordes/WMMLDL5VFWRVDSYV4BV7VGMXDE/* (accessed 20 January 2021).
36. M. Martina, J. Renshaw and T. Reid, 'How Trump Allies Have Organized and Promoted Anti-Lockdown Protests', *Reuters* (22 April 2020), *www.reuters.com/article/us-health-coronavirus-trump-protests-idUSKCN2233ES/* (accessed 20 January 2021).
37. Mark Bray, *Antifa: The Anti-Fascist Handbook* (Melbourne: Melbourne University Publishing, 2017), p. 15.
38. N. MacFarquhar, A. Feuer and A. Goldman, 'Federal Arrests Show No Sign that Antifa Plotted Protests', *New York Times* (11 June 2020), *www.nytimes.*

com/2020/06/11/us/antifa-protests-george-floyd.html/ (accessed 20 January 2021).

39. C. Weaver, 'Trump Blames "Antifa" for Protests Despite Lack of Evidence', *Financial Times* (4 June 2020), *www.ft.com/content/04ba905f-f965-4f7b-80ab-cccb0f912ddc/* (accessed 20 January 2021).

40. Bray, *Antifa*, p. 15.

41. Armstrong, 'A Nation Reborn', 380.

42. Abbott, 'James DeMonaco's *The Purge Anarchy* (2014) – Post-Millennial Horror', p. 124.

43. Armstrong, 'A Nation Reborn', 377.

44. Abbott, 'James DeMonaco's *The Purge Anarchy* (2014) – Post-Millennial Horror', p. 121.

45. M. Clarke, '*The First Purge* is the Perfect Political Commentary on the Trump Era', *NBC News* (7 July 2018), *www.nbcnews.com/think/opinion/first-purge-perfect-political-commentary-trump-era-ncna889511/* (accessed 20 January 2021).

46. S. Bacon, 'Introduction', in Simon Bacon (ed.), *Horror: A Companion*, p. 6.

9

Happy Death Day

Beyond the Neo-slasher Cycle

Sotiris Petridis

CINEMATIC HORROR is an important genre with a plethora of subcategories and cycles. One of the most well-known subgenres of cinematic horror is the slasher film with its narratives about a serial killer that usually uses bladed weapons, who is spreading fear and death in a middle-class community by killing innocent people. At the end, the killer is often temporarily defeated and the main character (or in some cases, more than one) survives. Blumhouse has created a contemporary comeback of the subgenre with original films such as *Truth or Dare* (2018) and *Thriller* (2018), and revivals of famous franchises such as *Halloween* and *Black Christmas* (2019).

In 2017, Blumhouse released *Happy Death Day*, an innovative slasher film that reimagined the narrative formula of the subgenre. This chapter examines the relationship of this film's formula with the structures of the subgenre's cycles. *Happy Death Day* abandons the legacy of previous films of the new millennium by establishing new norms based on the peculiar time construction of its narrative and by bringing the character that survives to the fore.

Slasher Film: The Formula

Although the origin of the slasher is highly contested, hundreds of such films have been produced that shaped, evolved and rejected conventions of the subgenre. In *Anatomy of the Slasher Film*, I created a corpus of films, which was the basis of my attempt to study and define the narrative formula of the slasher subgenre.[1] More specifically, I created a list of semantic and syntactic elements that characterise the films of this subgenre. The semantics refer to a list of common elements that exist in the audiovisual works (e.g., characters, shots, locations), while the syntax refers to specific constitutional relationships, based on how the elements are placed in the narrative by means of the particular fundamental structure of the genre.[2] In slasher films, the semantic elements are four umbrella terms, which were identified after the systematic reading of the corpus films: normality; others; final survivors; and victims.

In every slasher film there is a selection process among the characters indicating who will be murdered and who will survive. This selection is not random, but relies on rules that change over time. These rules form the 'normality' of the fictional world, which varies according to the needs and fears of the society in question. This code is closely related to the notions of 'normality' and 'other', which Robin Wood mentions in his theory where any person who does not obey the rules of society must be either eliminated or changed according to the community rules.[3]

Another important element of horror films is the 'monster' of the narrative. The monster can take various forms: metaphysical (e.g., vampire, werewolf); human (e.g., insane scientists, murderers); or forms related to nature (e.g., animals, extreme weather). As Cary Morrison states, '(the monsters) reflect the deepest fears of a culture, mirroring those issues that confront us on primal levels'.[4] The term 'other' is an umbrella term that can cover all aspects of evil, while this approach can be generalised and applied to our case too, where the 'other' does not necessarily have a human form. Each narrative also has at least one 'final survivor'. The 'final survivors' along with the 'others' are a dynamic duo of the subgenre's narratives; when there is a change in one of the two, this automatically implies the influence of the second pole.[5]

The last semantic element of the subgenre is the 'victim'. Victims are closely linked to the three above-mentioned semantic elements. The code that dominates the society represented and forms the 'normality' sets certain rules that its members must obey. The 'other' is the one who will apply the punishment to those who do not obey. Through the narrative, comes the reward of the members of the society that they obeyed, and thus the 'final survivors' are created, but there are always members who do not come into complete harmony with 'normality'. These members are the 'victims', which, as it is logical from the above analysis in relation to the other elements, are the exact opposite of the 'final survivors'. 'Victims' are among the first characters that the public are urged to identify with, and although there is no time to develop, it is usually achieved through the common cultural identity with the viewers.[6] This is often accomplished by showing the victims engaged in the typical leisure activities of middle-class youth, such as partying, sex and pranks.

The syntax of the subgenre is divided into three major categories: the backstory of the 'other'; the connection of the 'other' with the 'final survivors'; and the relationship of 'normality' with the remaining three, separate, semantic elements.

From something simple to something more complex that involves interpersonal and/or family relationships with the other characters, there is almost always a reason why the 'other' is killing innocent people.[7] These reasons form a backstory, which does not necessarily have to be represented on screen; it is merely the set of actions that have made the 'other' what it is in the narrative present. The relationship of the 'other' with the 'final survivors' can take various forms: a relationship may range from being totally unknown to being connected by the events and the backstory of the 'other' (*The Texas Chain Saw Massacre* [1974], *Friday the 13th* [1980] and *A Nightmare on Elm Street* [1984]), a family connection (*Halloween* [2007] and *Texas Chainsaw 3D* [2013]) or even a sexual relationship (*Scream* [1996] and *Valentine* [2001]). This syntactic connection of the two semantic elements is important for the narrative, as the whole story of each film is based on this quest for assassination-survival.[8] Although 'normality' is an element determined on the basis of a sociopolitical context, the three other elements are personified within the narrative and therefore the characters embodying them are directly affected by 'normality'.[9] In other words, the code of each 'normality' contributes to the expression, positioning and interaction of the characters that express the three other semantic elements.

These three syntax categories along with the four semantic elements structure the identity of the subgenre. Even though the semantic elements remain stable throughout the lifetime of the subgenre, the syntax changes from time to time and create new cycles within the slasher film. According to Leger Grindon,[10] a cycle is a series of films of a limited period and linked by a dominant trend in their use of the genre's conventions. Genres are dynamic texts that are constantly developing and adapting their conventions to circumstances because they are better understood when viewed as evolutionary processes.[11] The slasher film has experienced three cycles: the classical (1974–93); the self-referential (1994–2000); and the neoslasher (2000–13).

The Three Cycles of the Subgenre

After *The Texas Chain Saw Massacre, Black Christmas* (1974) and *Halloween* (1978), slasher films began to be produced systematically and by the early to mid-1980s its classical formula had been established. By the end of the 1980s, the slasher-film subgenre was recognisable throughout the North American film industry, the media and with audiences.[12] The films' narratives are based on the representation of a community, which is centred on everyday middle-class anxieties or activities, such as babysitting or family events.[13] The 'normality' of the classical cycle is conservative, with adolescent characters having divergent behaviours and the 'other' being used as a means of compliance and enforcement with social norms until 'he' is punished ultimately too. The only character of the classical cycle that is considered a 'winner' is the 'final girl' – a term that was first introduced by Carol J. Clover – and she 'wins' because she follows, literally, the set moral and social rules without contradicting 'normality'.[14] The 'other' along with the 'final survivor' are linked through their sexual identities, while the relationship between 'normality' and the three other semantic elements is structured in such a way as to establish a code that serves a conservative 'normality'.[15]

Beginning in the 1990s, the only slashers that were able to find sizeable audiences were sequels to famous franchises; newer slasher films were made available through video only, unable to find national distribution.[16] Accordingly, the subgenre had to reinvent itself, which, in the early 1990s, it achieved through self-referentiality and parody. Kara Kvaran points out that the slashers of the 1990s demonstrate their success through their engagement in the game that they create with already known subgenre rules.[17] The backstory of the 'other' was redefined in relation to the classical cycle, and the 1990s brought us self-referential slashers with a narrative that developed around whodunit conventions – a structure centred around a possible answer to the question of 'who committed the crime?'.[18] While in classical-cycle films we often see the 'other' from the beginning of the narrative, in the majority of the films that belong to the self-referential cycle the backstory of the 'other' is revealed towards the end of the film in the unfolding of a whodunit plot. These conventions, in combination with the relationship of 'normality' with the three other semantic elements, bring to the fore the self-referentiality and notion of parody by creating a humour that aims to convey our fears.[19] Hence, the connection of the 'other' with the 'final survivor' changes its form and often becomes 'opposite' when compared to the classical filmic texts, establishing an erotic relationship between them, such as in the first instalment of the *Scream* franchise.[20]

The self-referential cycle was a reaction to the standardisation of the classical formula, but it was short-lived and the new millennium brought new conventions. Neoslashers began to focus more on identifying the causes of the development of violence and terror rather than the graphic representation of unjustifiable violence. According to J. P. Telotte, horror films usually achieve their goals by creating a sense of the fact that we – the audience – are also involved in the increase of horror, since we witness the causes of its spreading.[21] The backstory of the 'other' is now structured in a way that the 'other' is the main protagonist and the narrative attempts to represent 'him' as a three-dimensional character rather than a merely stereotypical one. Regarding the connection between the 'other' and the 'final survivor', there is a tendency to strengthen the causal relationship between the two characters, establishing interpersonal, family, love or even cause-and-effect relationships established between them. Finally, even the third category of the syntax focuses on an extensive justification of narrative connections, with 'normality' being linked to more solid structures with the other three semantic elements.[22]

After 2013, the slasher film subgenre went through a decline and the third cycle came to an end. During the period from 2014 to 2016, no slasher film managed to get into the top 100 domestic box office – but this can be justified by new forms of video-on-demand distribution services that commonly carry slasher films, as well as the expansion of the subgenre on television, with examples such as *Scream: The TV Series* (MTV, 2015–present) and *Scream Queens* (Fox, 2015–16).[23]

Happy Death Day: A Slasher Film Beyond the Cycles

In 2017, a new slasher film revived the subgenre: *Happy Death Day* which premiered on 13 October and managed to break into the top 50 of the North American box office that year. The film is about a college student named Tree, who must relive the day of her murder over and over again, in a loop that will end only when she discovers her killer's identity. This day is her birthday, on which, after a night of drunken partying, she wakes up in the dorm-room of her classmate, Carter. Time and again, Tree realises that she is in a loop and attempts to avoid her murder, but she repeatedly fails and the figure wearing a mask of the school mascot always finds her and kills her. Eventually, Tree realises that her killer is her sorority housemate, Lori, who is having an affair with Dr Butler, whose preference for Tree drove Lori mad with jealousy. In a closing fight, Tree takes the poisoned cupcake that Lori tried to feed her and stuffs it in her mouth, then kicks her from a second-storey window to her death.

The film was both an economic and critical success, grossing $125 million worldwide on a $4.8 million budget and receiving mostly positive reviews. Reviewers saw the film as entertaining even though it had a familiar premise,[24] with some describing it as '*Groundhog Day* meets *Scream*'.[25] Although some critics claimed that it was a slasher with a familiar formula, this is far from the truth. The film employed a plethora of innovations to reinvent the slasher formula and to create a unique narrative. Even if *Happy Death Day* is the first economic success of the subgenre after the end of the neoslasher cycle, at its core it has many innovative elements that do not come from the previous slasher cycle. Subjecting the film to a semantic/syntactic analysis will afford a better understanding of its structure and demonstrate its divergence from the slasher formula.

The 'normality' of the film has as its basis a peculiar convention: the main character relives over and over again her final day before an unknown killer murders her. When the masked killer ends her life, Tree wakes up in the same place where she was in the morning and the day begins again. This is a convention that is not justified in the story of the film. From the audience to the main character, no one knows why this is happening, but it is assumed that if she finds her killer before she is murdered, the loop will end. Thus, the 'normality' of the film continues the neoslasher tradition that focused on finding the reasons for the creation of evil, but it does so in a more simplistic way, by restoring the whodunit structure from the self-referential cycle. The 'normality' of the film restores the humour from the second cycle and incorporates it with the main core of the third cycle to create an unusual 'normality' where the same day – and therefore the same events – happen over and over again. This means that the progress of the narrative develops around the question of 'who is the killer?' and consequently what his or her motives are.

With the semantic element of the 'other', the neoslasher cycle placed the 'other' as main character at the heart of the narrative. *Happy Death Day* changes this, since it creates a masked killer with no known motives. The 'other' is similar to the classic killers of the subgenre, such as Michael Myers and Jason Voorhees who are portrayed as relentless, impersonal, masked outcasts.[26] The only thing that the audience knows about the 'other' until the very end is that he or she wants only to kill Tree and that they will do whatever it takes to achieve it – the audience learns that the 'other' is Lori, Tree's roommate, and her motive was based on her love interest in Dr Butler. Even with the final scene of the 'other', we see that the narrative creates a two-dimensional character with stereotypical motivations that lead her to haunt and try to kill the 'final survivor'. The 'other' has swiftly changed in regard to the previous slasher films of the new millennium in order to be better suited for the aforementioned peculiar 'normality'. Since the narrative reproduces the same day from the 'final survivor's' point of view, there is no room for further development of the 'other'.

As a result, the 'final survivor' is the centre of the narrative, since the audience witnesses the story from her viewpoint. Even if the narrative consists of the repetition of the same day and the other characters are not structured based on a concrete arc development, Tree is the only character who maintains her consciousness and therefore can develop as the narrative progresses. She is the centre of the storyline and, as the main protagonist, she undergoes a transformation from the inner journey that she experiences during the course of the story. Thus, we see that the subgenre returns to its roots and, just like in the classical cycle, it creates a three-dimensional 'final survivor' who must confront a two-dimensional 'other'. However, the odd 'normality' complicates things and the film is not simply an ordinary homage to previous classical slashers, but an innovative narrative that stands out.

The final semantic element shows how the aforementioned choices alter the narrative and create a unique film. Since there is a repeatable day with an 'other' who wants only to kill the 'final survivor', the question that arises is which characters can be considered victims? In the entire film, eight characters are seen to be murdered: Tree (the 'final survivor' who dies multiple times); a male from a party; Danielle; Dr Butler; two officers; a nurse; and Carter. There are two main problems that can make their categorisation as 'victims' difficult. First, they do not all die through the agency of the 'other': Danielle dies in a bus accident, while the second officer, the nurse and Carter are murdered by John Tombs, a serial killer being held at the campus hospital whom Lori sets free in order to create a distraction and an alibi. This makes the number of victims four if one includes the 'final survivor', a small number for the subgenre.

The second problem is that these characters do not die in the same version of the repeated day. In each version, Tree attempts to change the events to avoid her murder, therefore different characters may die in the quest of the 'final survivor'. For example, the male from the party dies in the second version just because he is in the same room with Tree when the 'other' tries to kill her. Of course, this means that the same characters are still alive when the next version of the same day starts. Thus, the only character that truly fulfils the real purpose and meaning of the victims is Tree, because she is the only one that keeps dying in each version – except the last one – at the hands of the 'other'.

This creates a narrational anomaly, since the same character fulfils the purpose of two contrasting semantic elements – of the 'final survivor' and of the 'victim'. No matter the cycle, these two elements are contradictory: the 'victims' are being punished for breaking the code of 'normality', while the 'final survivor' is being rewarded for following it. In *Happy Death Day* the formation of its narrative and consequently its 'normality' makes it possible for the same character to simultaneously be the 'final survivor' and the 'victim' of the film. This anomaly does not break the rule of the four stable semantic elements of a slasher film, since all of them are present, but it creates new connections between them that are part of the film's syntax.

Having accounted for the four semantic elements, it is now necessary to examine the syntax of the filmic text. In the previous cycles of the subgenre, the backstory of the 'other' played a central role in the narrative. Here, the narrative is not built around the 'other', but based on the repetitive 'normality'. Therefore, the backstory of the 'other' is part of the whodunit narrative structure and the events of the past and the recurring present are loosely connected. Even if Lori, the 'other' of the narrative, has some motives to move against Tree, they are not enough to justify murder. In the present moment, there is no need for the subgenre to find the causes of evil, so the backstory of the 'other' is weak and serves only the coherence of the story itself.

This second syntactic category, the connection between the 'other' and the 'final survivor' is also weak, since the narrative wants the audience to be surprised by the revelation of the 'other's' identity. For much of the film's duration, Lori is a secondary character who Tree does not even consider as a possible killer. Even if she is part of the same sorority as Tree, she stands out since she is a working student and has different activities and a different appearance from the other sorority sisters. The only connection with the 'final survivor' seems to be their cohabitation, sharing the same room at their sorority house. The backstory of the 'other' is revealed at the very end, when the confrontation scene takes place, but there is no justification of the backstory throughout the narrative. Both the audience and Tree do not know that Lori is in love with Dr Butler, and this backstory seems to exist only to serve as connection point between the 'other' and the 'final survivor'. In other words, the first syntactic category is schematic and serves only the rudimentary and basic connection regarding the second syntactic category. Both categories reinforce the whodunit structure by hiding the backstory of the 'other' and building up the moment of discovery to create a surprise for the audience.

The key to the differentiation of the film's syntax is the third category. As mentioned before, its 'normality' has an atypical form, since it consists of a plethora of different versions of the same day. The connections between 'normality' and the other semantic elements expand this atypical form and transmit it to the core of the film's syntax. The connection between 'normality' and the 'other' is straightforward: in each version of the same day, Lori attempts to kill Tree. Each time the 'other' employs a different way to kill the 'final survivor', since the environment changes and the characters adapt to the repetitive 'normality'. Of course, this means that with the help of the characteristics of this 'normality', the 'other' mostly succeeds and kills the 'final survivor' – which is rather ironic, since Tree's main characteristic is that she does not die.

With this in mind, we can observe that 'normality' creates a dual connection with Tree. This connection serves as both 'final-survivor-normality' and 'victim-normality' links. Based on the narrational anomaly regarding the same character fulfilling the purpose of the two contrasting semantic elements, 'normality' forces the narrative to be structured around this and identifies Tree as both a 'final survivor' and the only real 'victim' of the film. No matter the cycle, in a typical slasher film the audience witnesses many murders of innocent characters, the so-called 'victims', before the final confrontation between the 'other' and the 'final survivor'. Here, the audience does not witness the murders of other characters but sees Tree repeatedly and in differing ways being murdered until she finally confronts the 'other' and ultimately transforms into the 'final survivor'. Therefore, *Happy Death Day* is based on a repetitive 'normality' that forces the syntax of the film to acknowledge the same character as both 'victim' and 'final survivor'. By doing this, the film returns to its roots about the representation of the 'other' – who is two-dimensional, with a loose backstory – and creates a whodunit structure with humorous elements that is taken from the self-referential cycle and therefore substantially separates itself from the neoslasher cycle.

Happy Death Day 2U: Beyond the First Instalment

With the success of *Happy Death Day*, a sequel was expected. Two years after *Happy Death Day* made its premiere, *Happy Death Day 2U* (2019) was released. The film again follows Tree, who is accidentally transported to another dimension where she must repeatedly relive a different version of the same day as she tries to return home while a new killer is on the loose.

The sequel gives the franchise a sci-fi twist to justify the creation of the time loop. Students working on an experimental quantum reactor are responsible for creating the loop. It is worth mentioning that the sequel brings in another character as the 'other' of this narrative. Most of the time, the killers are a constant element of the narrations between the sequels of the subgenre. In *Happy Death Day*, this is not the case, since 'normality' is the constant element between the two films. Even if the second instalment tries to find the reasons that caused the time loop, it still shares the same 'normality' with its predecessor. The sequel follows the syntax of the first film with the repetitive 'normality' at its centre, while the 'other' is only part of the progression of the story and Tree shares again the two identities: 'final survivor' and main 'victim'. Nevertheless, *Happy Death Day 2U* is not just a derivative work of the first film, it uses these norms as a bases and incorporates sci-fi elements allowing the sequel a uniqueness.

Since slasher films have a franchise legacy with a plethora of filmic texts, there are already discussions underway about a third film, with director Christopher Landon stating that he already has an idea for the third movie, while producer Jason Blum claims that 'enough people see this movie, we're gonna make a third movie, we want to make a third movie'.[27] After the average box-office gross of the sequel, Blum said a third film was 'not very [likely] but not impossible',[28] while Landon stated that he has an outline written with the title *Happy Death Day Tre3*.[29]

Conclusion

Among horror subgenres, Blumhouse has contributed to slashers. The subgenre counts hundreds of films over four decades, having conquered other mediums as well, such as television, video games and comics. In 2017, the company made history with the film *Happy Death Day*, the first film of the subgenre since 2014 that managed to reach the top 100 of the domestic box office. Before then, the subgenre had three cycles: classical, self-referential and neoslasher. The third cycle ended in 2013 and for three years the subgenre went into hibernation. *Happy Death Day* helped it to reinvent itself and place it back in the spotlight. By creating a peculiar 'normality' that is based on a repetitive day with different versions, the film's narrative uses different norms from the previous cycles and incorporates them into its core. The result is something new and refreshing, which helps the film to stand out and not be an excessively derivative homage to previous filmic texts. The film restores the 'final survivor' as the main protagonist and offers a narrational twist; the same character also fulfils the role of the main 'victim'. Therefore, 'normality' has a dual connection with this character and the syntax of the narrative forces the audience to identify Tree as the 'final survivor' and the only victim in all the versions of the repeatable day, except the last one that is dedicated to the final confrontation of the 'other'.

Of course, *Happy Death Day* and its sequel offer just one particular case study of the contemporary situation regarding slasher films and the aforementioned analysis does not mean that this is the start of a new cycle. Nevertheless, this chapter has suggested a possible new diegetic form to slasher films. Even if there were earlier films that played with the slasher formula, this is the first example to experience mainstream success. It differentiates itself from the previous cycles and adds a novel tone to the subgenre; however, to be considered the beginning of a new movement within the subgenre, it must be reproduced by several other filmic texts that incorporate and expand these characteristics.

Notes

1. For more, see Sotiris Petridis, *Anatomy of the Slasher Film: A Theoretical Analysis* (Jefferson NC: McFarland, 2019), pp. 7–10.
2. R. Altman, 'A Semantic/Syntactic Approach to Film Genre', in B. K. Grant (ed.), *Film Genre Reader IV* (Austin TX: University of Texas Press, 2012), pp. 31–2.

3. Robin Wood, *Hollywood from Vietnam to Reagan . . . and Beyond* (New York: Columbia University Press, 2003), pp. 65–6.

4. C. Morrison, 'Creature Conflict: Man, Monster and the Metaphor of Intractable Social Conflict', in P. L. Yoder and P. M. Kreuter (eds), *Monsters and the Monstrous: Myths and Metaphors of Enduring Evil* (Oxford: Inter-Disciplinary Press, 2004), p. 172.

5. Petridis, *Anatomy of the Slasher Film*, pp. 28–9.

6. Petridis, *Anatomy of the Slasher Film*, p. 29.

7. Petridis, *Anatomy of the Slasher Film*, p. 32.

8. Petridis, *Anatomy of the Slasher Film*, p. 33.

9. Petridis, *Anatomy of the Slasher Film*, p. 33.

10. L. Grindon, 'Cycles and Clusters: The Shape of Film Genre History', in *Film Genre Reader IV*, p. 44.

11. R. Cohen, 'History and Genre', *New Literary History*, 17/2 (1986), 205–6.

12. R. Nowell, *Blood Money: A History of the First Teen Slasher Film Cycle* (New York: Continuum, 2011), p. 18.

13. N. S. Fhlainn, 'Sweet Bloody Vengeance: Class, Social Stigma and Servitude in the Slasher Genre', in Marlin C. Bates (ed.), *Hosting the Monster* (New York: Rodopi, 2008), pp. 184–5.

14. C. J. Clover, 'Her Body, Himself: Gender in the Slasher Film', *Representation*, 20, 200–4.

15. Petridis, *Anatomy of the Slasher Film*, p. 35.

16. Adam Rockoff, *Going to Pieces: The Rise and Fall of the Slasher Film, 1978–1986* (Jefferson NC: McFarland, 2002), p. 177.

17. K. M. Kvaran, '"You're All Doomed!" A Socioeconomic Analysis of Slasher Films', *Journal of American Studies*, 50/4 (2016), 964.

18. Charles Derry, *The Suspense Thriller: Films in the Shadow of Alfred Hitchcock* (Jefferson NC: McFarland, 2001), p. 59.

19. Paul W. Kahn, *Finding Ourselves at the Movies: Philosophy for a New Generation* (New York: Columbia University Press, 2013), p. 169.

20. Petridis, *Anatomy of the Slasher Film*, pp. 38–9.

21. J. P. Telotte, 'Faith and Idolatry in the Horror Film', in B. K. Grant (ed.), *Planks of Reason: Essays on the Horror Film* (London: Scarecrow Press, 1984), p. 26

22. Petridis, *Anatomy of the Slasher Film*, pp. 40–5.

23. Petridis, *Anatomy of the Slasher Film*, p. 9.

24. J. Giles, '*Happy Death Day* is Familiar but Fun', *Rotten Tomatoes* (12 October 2017), *https://editorial.rottentomatoes.com/article/happy-death-day-is-familiar-but-fun/* (accessed 10 November 2019).

25. A. D'Alessandro, 'Blumhouse has Plenty to Smile about as *Happy Death Day* Scares Up $26M+ Opening', *Deadline* (15 October 2017), *https://deadline. com/2017/10/happy-death-day-blade-runner-2049-weekend-box-office-the-foreigner-jackie-chan-1202187771/* (accessed 10 November 2019).

26. M. Hills and S. J. Scneider, '"The Devil Made Me Do It!" Representing Evil and Disarticulating Mind/Body in the Supernatural Serial Killer Film', in M. F. Norden (ed.), *The Changing Face of Evil in Film and Television* (New York: Rodopi, 2007), pp. 71–87.

27. D. Salemme, 'Jason Blum Has Plans to Create a Shared Universe for Blumhouse', *Screen Rant* (2 February 2019), *https://screenrant.com/blumhouse-shared-universe-jason-blum-plans/* (accessed 2 November 2019).

28. S. Schaefer, 'Jason Blum: *Happy Death Day 3* isn't Likely to Happen', *Screen Rant* (2 November 2019), *https://screenrant.com/jason-blum-happy-death-day-3-not-happening/* (accessed 2 November 2019).

29. P. Cavanagh, '*Happy Death Day* Director Addresses the Franchise's Possible Future', *ComicBook* (15 August 2019), *https://comicbook.com/horror/news/happy-death-day-3-details-christopher-landon-sequel-details/* (accessed 4 November 2019).

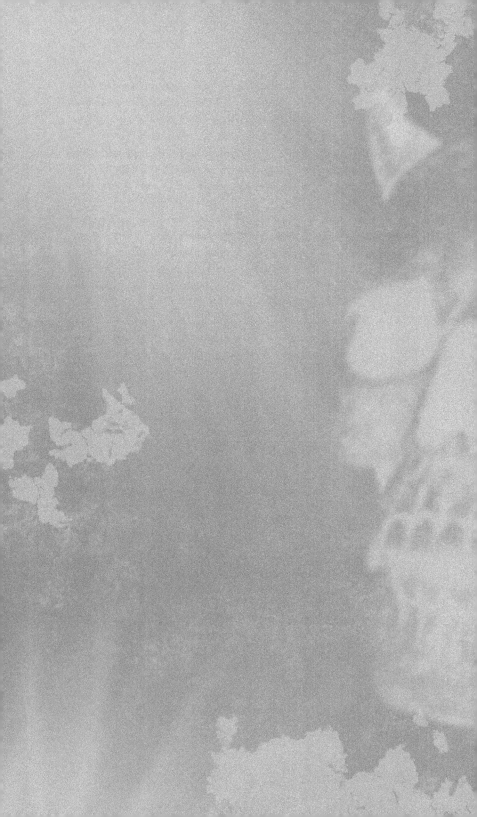

10

Haunted Networks

Transparency and Exposure in *Unfriended* and *Unfriended: Dark Web*

Zak Bronson

WHILE DEPICTIONS of technological horror have always been a central component of the horror genre, the recent releases of *Unfriended* (2015) and *Unfriended: Dark Web* (2018) mark a new direction for the tradition. Both films are part of a recent cinematic subgenre known as 'screencast' films – or what *Unfriended* producer Timur Bekmambetov calls 'screenmovie' – in which the entire narrative transpires through the protagonist's computer screen and the action unfolds across multiple social media platforms, including chat-based messaging, browsers and websites.[1] In addition to the *Unfriended* films, this subgenre includes films such as *Open Windows* (2014), *Sickhouse* (2016), *Searching* (2018), *Unsubscribe* (2020) and *Host* (2020). Among these films, however, the *Unfriended* films warrant special attention for the ways in which they narratively and stylistically engage with digital anxieties to construct horrific narratives that depict characters who are stalked by mysterious and unknown forces. In *Unfriended*, six friends chatting online are suddenly attacked by a vengeful ghost that haunts them through Skype, Facebook and other online messaging services. In *Dark Web*, five friends become unexpectedly entangled with a covert darknet community that hacks into their computers, discovers their personal information and viciously attacks them. Situating these narratives through screens and platforms, both films capture a sense of the anxiety and intimacy associated with the widespread growth of information technologies and their integration into everyday life. In doing so, both films reveal fears not just around modern technologies, but also around the ways in which they remain closely linked to wider networks of power, visibility and control.

Through their unique engagement with computer-mediated images, *Unfriended* and *Dark Web* contribute to a growing number of digital horror films that have emerged over the past two decades in response to the birth of the 'networked' society and the growth of information and communication devices such as handheld cameras, digital editing software and high-speed computers. Over this period, films such as *The Ring* (2002) and *Pulse* (2006), and 'found-footage' films such as *Paranormal Activity* (2009), *[•REC]* (2007) and *Cloverfield* (2008), have each responded to these social and cultural conditions by adopting highly self-reflexive narratives that simultaneously reflect on these developments.[2] In each of these films, the horror resides not only in their storylines, but also in the process of mediation captured through their use of handheld cameras, computers and mobile phones. As Linnie Blake and Xavier Aldana Reyes argue, this unique combination has made digital horror:

> an exceptionally anxious cinema, preoccupied with the dangers of digital technology, specifically its proliferation of mediated images of real-world violence, its capacity to bring surveillance societies into being, its exposure of the user to the uninvited attentions of strangers 'from beyond' and its impact on human identity.[3]

The *Unfriended* films are the latest iteration of this trend. Cleverly building on the tropes and conventions of the found-footage genre, the films integrate a host of modern technologies, including computers and webcams, websites like Facebook and Google, applications such as Skype and iMessage, and various 'unseen' intruders including trolls, hackers, viruses and glitches. In combining these elements, both films capture something uncanny about our dependence on these machines, while also suggesting that there is something lurking 'behind the screen' watching us and threatening to remove our agency and power. If horror film has always demonstrated an ongoing concern with modern technologies, then both *Unfriended* and *Dark Web* expand on these ideas to illustrate the increasing anxieties associated with information and communication technologies in the twenty-first century.

In the past decade, the rapid proliferation of new media devices, social media and surveillance technology has resulted in the emergence of what Bernard Harcourt terms the 'society of exposure', a new era of public visibility in which powerful new devices such as smartphones, cameras and social media sites continually track, store and expose private information to digital networks. According to Harcourt, this expository society has resulted in unprecedented levels of public transparency that have fundamentally altered the lines between public and private space: social media sites such as Facebook and YouTube accumulate massive amounts of personal data on users; websites such as Google and Amazon record every keystroke and movement users make; smartphones collect geolocation data that can identify where individuals travel. And much of this information is accessible to government, corporate and peer surveillance.[4] This type of surveillance, however, differs from disciplinary models of surveillance captured in Michel Foucault's discussion of the Panopticon. In the society of exposure, 'we have brought this upon ourselves willingly, enthusiastically, and with all our passion: through our joyful and fulfilling embrace of social media and online shopping, through our constant texting to loved ones and our Google searches'.[5] Certainly, this new era of visibility is not only drastically eroding the lines between public and private space but is also threatening to undermine traditional notions of agency and privacy. As Harcourt summarises, this 'new expository power constantly tracks and pieces together our digital selves. It renders us legible to others, open, accessible, subject to everyone's idiosyncratic projects – whether governmental, commercial, personal, or intimate'.[6]

As films that emerge in response to these ongoing transformations, *Unfriended* and *Dark Web* embody the concerns around exposure, desire and fear that make up the conditions of an increasingly transparent and visible society. By narratively foregrounding new technologies, each of these films illustrate the increasing ubiquity of new media devices within everyday life and the ways in which these technologies routinely 'expose' personal information and make it accessible to public networks. Since both films focus on characters who are attacked by mysterious figures that have access to personal information and threaten to use it for horrific ends, they each illustrate a profound cultural anxiety around these changes and the ways in which they erode the boundaries between public and private space. In doing so, both films depict what I call 'haunted networks', information and communication networks that remain possessed by unknown and unseen forces and that reflect the numerous anxieties associated with an era of increasing public visibility. Within both films, the image of the haunted network symbolises the proximity and intimacy of modern information and communication networks, and the ways in which digital technologies threaten to undermine traditional notions of agency and privacy. In utilising these haunted networks, *Unfriended* and *Dark Web* capture the dystopian side of contemporary life in an era where everyone and everything is subject to continual monitoring, tracking and exposure. Taken together, the two films are not direct sequels as much as they are disturbing and frightening explorations of the underlying fears associated with an expository society in which personal information is continually threatened to become publicly exposed to unknown audiences.

Social Networks and Spectral Figures

Released in 2015, *Unfriended* provides an exemplary depiction of networked haunting that perfectly captures the anxieties associated with the widespread proliferation of new media technologies such as smartphones, digital cameras and social media. The film's narrative focuses on Blaire, a female high-school student still mourning the death of her best friend Laura, who committed suicide after experiencing online bullying when an embarrassing video of her was posted on YouTube. On the night of the one-year anniversary of Laura's death, Blaire meets with five friends on Skype to do homework together. However, as they chat, their conversations are interrupted by an unknown user named 'billie227' who joins their conversations and posts harassing comments and embarrassing images online. As these attacks continue, billie227 forces each of the friends to admit to their own participation in Laura's bullying, and near the film's end, it is revealed that billie227 is actually Laura's ghost who has returned on the anniversary of her death to punish each of her close friends for their own involvement in her online abuse. Through this modern variation of the ghost narrative, *Unfriended* offers a potent exploration of the ways that digital networks not only expose private information, but do so in ways that threaten the possibility of self-definition. If the society of exposure is one which undermines traditional notions of public and private space, then *Unfriended* offers a horror dealing with the ways in which our private lives have been increasingly mediated, monetised and shared for public consumption in ways that contribute to a loss of self-identity.

At its core, *Unfriended* is a cautionary tale about the nature of social media, and the film taps directly into media panics surrounding the ways that sites such as Facebook and Twitter have led to an increase in online bullying and cyberbullying. Many of these ideas are indicated in the film's title and tagline ('This April, Revenge Comes Online'), which both allude to the problems that have emerged due to social media abuse. However, the film goes beyond these issues to illustrate a generalised concern with how contemporary technologies enable new forms of public visibility that undermine self-identity. Immediately following the film's opening credits, viewers see Blaire's computer as she watches two videos that provide detail into Laura's suicide. The first video, posted to the website LiveLeak, shows a distraught Laura as she stands in an outdoor high-school basketball court and shoots herself, while onlookers stand by and record her with their smartphones. Right after this, Blaire watches a video on YouTube entitled 'LAURA BARNS KILL URSELF' which provides more information about the events that caused Laura's suicide. In the video, an inebriated Laura stumbles through an outdoor party where she fights with friends, plays drinking games and passes out drunk covered in her own faeces. Posted to YouTube, then shared through social media platforms, the video received more than 75,000 views and thousands of dislikes from online viewers, many of whom posted harassing comments such as 'kill urself', 'no one likes u' and 'u should just die'. Being shared across digital platforms and endlessly replayed by viewers, the videos of Laura become public data that endlessly recirculates across social media sites and shared among friends, ultimately creating a public image of Laura that directly challenges her own means of self-representation. In this way, Laura's embarrassing moments are not just captured on camera but are also endlessly replayed as a new form of amusement and monetisation that undermine her own ability to define herself.

The film's concerns with digital technologies and the erosion of public and private space also work in tandem with the film's style, which deliberately highlights the voyeuristic nature of the viewing experience. Horror cinema has long demonstrated an ongoing concern with voyeurism and, as Isabel Pinedo notes, frequently utilises a 'series of voyeuristic shots, either tracking or stationary, taken from assorted angles and points in the narrative space, or other framing devices to create the keyhole effect of surveillance by an unseen or partially seen other'.[7] While films such as *Halloween* (1978) have commonly done this by relying on point-of-view shots, *Unfriended* exploits the screencast style to place audiences as participatory voyeurs watching the narrative unfold. Indeed, right after the opening scenes, viewers watch as Blaire and her boyfriend begin to chat on Skype and, as they do so, their conversations quickly become sexual. Blaire begins by telling Mitch 'I've got something to show you', and she reveals her freshly painted toenails. Mitch replies that 'there's other things I want to see more of', and 'why don't you take that shirt off'. As the two flirt, Blaire begins to seductively unbutton her shirt; however, just as she begins to remove it, she receives a Skype call from their friends requesting to join their conversation. Blaire attempts to reject the invitation, but a computer glitch accepts the call and her friends suddenly see them in various states of undress. This scene not only highlights directly how technologies expose private information, but the film's framing – including the laptop screen backdrop, the constrained viewing space of the Skype window and the camera's gaze upon Blaire and Mitch's bodies – taps into cinema's history of voyeurism in ways that place audiences as cinematic 'lurkers' who are invading the characters' privacy. The imagery of this scene directly calls to mind the 'peep hole' gaze of Norman Bates watching Marion Crane in *Psycho* (1960), and much like that film, *Unfriended* uses framing and images to make audiences complicit in this crossing of private boundaries.

Throughout the film, this voyeurism is paralleled with another type of intrusion, that of billie227 – the digital ghost that invades their network. As a digital revenant, billie227 represents a variation of what Neal Kirk terms 'networked spectrality', the unique image of disembodied ghosts that have emerged in the digital era through films such as *Pulse*, *In Memorium* (2005) and *Paranormal Activity*. According to Kirk, networked spectrality identifies the ways in which digital technologies create a profound sense of unease stemming from how they remove materiality from communication, and ultimately cast doubt about who could be on the other side of the machine.[8] Appearing to be both real and virtual, billie227 captures this eerie manifestation of digital haunting. What is so notable about billie227's presence is the way that it almost goes unnoticed altogether. Originally believed to be simply a technological glitch of a nefarious hacker, Blaire and her friends decide to simply ignore billie227. It is not until billie227 admits to posting embarrassing images online that Blaire begins to become suspicious of its presence, and suddenly discovers that the online profile belongs to Laura. As she does so, Blaire also discovers that billie227 has managed to steal private videos and images that depict Blaire sleeping with Mitch's best friend Adam, and that reveal her own participation in bullying Laura online. In this manner, billie227 provides an overt symbol for the anxiety associated with public visibility and the threats of having one's private details exposed.

Of course, the anxiety that billie227 provokes is not simply a fear around digital exposure, but also around the ways that personal information is shared and distributed through digital networks in a manner that threatens personal boundaries. As Kirk explains, networked spectrality replaces the singular attacks commonly depicted in horror narratives with networked attacks in which ghosts can torment victims by rapidly distributing images and videos online. 'In other words,' writes Kirk, 'ghosts have, in internet parlance "gone viral" as haunting becomes conflated with endemic apocalyptic contagion.'[9] Fittingly, billie227's attacks resemble the nature and ubiquity of social networks themselves. Indeed, shortly into the film, billie227 accesses Jess's Facebook account and uploads an album of photos that depict Val drinking, doing drugs and passed out on the floor. Jess repeatedly attempts to delete them from her account, but a technical glitch prevents her. When she eventually manages to erase them, billie227 immediately accesses Adam's Facebook and reposts them there. As they are reposted, they attract more and more attention and comments from Facebook friends, which directly results in the friends breaking into a fight by calling one another 'slut', 'whore' and 'trashy'. These scenes draw direct parallels with Laura's experiences depicted earlier in the film, and she replays these attacks as a form of retaliation against Val. The gendered dimensions of these attacks are unmistakable, as the revelation of these images cause Val to experience the same type of 'slut shaming' and abuse directed at Laura. In this respect, billie227's presence reveals the underlying anxiety associated with having one's most intimate details publicly revealed. This is not simply a fear of digital technologies, but a particular fear around the ways that these devices increasingly creep into private spaces and threaten to expose private details.

This anxiety around digital exposure is cleverly revised as it is eventually revealed that Blaire and her friends each took part in posting harassing statements about Laura online, and that Blaire was the one who posted the original video to YouTube. Given this new context, billie227 is not simply a digital ghost, but an avenging spirit that has returned from the grave to punish and confront her online harassers. Attacking them through social media and platforms, billie227 utilises the same methods and approaches used on her to attack her friends. In this respect, the film demonstrates a close connection to the 'vengeful spirit' narrative popularised in films such as *Ringu* (1998), *Ju-on: The Grudge* (2000) and *One Missed Call* (2003), which each used the image of the vengeful spirit to confront the repressive social and gender codes by which women are subjugated.[10] In this same way, *Unfriended*'s narrative reversal – in which billie227 goes from haunting figure to avenging spirit – forcefully articulates the restrictive codes and standards to which women are held, particularly in online spaces. Indeed, one of the film's most provocative scenes appears shortly after the attacks begin, when Blaire watches a YouTube video made by Laura just prior to her suicide. Filmed entirely in black and white, the video depicts Laura holding up cue cards that express her anger and resentment at her online attackers for the ways in which they harassed her. The imagery of the video, including the black and white images, handwritten cards and folksy music, mirrors a similar video produced by teenager Amanda Todd in 2013, in which she released a YouTube video where she detailed her experiences of being harassed for years after a sex tape was posted of her online.[11] Drawing on these same types of image, Laura's videos articulate her own pain around the discovery that she has lost control over her own mediated image and the abuse she has endured from a patriarchal society in which women are punished for their sexuality.

Viewed in this context, *Unfriended* can be seen as a feminist revenge narrative in which Laura's ghost repurposes the tools of abuse lobbed at her by redirecting these same forms of violence against her online attackers. If, as Robin Wood has famously argued, the 'true subject of horror is the struggle for recognition of all that our civilization represses or oppresses', then billie227's act of revenge can be read as a symbolic act of resistance in which Laura returns from the grave to challenge the oppressive patriarchal standards to which women are held.[12] Hannah Bonner notes that the film demonstrates a close similarity to Brian De Palma's *Carrie* (1976) and that much like that film, 'Laura, too, is relentlessly bullied, albeit online, urged to kill herself for such a bodily affront to female decorum. Subsequently, Laura punishes the purveyor of the surveillance footage (Blaire) by utilizing surveillance footage to achieve her own ends'.[13] In doing so, billie227 uses the revelation of private information to subject all her friends to the same types of punishment and attack online that she experienced. Indeed, after Blaire eventually confesses to her complicity in Laura's bullying, Blaire believes that she has been saved and attempts to repair her relationship with Mitch. However, just as she closes her laptop, Blaire looks up and sees Laura's ghost who suddenly leaps at Blaire and instantly kills her. Although this ending completes Laura's act of revenge, this final resolution denies Laura the ability to recover her online image. Even after Laura publicly shames and attacks her online harassers, her embarrassing videos and harassing comments remain uploaded and circulating the internet, endlessly shared and distributed through digital networks. Unable to fully remove these images online, Laura's story speaks to a contemporary moment in which private images and videos endlessly haunt our digital networks and frighteningly expose our most intimate details. In this respect, the film not only reveals the restrictive gender standards to which women are held, but also exposes the ways in which these forms of online harassment and bullying are monetised and exploited by digital networks that capture and expose private events and behaviour while being indifferent to the effects of such abuse.

Cryptic Networks and Dark Webs

Unfriended's image of digital haunting lays the foundations for *Dark Web*, which expands on the tropes of the earlier film to explore the anxieties associated with digital technologies and the ways in which they are linked to networks of surveillance, monitoring and control. Whereas *Unfriended* illustrated the nascent anxieties of the networked society and its blurring of public/private boundaries, *Dark Web* can be read as demonstrating an encroaching paranoia associated with digital surveillance, stemming from the covert ways that digital devices continually track, monitor and store personal information and make it accessible to digital networks. The film was released several years after Edward Snowden's revelations regarding the coordination of government and corporate surveillance, and two years after the 2016 Facebook data breach, and the film seems to directly respond to the growing anxieties associated with the internet as a massive surveillance network, or what media theorist Siva Vaidhyanathan terms the 'Cryptopticon': 'an inscrutable information ecosystem of massive corporate and state surveillance.'[14] According to Vaidhyanathan, modern information networks rely on dozens of covert methods of tracking users through computers, mobile phones and webcams, which means that users 'can never be sure who is watching whom and for what purpose. Surveillance is so pervasive and much of it is so seemingly benign . . . that it's almost impossible for the object of surveillance to assess she is manipulated or threatened'.[15] In exploring these concerns, *Dark Web* associates this pervasive surveillance with digital haunting to capture the lingering anxieties associated with modern technologies that constantly track and expose personal information with very little public awareness. In doing so, the film's haunted networks speak to the 'behind-the-scenes' activities that occur online and which simultaneously open up individuals to new levels of manipulation, invasion or risk.[16]

Dark Web taps into these surveillant anxieties by dealing with the threats of being attacked and monitored by unseen and unknown forces whose perceptual threat remains beyond complete and total comprehension. The film's narrative focuses on Matias, an amateur computer programmer who steals a laptop from a nearby coffee shop in order to develop a language application program that enables him to better communicate with his deaf girlfriend Amaya. As he and his friends chat together on Skype, Matias discovers the previous owner of the computer (known only as Charon IV) is a member of a darknet community known as The River, where users take part in the production and sale of graphic torture videos. Matias also discovers that Charon IV has recently kidnapped a young woman named Erica and is currently auctioning off her murder to the highest bidder. After discovering this, Matias and his friends attempt to save Erica, however, in doing so, they rouse the attention of the entire darknet community (known as The Circle), who coordinate a plot to target Matias and his friends by using the internet to uncover each individual's personal information, find their home addresses and then kill them in attacks designed to resemble accidents. After Matias and each of his friends are killed, the film camera pulls back to reveal that audiences have not been watching Matias' laptop, but have actually been watching the computer screen of Charon I, the leader of the darknet community, who has orchestrated the entire event as a game in which members of the community pay money to watch each of the players be murdered. Relying almost exclusively on their computers, The Circle has exploited the internet's elaborate surveillance network in order to monitor, track and target Matias and his friends, and to do so without leaving any physical traces.

Although the narrative centres on the darknet, the film makes a number of connections to suggest that it is about internet surveillance as a whole. Many of these ideas are addressed by Matias' friend A.J., an amateur conspiracy theorist and YouTube personality, who routinely warns his friends about the nature of modern surveillance and at one point in the film explains to them that it is not just the government that spies on individuals:

it's the Cicadians, and the Bilderbergs, and the Illuminati, and corporations. Why do you think Facebook and Twitter are free? Because you're the product. They own every single thing you post. Everybody assumes it's just pictures and shit and all they care about is targeted marketing, but the Internet, as you know it, is just the surface . . . it's the total integration of Wi-Fi, cell towers, GPS, IP address detection, Bluetooth device tracking, even those FitBit devices you like to run around with, they can track you through that.

A.J.'s slightly paranoiac ramblings, including his bridging together of well-known facts about Facebook's targeted advertising and blatant conspiracies about the Illuminati, nicely captures the cryptic nature of modern surveillance and the ways in which devices such as FitBits, Bluetooth and GPS are closely integrated together through global surveillance networks. Indeed, right after A.J. says these words, Matias discovers that his new computer contains dozens of private home surveillance camera videos that Charon IV recorded by hacking into neighbours' WiFi networks and recording them in their homes. Moreover, as Matias discovers, Charon IV then uses this information to breaks into victims' houses, kidnap them and auction off their torture on The River. This overt connection between the darknet community and surveillance as a whole illustrates the ways that digital technologies are interwoven with tracking tools that simultaneously expose private information to unknown attackers.

Much like *Unfriended*, the film also strategically exploits the screencast framing to examine – and undermine – traditional notions of cinematic voyeurism. After Matias discovers the hidden videos on his computer, he and his friends begin to watch a number of videos that depict individuals chained in empty, abandoned warehouses, who are tortured through horrific forms of violence. These scenes not only convey the anxieties associated with digital technologies to record and distribute horrifically violent acts, but they also self-reflexively comment on the act of watching, especially since the film screen is intentionally reminiscent of the experience of watching videos on one's laptop. This video's grainy images and reduced framing intentionally call to mind the videos and images commonly shared on websites such as LiveLeak. Through these images, the film exhibits a self-reflexivity that simultaneously raises questions regarding the nature of cinematic horror and its capacity to elicit pleasure from sadistic images. Not only do these images directly call to mind Laura's suicide in *Unfriended*, but the imagery of these videos – including the warehouse settings, grainy images and graphic displays of violence – all draw close connections to the graphic displays of violence commonly seen in the 'torture porn' genre, including films such as *Saw* (2004) and *Hostel* (2005). *Dark Web*, however, disrupts the experiences of pleasure commonly associated with cinematic violence by avoiding the exploitation-style effects and spectacularised displays of violence apparent in those films. Instead, by revealing the disturbing nature of this violence and making audiences complicit with it, *Dark Web* avoids depictions of gore to more fully articulate an anxiety around how digital technologies can lead to a loss of personal agency and self-control.

This emphasis on watching is further refined as the film repeatedly suggests that there remains something lurking on the other side of the screen watching Matias and controlling his actions. Early in the narrative, Charon IV sends Matias messages telling him to return the laptop, but when Matias fails to do so, Charon IV decides to attack Amaya. Finding her information online, Matias arrives at Amaya's house with plans to kidnap her, but in a rush ends up killing Amaya's sister. Sitting in his apartment, Matias watches the entire event unfold on his computer screen, which Charon IV has managed to make accessible for Matias to watch. However, every time that Charon IV walks in front of the camera, it causes a technological glitch that conceals his identity. Appearing only as a series of scrambled images and pixelated frames, Charon IV resembles a type of digital ghost that haunts his machine. Although this effect is likely due to some sort of concealed technological device, the film's lack of explanation articulates the anxiety around the ways that computers and machines are similarly 'haunted' by external forces, and which closely connects with the anxieties associated with internet surveillance. If, as Kirk argues, networked spectrality articulates the underlying anxieties around how digital technologies can be 'possessed' by unknown individuals, then these scenes articulate a feeling of dread associated with the imbalances of power produced by new media devices and the ways that they can be taken over and controlled by unknown powers.

Despite the threat that Charon IV wields, Matias and his friends attempt to use their technological knowledge to save Erica. To do so, Matias blackmails Charon IV by stealing his bitcoin, which unintentionally attracts the attention of The Circle, who have been tracking his every action and move. Although Matias manages to throw them off, each of his friends suddenly find themselves as the targets of The Circle's vicious 'game'. Their attacks begin by targeting Lexx. First, they find her Facebook page to discover her alma mater, then hack into the university's database to uncover her home address, and then arrive at her home and kill her by pushing her off of her apartment roof; and all of this is shared through a YouTube video that is spread virally online. Following Lexx's death, The Circle targets A.J. by carefully editing together a series of his YouTube videos to make a police phone call that convincingly sounds like a terrorist attack. As the police storm into his home, A.J. attempts to warn the police that he is unarmed, but a quickly edited sound effect makes it sound like he has a weapon, and the police gun him down instantly. These scenes perfectly illustrate the threats of public visibility provided by social networks that contain personalised information, while also demonstrating a more general anxiety about the loss of autonomy and agency in the face of increasingly vast digital networks that can be easily accessed and manipulated. In an age when personalised information is tracked, collected and stored through obscured forms of digital surveillance, *Dark Web* articulates the ways that this digital exposure renders us susceptible to new levels of risk and harm.

This sense of powerlessness is aided by the stylistic and thematic framing of these deaths. As The Circle targets each individual, Matias and audiences are forced to watch as the elaborate deaths take place with little ability to prevent them. Even though characters – and audiences – remain aware that an attack is coming, each death is drawn out in extreme detail, which emphasises the feeling of helplessness against the attacks. Right after the darknet community kills Lexx and A.J., they attack Serena and Nari by going to the hospital where Serena's mother remains on life support. The Circle forces Serena to choose between saving Nari or saving her mother. Unable to make a choice, Serena simply refuses to decide, and, as a result, all three are killed. The long drawn-out nature of these deaths draw close connection to tropes used in films such as *Final Destination* and *Saw*, which offer elaborate and protracted tortures where characters have little to no agency to prevent their eventual deaths.[17] However, whereas *Final Destination*'s elaborate deaths illustrate the cruel hand of fate and the inability to escape it, *Dark Web* conveys the erosion of individual agency against a larger digital network that seems to control individuals' lives and abilities. Moreover, aside from Matias's act of stealing the computer, each of his friends are innocent bystanders who are unfairly drawn into his actions through their attempts to save Erica. Yet despite their innocence, each of them becomes inevitably drawn into this sadistic game with no means to prevent it. The darknet community is so fully in control of the 'game' that each friend is killed easily without any ability to escape their attacks.

After each of his friends are killed, Matias attempts to save Amaya by covertly messaging her to meet in a place that only they know about. However, as Matias bikes to meet her, he discovers that The Circle have redirected her to an alternate location where she is quickly and savagely killed in front of the camera. Forced to watch her die on his phone, Matias suddenly asks The Circle why they did this. 'It was game night', the leader Charon I explains. As he does so, Charon I launches a poll on his computer that asks other participants 'Should Matias Live?'. After The Circle overwhelmingly votes 'No', Matias is suddenly struck and killed by a large cargo van that kills him instantly. As it does so, the film slowly pulls back from the computer screen to reveal that Charon I sits behind a military-style computer command centre, watching the entire situation unfold while accepting money from other members of The River. As it turns out, the entire series of events was an elaborately orchestrated game coordinated by The Circle for entertainment. As the camera pulls back from the frame, the film highlights the extent to which modern surveillant structures have enabled a massive and complex form of individualised monitoring and tracking. Yet, even as it does so, this final scene also contains a self-reflexive element that implicates the audience for also participating in watching this game unfold. Given the film's larger context, this ending suggests that we ourselves have been integrated into this large surveillance network which continually lurks behind the screens that we use, and which works within the dominant systems in which we live, work and play.

Despite their narrative differences, *Unfriended* and *Dark Web* both illustrate profound anxieties associated with life in the digital age and the ways in which modern technologies have restructured the lines between public and private space. In doing so, both films build on the tropes of digital haunting conveyed in films such as *The Ring*, *Pulse* and *Paranormal Activity*. However, whereas those films addressed the underlying threats associated with the emergence of new media devices such as cameras, smartphones and the internet, the *Unfriended* films draw attention to the new systems of power and exploitation that exist within information and communication networks that enable the ability to track and monitor individuals' actions. In a digital society where private information is recorded, shared and accessible on digital networks, *Unfriended* and *Dark Web* articulate the underlying anxieties associated with the ways that communication devices 'leak' private information and threaten to undermine personal ideas of agency and individuality. As contemporary society still reels from the impact of these social and technological transformations, and as governments grapple with questions around privacy in the digital era, who knows what new horrors await behind the screen.

Notes

1. T. Bekmambetov, 'Rules of the Screenmovie: The *Unfriended* Manifesto for the Digital Age', *Movie Maker* (22 April 2015), *www.moviemaker.com/unfriended-rules-of-the-screenmovie-a-manifesto-for-the-digital-age/* (accessed 31 January 2021). For a discussion of the screencast subgenre, see J. Tram 'Digital Disquietude in the Screencast Film', *Senses of Cinema*, 92 (2019), *www.senses ofcinema.com/2019/cinema-in-the-2010s/digital-disquietude-in-the-screen-cast-film/* (accessed 31 January 2021).

2. L. Blake and X. Aldana Reyes, 'Introduction: Horror in the Digital Age', in L. Blake and X. Aldana Reyes (eds), *Digital Horror: Haunted Technologies, Network Panic and the Found Footage Phenomenon* (London: I. B. Tauris, 2016), p. 3.

3. Blake and Aldana Reyes, 'Introduction', p. 3.

4. Bernard Harcourt, *Exposed: Desire and Disobedience in the Digital Age* (Cambridge MA: Harvard University Press, 2015), pp. 1–28.

5. Harcourt, *Exposed*, p. 13.

6. Harcourt, *Exposed*, p. 15.

7. Isabel Cristina Pinedo, *Recreational Terror: Women and the Pleasures of Horror Film Viewing* (Albany NY: State University of New York Press, 1997), p. 52.

8. N. Kirk, 'Networked Spectrality: *In Memorium, Pulse* and Beyond', in *Digital Horror: Haunted Technologies*, p. 59.

9. Kirk, 'Networked Spectrality', p. 59.

10. Valerie Wee, *Japanese Horror Films and Their American Remakes: Translating Fear, Adapting Culture* (London: Routledge, 2014).

11. Wendy Chun, *Updating to Remain the Same* (Cambridge MA: The MIT Press, 2016), pp. 135–65.

12. Robin Wood, *Hollywood from Vietnam to Reagan . . . and Beyond* (New York: Columbia University Press, 2003), p. 68.

13. H. Bonner, '#Selfveillance: Horror's Slut Shaming Through Social Media, Sur- and Selfveillance', in Samantha Holland, Robert Shail and Steven Gerrard (eds), *Gender and Contemporary Horror in Film* (Bingley: Emerald Publishing, 2019), p. 91.

14. Siva Vaidhyanathan, *Antisocial Media: How Facebook Disconnects Us and Undermines Democracy* (Oxford: Oxford University Press, 2018), p. 67.
15. Vaidhyanathan, *Antisocial Media*, p. 67.
16. Sun-ha Hong, *Technologies of Speculation: The Limits of Knowledge in a Data-Driven Society* (New York: New York University Press, 2020).
17. I. Conrich, 'Puzzles, Contraptions and the Highly Elaborate Moment: The Inevitability of Death in the Grand Slasher Narratives of the *Final Destination* and *Saw* Series of Films', in W. Clayton (ed.), *Style and Form in the Hollywood Slasher Film* (London: Palgrave Macmillan, 2015), pp. 105–17.

11

Shifting Shapes

Blumhouse's *Halloween* (2018) and the New Ethos of Slasher Remakes

Guy Spriggs

L ET US START with a recognisable scene from a slasher film: Jason Voorhees brutally murders scores of young people in the vicinity of Crystal Lake, only to re-encounter the one girl who has been able to avoid his rampage. After the miraculous reappearance of a male friend, this 'final girl'[1] is able to fight off Jason and render him lifeless with a mortal wound from his own blade. However, in the brief calm following his spree-killing, Jason explodes back to life, making one last attack on the survivors and giving the audience one final scare. To slightly complicate things: which *Friday the 13th* instalment ends this way? Including the 1980 original film (in which Jason only appears as a child in the coda), the 2003 fantasy mashup *Freddy vs. Jason* and the 2009 remake, exactly half of the twelve instalments in the franchise follow this rather specific formula[2] for their conclusions.

But the remake of *Friday the 13th* (2009) features a particularly striking addition to this established sequence that signifies more than a simple narrative or technical departure. Before the final blow that renders him lifeless (and the obligatory resurrection minutes later), Jason struggles to escape from a chain that pulls him slowly towards the spinning blades of a piece of farm equipment. Unable to free himself, Jason reaches out in desperation, but not to drag someone to join his doomed fate or to lash out with one final blow as seen consistently in previous iterations of his character (and others like him). Instead, his reach has a clear sense of panic and concern as he tries to grasp a locket containing a photograph of his dead mother, whose voice encourages Jason to kill throughout the film as he protects her place of death as a sacred memorial.

This image – which lasts for only two seconds – noticeably reorientates the ethical positioning of the film, dramatising a profound shift in the conventions and moral dimensions of slasher film. Jason's grasping is instantly recognisable as a gesture seeking sympathy, yet the film deploys this easily readable sign of loss and longing on behalf of a ruthless, remorseless mass murderer. In this moment Jason stops trying to kill anyone and simply tries to regain a connection with his mother, transforming him from a cruel monster to a goal-driven character with motivations that we recognise as something other than evil. Perspective is particularly important here: *Halloween* (1978), *Friday the 13th* (1980) and *Friday the 13th, Part II* (1981) are remembered for letting the audience see through the eyes of their killers,[3] but here we are decidedly separated from Jason. Instead, he reaches *towards* us – the camera points straight into the empty eyes of his mask – as if asking for recognition of his humanity from forces transcending the world of the film. This brief moment crystallises a central facet of twenty-first-century approaches to revisiting established horror stories and conventions. As also evidenced by remakes of other popular franchises, films like *Friday the 13th* (2009) encourage a new and disturbing sense of empathetic identification, a feature largely absent from American slashers. While the broader legacy of horror features plenty of misguided and misunderstood monsters, slasher films in particular are very rarely built around such sympathy. However, this newfound compassion is not directed towards the films' victims as a way of counteracting the horror genre's degradation of its human subjects, but rather towards the murderers and torturers who do the degrading. This shifting framework expands slasher films' ever-present empathy gap, offering defence and exoneration for the literal monsters whose acts are meant to be as shocking, graphic and morally cautionary as possible. The resonance of these shifts is further exposed by ongoing developments of empathy seen in the 2018 Blumhouse Productions *Halloween*, which directly challenges the drive to understand on-screen killers such as Michael Myers. *Halloween* (2018) pushes back against this compulsion in clear and purposeful ways, counteracting the troubling moralistic configurations seen in previous iterations of what can be called the 'Halloween cinematic universe' and the previous generation of slasher films. While the work of scholars such as Robin Wood insightfully demonstrates how horror is built around exploring the nature of the monster, Blumhouse's Halloween (2018) reorientates this understanding by privileging the question of how human characters live and survive, rather than if they do and why. This new ethos offers compelling, needed and timely legitimacy for the trauma of female victims, renewing the potential for capturing the spaces of gendered power in horror film theorised in previous generations of film and horror scholarship.

As centrepieces of American horror film, slasher franchises such as Halloween, Friday the 13th and Nightmare on Elm Street have become exemplars of the genre's penchant for moralism. Their shared interest in super-powered, unapologetic murderers stalking and killing predominantly young, wayward victims offers clear and consistent insight into the genre's broader ideological investment in regressive institutionalised standards, such as corralling sexuality. As Robin Wood simply but famously suggests, 'What escapes repression has to be dealt with by oppression',[4] illustrating horror film's drive to punish rather ordinary behaviours that are troublingly identified as abnormal or threatening. Wood also notes the 'protean' nature of the horror Monster, which changes along with 'society's basic fears',[5] and the Halloween franchise has a distinct capacity to reflect such cultural transformations. This capacity is situated in its killer's true identity as The Shape – the way he is credited in in Halloween (1978) and Halloween (2018) – making him particularly susceptible to shift and change. The monster in these films is not simply Michael Myers but is instead a more abstract, transcendent idea, filling gaps and existing in the shadows where it cannot be measured. Being 'The Shape' means being simply a form, edges and boundaries that defy complex interiority and definition beyond what we can see. This is reflected most clearly and dramatically by The Shape's face, which is distinct from those of other slasher film icons. Freddie Krueger's face is scarred but expressive in the extreme, seen even when transforming into the fantastical monsters he creates in dreamscapes. Jason Voorhees infamously wears a hockey mask but is first seen as a disfigured child and regularly (and willingly) removes his mask as an adult thereafter. Leatherface's mask in The Texas Chain Saw Massacre (1974) is made of the yellowed, sewn-together skin of previous victims. But The Shape distinguishes Halloween from other slasher franchises: his mask is not expressly meant to terrify but rather to allow victims to be terrified by their own fears, anxieties and imagination. It is the same as

Michael Myers's expression after killing his sister as a child, the 'blank, pale, emotionless face' with 'the blackest eyes' of humanity at its most unknowable, unpredictable and unexpected. The 2018 film pushes this dynamic further, suggesting a more meaningful, powerful, even symbiotic relationship between Michael and his mask. The opening scene of *Halloween* (2018) ends with Michael being reconnected with the mask that he wore when committing the murders of the original film forty years earlier. He visibly reacts to being in the presence of the mask despite not seeing it, and the reporter who brought the mask encourages Michael to break his decades-long silence, saying: 'You feel it, don't you Michael? You feel the mask . . . It's a part of you, Michael.' Whereas slasher masks are typically obtained through less deliberate means – Michael steals his from a pharmacy in *Halloween* (1978) and Jason's hockey mask is taken from a victim in *Friday the 13th, Part III* (1982) – here Michael's first act after escaping from custody is to track down his mask and properly reunite with his true face.

The portrayal of unreasoning evil is at the heart of how *Halloween* (2018) moves away from any attempt to exonerate its monster. Framed as a direct sequel to Carpenter's 1978 film – thereby erasing the other seven sequels in the original franchise and undoing much of their mythos – the Blumhouse *Halloween* also embraces a distinct turn towards empathy in its ethical framework. Michael Myers is returned to his original form: a brutal, unyielding and remorseless killer with no motivations beyond the expression of evil, stripped of all qualities that might make him more sympathetic or human. In this way, he reflects the first characteristic Robin Wood associates with 'reactionary horror', namely that 'the *dominant* designation of the monster must necessarily be "evil"'.[6] Just as importantly, Laurie Strode – Michael's original target and final girl of the 1978 *Halloween* – is neither a helpless, fleeing teenager nor a stereotype of the crippled neurotic. In fact, with the exception of one scene, all the women of *Halloween* (2018) demonstrate levels of resolve and resistance rarely seen in the slasher genre. These qualities are coalesced in Strode, who is now not only a mother, grandmother and protector, but is a protagonist in the purest narrative sense: she is the one with goals and desires, pushing the story forward and pursuing resolution against the resistance of obstacles. This addition to the story noticeably privileges the psychology and human value of female victims rather than absolving the violence of its male villains, offering a noticeable response to the values driving the previous generation of slasher remakes.

The engagements with gender, trauma and morality running through *Halloween* (2018) suggest further influence of important contemporaneous cultural events: star Jamie Lee Curtis (who returns as Laurie Strode) suggests in various outlets that the film is clearly connected to a 'shift in thought and action' related to the social upheaval of the #MeToo movement.[7] Multiple reviews echo Curtis's impression, referring to the film as 'made for the #MeToo era' as Strode seeks 'to make the villain the final male predator'.[8] Several horror and media scholars point out the influence of 9/11[9] and increasing inescapability of the 24-hour news cycle on the previous decade of horror and slasher films, which generated uncomfortable justification for the shocking and horrible actions taken by their killers instead of the rather ordinary behaviour of their victims. *Halloween* (2018), then, grows out of both contexts, simultaneously responding to the troubling application of empathy that predates it and reflecting new movements in recognising gendered trauma. The film's shifting investments expose the slasher genre's difficulty in engaging with politics, anxieties and ideologies in non-regressive, non-disciplinary ways. If horror can offer functional value as a method of therapeutic resolution, as philosopher Cynthia Freeland suggests, the slasher remakes predating *Halloween* (2018) demonstrate how displacement can cause this process to go awry.

Take the original *A Nightmare on Elm Street* (1984), for example. Freddy Krueger is a sort of vengeful ghost, attacking teenagers in their dreams as punishment for his death at the hands of their parents. Importantly, Freddy is presented as simply and unquestionably evil: he is introduced as a 'filthy child murderer who killed at least twenty kids in the neighborhood', with the film never attempting to redeem him or explain away his horrific behaviour. The film offers no measurable criticism of the parents' decision to punish him themselves through vigilantism, and there is no indication within the world of the film that Freddie is meant to be understood as any sort of righteous avenger. The same basic elements are true of the 2010 remake, but the portrayal of Freddy and his victims is far more opaque and morally grey. Instead of a filthy child murderer, Freddy is shown through flashbacks, dialogue and visions to have been a well-liked groundskeeper at a preschool, playing with and beloved by children. Main characters Nancy and Quentin eventually find some evidence that Krueger sexually abused students in their kindergarten class – an important step in re-establishing Freddy on the side of evil – but only after spending the entire second act of the film expressing outrage at their parents for killing 'an innocent man'. Interestingly, the teenagers in *A Nightmare on Elm Street* (2010) are the actual victims of Freddy's crimes, and yet appear mostly free from trauma through a sort of shared memory loss engineered by their parents. Quentin eventually learns of the mob led by his father that killed Freddy, and the scene of Freddy's death is haunting and even sympathetic, as he pleads with the parents and asserts his innocence, saying they have no evidence as his attackers insist they cannot and will not just leave things to the police. Freddy is a horrible monster who does horrible things in this remake, but the audience is nevertheless left with a composite image of him as being something other than totally bad – something less than the simple, shocking evil of the 1984 Freddy and his original slasher counterparts.

The shift in ethos that can be seen in the muddying of Freddy's guilt, or the sympathetic longing of Jason Voorhees's outstretched hand, creates a striking departure from the moral systems and unflinchingly evil monsters established in the original films of these core slasher franchises. Media and culture scholar Isabel Cristina Pinedo associates this kind of muddiness with the post-1968 era of horror film that gave birth to these slasher franchises, observing a postmodernism that breaks down 'moral clarities' and renders good and evil 'virtually indistinguishable',[10] even offering *Halloween* (1978) and *A Nightmare on Elm Street* (1984) as exemplars of this phenomenon.[11] But Pinedo's framework can be seen much more clearly in early twenty-first-century slashers, and Rob Zombie's 2007 adaptation of *Halloween* offers the most profound example of the ethically problematic breakdown of the division between good and evil she observes. *Halloween* (2018) does not begin with Michael Myers as a child; it does not begin with Michael Myers at all, and when we see him, he's a man beyond middle age. Instead, it starts with an investigative podcast team pursuing interviews with Michael, his new psychiatrist Dr Sartain and the reclusive victim Laurie Strode. Their stated mission is to understand who Michael is, what makes him so violent and why he killed so many people on Halloween in 1978. The podcasters' desire is seemingly the same as Zombie's *Halloween* (2007) itself, which frames Michael Myers as an extreme but still recognisable psychopath rather than as the pure, unmatched evil with the devil's eyes described in the original. Eyes offer more than a casual metaphor here: the very first images of *Halloween* (2018) intercut extreme close-ups of roving eyes with inmates and interiors of Smith's Grove Sanitarium, misdirecting our first impression through this seeming pursuit of psychopathy or other psychological phenomena.

Film and media scholar James Kendrick associates this reductive tendency to pursue psychological explanation with an 'incessant desire to explain' in post-9/11 horror, and offers *Halloween* (2007) as an illustration of how films of this era became 'consumed with showing us how and why'.[12] Indeed, *Halloween* (2007) frames Michael's acts as diagnosable and pathological: his character and the entire first act of the film are built around an exhaustive list of pop-psychology indicators for psychopathy, including bullies, a fatherless, hyper-sexualised household and fascination with dead animals and masks. This search for explanation builds curious sympathy for Michael, suggesting that he might be the true victim and that his attacks have motivations we might understand or even excuse and defend. The result is a curious relationship between the monster and the scores of people that he harms: while this version of Michael is protective of his baby sister (as a child), his greatest acts of brutality are saved for those who show him the most kindness and who demonstrate the most strength and resolve. Kendrick associates this tendency to explain with a cultural longing for understanding in the wake of 9/11, but *Halloween* (2007) provides more confusion than clarity, consistency or comfort. Robin Wood importantly notes that horror monsters 'are by definition destructive, but their destructiveness is capable of being variously explained, excused, and justified'.[13] *Halloween* (2007) clarifies that it is precisely this problematic transition from explanation to excuse and justification that characterises the first wave of twenty-first-century slashers.

In spite of the probing eyes of its opening, *Halloween* (2018) noticeably does not pursue such explanations, and instead frames Michael's murders and their lasting effects in simple, damaging terms that do not demand or ask for further examination of his motivation or mind. The reboot/sequel goes further than that as well, demonstrating a noticeably dismissive tone towards previous engagements with the franchise and its monster's mythology. Like the podcasters that open the film, Michael's new psychiatrist Dr Sartain frames the relationship with his patient in terms of understanding. He says Michael was kept at the centre to be studied, but bemoans his patient being transferred because 'the state has lost interest in learning anything further'. Sartain later reveals his depraved, decidedly non-therapeutic interest in Michael, who he sees as the ultimate predator and desires to see in action. After killing a police officer and preventing Michael from being captured, Sartain tells Laurie's granddaughter Allyson that his desire is to more directly see how crime affects Michael so that he can better 'understand the mind of evil'. But the film consistently shows that there is nothing to be learned, and Laurie's opposition to this mindset could hardly be stronger or clearer: when confronted by the inquisitive podcast team, Laurie responds with bewilderment, saying, 'Michael Myers killed five people . . . and he's a human being we need to understand?'. Her question suggests its own answer; namely, that we *do not* need to understand Michael. The film establishes its intolerance for this misguided sympathy shortly thereafter, as the podcasters are among Michael's first victims – there is no room for those who want to understand or humanise the monster. In this way, *Halloween* (2018) restores important elements of the original film, which 'identifies the killer with "the Bogeyman", as the embodiment of an eternal and unchanging evil which, by definition, can't be understood'.[14] The film further rejects other attempts to under-stand Michael's behaviour, such as the suggestion that he and Laurie are siblings (unbeknownst to her), an addition explaining Michael's motives and establishing him as a would-be family annihilator in *Halloween II* (1981). *Halloween* (2018) introduces this dynamic in dialogue only to disregard it as folklore, offering no replacement justification for Michael's previous crimes or his new rampage. Michael is not sick or treatable, and he certainly isn't a troubled mind yearning for understanding. Instead, he is again a true monster, having an impact on the story, environment and characters by what he does rather than who he is. And, just as impor-tantly, this shift away from justifying the slasher monster creates a sort of empathy vacuum – one that *Halloween* (2018) fills through its conscious investment in the survivors of Michael's murderous legacy.

From the outset of *Halloween* (2018), 'The Shape' does not appear as the same arbiter of regressive morality that we have come to expect from slashers. Instead, he seems to be a less discriminating – if not random – force of nature, and the absence of such moralism reinforces the impor-tance of Michael's victims instead of his own motivation or humanity. The film's first on-screen kill is a pre-teen boy who runs from the scene of the patient transport bus crash and is strangled by Michael as he tries to call the police. The most cinematic sequence of *Halloween* (2018) follows 'The Shape' for three minutes through two long takes as he weaves in and out of homes on a crowded street, murdering women without detection thanks to the cover provided by trick or treating and costumes. The deaths in this sequence are noticeably quick and brutal, and these victims' unawareness of their fates is a significant departure for slashers, where characters are almost always made to recognise what is happening to them and what monster is doing it. On his way to a renewed showdown with Laurie,

Michael also murders Allyson's goofy, awkward father and a genial police officer who tries to introduce his partner to Vietnamese food. Interestingly, though, Allyson's boyfriend escapes any sort of moralistic punishment despite kissing another girl in front of Allyson, attempting to gaslight her and destroying her mobile phone, which makes her particularly vulnerable since she can't be told about the threat posed by Michael's escape. These departures from slasher formulas reinforce the essential unknowability of earlier generations of horror monsters, whose motives and actions are not nearly as muddied by ambiguity in spite of a detachment from a consistent moral 'code'.

The lack of uniform ideological punishment in Michael's behaviour and the film's dismissal of explaining his motives make the monster's actions appear more depraved and his innocent victims' suffering more evident and affecting. The dynamics of *Halloween* (2018) establish its perspective on the complicated legacies and impacts of trauma from the start: Laurie managed to escape Michael's murderous rampage forty years earlier but admits that it has left her a 'basketcase', and we see how her daughter, granddaughter and son-in-law have also suffered as a result of the psychological scars left behind. Previous *Halloween* films show characters managing the purely physical damage resulting from encounters with Michael, but Laurie's only physical limitation is age – something she doesn't appear to share with Michael, who has retained all his superhuman strength, mobility and stamina. Yet while she maintains a connection with granddaughter Allyson, Laurie is estranged from her daughter Karen as a result of years of overbearing concern over Michael's potential return. Karen expresses this most cogently, saying she's had to get over the 'paranoia and neuroses' that her mother projected onto her. But the film's climax shows Karen has also gained resolve, her greatest expression of the survival training she begrudgingly received from her mother. After his battle with Laurie, Michael uncovers the basement panic room where Karen and Allyson have been hiding. Karen is armed with a rifle, but is unable to hold it steady, whimpering 'I can't do it . . . I'm sorry, I can't do it' as she is overwhelmed by the reality of what she previously felt were simply her mother's misguided fears. However, as Michael appears at the top of the stairway – seeming to recognise Karen's display of weakness – she snaps into form, straightening her posture and aiming the rifle purposefully as she confidently says, 'Got you'. This apparent manipulation allows her to shoot Michael in the face – what might be a mortal wound for anyone but 'The Shape' – and begin the final sequence of attacks that ends with Michael trapped in the basement. There is even a sense of inherited, activated resolve in Allyson, who is both further removed from and more directly exposed to the true evil of 'The Shape' than her mother. Allyson can seek closeness with Laurie that Karen cannot because the effects of Michael's murders are largely theoretical to her, but she also sees her friend's dead body and comes face to face with the monster multiple times while her mother is locked away in the basement and witnesses no violence first-hand for the entire film. Importantly, while she is at first overwhelmed and justifiably hysterical when confronted by 'The Shape', by the end of the film Allyson grabs a knife and attacks him, freeing mother Karen from his grasp even as her family shouts at her to leave and save herself.

This complexity regarding the lasting impact of Michael's crimes is introduced by the investigative podcasters at the film's outset, as they openly ask if Laurie's troubled life as a survivor means that one monster has created another. *Halloween* (2018) further plays with this sort of displacement or transformation in visual ways, recreating iconic imagery from Carpenter's original film with Laurie in the spaces previously occupied by the monster that terrorised her. Early in the film, Allyson glances out the window while sitting in class listening to a lecture on fate – just as Laurie did in 1978 – but sees her grandmother rather than 'The Shape'. During her final showdown with Michael, it is Laurie who disappears from the ground after falling and being left for dead and who emerges from perfect darkness to attack 'The Shape' with a knife, not the other way around. It is clear, however, that Laurie has not become a monster herself – she has been shaped by Michael but has not become him. When she appears from the shadows to surprise Michael as he did to her forty years earlier, she still occupies her original on-screen space. Laurie's life has been shaped by a monster's evil and in her active pursuit of Michael she may even appear as a monster to him, but she is never truly incorporated into the position suggested by the podcasters on ethical or cinematic/visual grounds.

The result of these overlapping dynamics of trauma and empathy is that *Halloween* (2018) engages less with the question of whether the monster's victims deserve to die, instead making it absolutely clear the monster himself *must* die. Kendrick notes a similar necessity in Carpenter's original vision that pushes past Robin Wood's discussion of the unknowable monster, recognising Michael Myers as 'a complete breakdown of rationality, a figure of menace we cannot explain or understand *and must simply destroy, even as he resists destruction*'.[15] Or, as Brian Tallerico more simply suggests in his review, the film shows that when confronted with the monster,

'Don't try and study it, or understand it – just kill it'.[16] To paraphrase critic Monica Castillo, for *Halloween* (2018), trauma is not a plot device but an explicit subject:[17] the film is not just about violence and pain, it engages with the ways horror as a genre is itself inextricable from these forces. More than that, the film shows how trauma demands decisive closure rather than mitigation. The podcast team and Dr Sartain pursue separate talk-based solutions to trauma and evil, the former encouraging Laurie by saying she should 'sit down and say the things you've been longing to say' and the latter begging for Michael himself to speak.[18] Notably, Sartain's last words in the film are 'Say something', which he utters just before Michael silently stomps him to death. In *Halloween* (2018), not only is the desire to understand and redeem killers such as Michael Myers misguided, but the pursuit of such ends makes one a far more suitable target for punishment than the general waywardness seen in most slashers.

Instead of more mediated solutions, the tape-recorded voice of Michael's original psychiatrist Dr Loomis reminds us from beyond the grave that the only course of action for 'The Shape' is 'Termination . . . death is the only solution'. Laurie does not deal with her unshakeable fear and trauma by talking – or by running away, self-medicating with alcohol or becoming institutionalised, as in previous iterations of her character – but rather she says she prayed every night for Michael to escape so that she could kill him. Not only does Laurie roam the streets with a gun and a police scanner looking for Michael after his escape, but the film's ambiguity allows us the possibility to imagine (however unlikely it may be) that she might have even caused the bus crash that set him free, seeing it as her only opportunity to actually stop him. Laurie has not been hiding since the original attack, and it is no accident that she has remained in the area where her would-be killer is institutionalised. Her home is now a training ground and fortress, filled with weapons and covered in surveillance equipment, outfitted with a hidden basement bunker and sliding gates that can seal off any room. But Laurie's house is not meant for protection and safety: as Karen tells Allyson while locking Michael in the basement, 'It's not a cage, baby . . . it's a trap'. Laurie has spent forty years channelling her trauma and loss into the creation of an inescapable tomb for Michael, a place she is certain he will come to but knows she cannot allow him to leave. In *Halloween H20* (1998), Laurie is confronted by Michael for the first time in twenty years and tells those around her that their goal is simply to 'Try to live'. In *Halloween* (2018), Laurie has been trying to survive for four decades, and it is clear that mere survival or attempts at rehabilitating 'The Shape' and herself are not enough. Michael – a true Bogeyman – must be killed, and the ideological shift is clear: the slasher's empathy gap is most valuably addressed not by better understanding its monsters, but by acknowledging the humanity and agency of those hurt by them. As a result, *Halloween* (2018) is something decidedly other than an exercise in witnessing superhuman judges punish questionable behaviour; rather, it is the familiar but novel opportunity to witness the direct and indirect victims of violence pursue final resolution in the face of true evil. When Laurie, her daughter and granddaughter – three generations of women carrying the direct and indirect wounds from one night of unimaginable evil – stand tall over Michael at the end of *Halloween* (2018), we see a familiar dynamic: the unrepentant monster at the end of his killing spree, confronted by the ones who have foiled him. Michael is trapped in the basement of Laurie's fortress, but as he watches his would-be victims escape, 'The Shape' does not reach out as Jason does in *Friday the 13th* (2009): there is no appeal to his essential humanity, no sense of knowable psychology, no attempt to cultivate empathy or understanding. And the reverse image is just as important, showing the Strode women – together, strong and aware – dropping a flare onto a man that they know will burn to death with no hope of escape. There is no rejoicing or fanfare, simply the recognition of the Strodes' suffering, the necessity of Michael's fate and the resolution that can only be provided by the eradication of evil.

But slasher monsters always return. On 7 July 2020, Blumhouse released the first-look teaser for *Halloween Kills*, released in October 2021. In it, survivors Laurie, Karen and Allyson are riding in the back of a truck, escaping the burning house fire where they left 'The Shape' to die. Their sense of relief is broken, however, by the sound of sirens – first responders rushing to the scene of the fire. The Strode women cry out at the realisation that there is hope for Michael's escape after all, and Laurie screams desperately for the firefighters to 'Let it burn'. The cruel brevity of their closure foregrounds their new trauma: Karen has lost her husband and Allyson has lost her father and best friend, victims of a monster that they could previously dismiss as an imaginary Bogeyman. *Halloween* (2018) shows us, however, that the return of the monster is not just a return of the repressed but also a renewed opportunity for resolution. The monster also returns for the purpose of being killed, legitimising the trauma of those he has hurt and giving victims a mechanism for resolution that transcends mitigation, mediation or empathetic understanding.

Notes

1. Although Carol Clover's canonical *Men, Women, and Chain Saws* enjoys a tremendous legacy through this term, this chapter is more engaged with her extensions of Laura Mulvey's influential work on gendered cinematic perspective.

2. Formulas in the slasher genre are commonly approached in archetypal and characteristic terms rather than those of narrative structure where examinations reveal the moral dimensions and foundational nature of formulas in the genre, primarily in determining the likelihood of a character's survival based on their behaviour. See, A. D. Weaver, D. Ménard, C. Cabrera and A. Taylor, 'Embodying the Moral Code?: Thirty Years of Final Girls in Slasher Films', *Psychology of Popular Media Culture*, 4/1 (2015), 37–43.

3. In all three examples the first-person perspective is not used to encourage identification with the killers but rather to keep their identities hidden, building a certain sense of mystery.

4. R. Wood, 'An Introduction to American Horror Film', in J. A. Weinstock (ed.), *The Monster Theory Reader* (Minneapolis MN: University of Minnesota Press, 2020), p. 110, emphasis in original.

5. Wood, 'An Introduction to American Horror Film', p. 110.

6. Wood, 'An Introduction to Horror Film', p. 129, emphasis in original.

7. C. Collis, 'Jamie Lee Curtis Says the new *Halloween* is a #MeToo Movie', *Entertainment Weekly* (27 September 2018), *https://ew.com/movies/2018/09/27/jamie-lee-curtis-halloween-metoo/* (accessed 15 January 2021).

8. J. Joho, 'Why 2018's *Halloween* is the Slasher Movie Made for the #MeToo Era', *Mashable* (26 October 2018), *https://mashable.com/article/2018-halloween-reinvents-final-girl-feminist-horror-trope/* (accessed 15 January 2021).

9. See, for example, Kevin J. Wetmore Jr, *Post-9/11 Horror in American Cinema* (New York: Continuum, 2012), p. 2; Cynthia Freeland, 'Horror and Art-Dread', in Stephen Prince (ed.), *The Horror Film* (New Brunswick NJ: Rutgers University Press, 2004), p. 190.

10. I. C. Pinedo, 'Postmodern Elements of the Contemporary Horror Film', in S. Prince (ed.), *The Horror Film* (New Brunswick NJ: Rutgers University Press, 2004), pp. 85–6.

11. Pinedo applies this label based largely on the lack of 'narrative closure' and 'closed endings' resulting from the inability to defeat the monster through 'human action'; see Pinedo, 'Postmodern Elements of the Contemporary Horror Film', p. 90.

12. J. Kendrick, 'The Terrible, Horrible Desire to Know: Post-9/11 Horror Remakes, Reboots, Sequels and Prequels', in T. McSweeney (ed.), *American Cinema in the Shadow of 9/11* (Edinburgh: Edinburgh University Press, 2016), p. 251.

13. Wood, 'An Introduction to Horror Film', p. 130.

14. Wood, 'An Introduction to Horror Film', p. 132.

15. Kendrick, 'The Terrible, Horrible Desire to Know: Post-9/11 Horror Remakes, Reboots, Sequels and Prequels', p. 266, emphasis added.

16. B. Tallerico, 'Review of *Halloween*', *Roger Ebert* (19 October 2018), *www.rogerebert.com/reviews/halloween-2018/* (accessed 20 January 2021).

17. M. Castillo, '*Halloween*: This Time, Laurie Strode is Locked and Loaded', *NPR* (18 October 2018), *www.npr.org/2018/10/18/656992437/halloween-this-time-laurie-strode-is-locked-and-loaded/* (accessed 20 January 2021).

18. This is another major divergence from the *Halloween* films of the 2000s, in which Michael repeatedly grunts 'Die' while killing one of his victims. Multiple characters in *Halloween* (2018) are desperate for Michael to talk, but he nevertheless remains the silent, unknowable killer from the 1978 original film.

12

'Disobedient Women' and Malicious Men

A Comparative Assessment of the Politics of *Black Christmas* (1974) and (2019)

John Kavanagh

B ASED ON REVIEWS, *Black Christmas* (2019) appears to be a polarising film that inspires little debate. Most reviewers avoid the pretence of a film critique and either praise or dismiss it based on its feminist values and politics. The positive reviews tend to disregard the horror elements of this slasher film with statements such as, 'Sophia Takal's film isn't particularly scary, but it has plenty on its mind',[1] 'in this case the novelty being that the movie . . . is actually rooted in something relevant and interesting',[2] and 'this . . . is a strong attempt at a feminist statement that often goes either haywire or not far enough'.[3] The negative reviews dismiss both the horror and politics with statements such as, 'it's ultimately less of a horror film and more of . . . a hodgepodge of buzzwords',[4] 'a feminist horror flick that lacks nuance in its feminism and thrills in its horror',[5] 'despite its desperate efforts to justify the homicides, there's nothing remotely innovative or even goofily satirical about it'.[6] There are even reviews on the negativity of the reviews, which Michael Kennedy puts down to 'plain old sexism'.[7] The purpose of this chapter is to examine this feminist text that has angered fans and divided critics by comparing the politics and subtext of *Black Christmas* (1974) and *Black Christmas* (2019). This analysis will help to contextualise the backlash against one of the most polarising films of 2019.

Disobedient Women

Black Christmas (1974) introduces us to a sorority house filled with women that do not conform to the traditional concepts of femininity in the horror genre. Director Bob Clark intended to avoid the typical tropes and clichés in favour of depicting these women as 'real college students',[8] something replicated in *Black Christmas* (2019).

The opening sequence of *Black Christmas* (1974) presents an intertwined prologue that intercuts scenes of the sorority house's microcosm, consisting of Barb, Clare, Jess and Phyl, and Billy invading their insular community. Barb's presence is felt immediately with her loud and boisterous demeanour. Her personality is contrasted by Clare who speaks softly and is drowned out by Barb calling her mother a 'gold-plated whore'. Phyl blends into the background of this sequence, but she is shown to disagree with Barb over her reaction to 'the moaner' and to her friends. Jess is presented as an all-round average woman, but not in the typical girl next-door manner, and her strength is revealed over the course of the film.

Already, there is a political element to this film as its protagonists are shown to be reflections of their era.[9] These are women who have matured in a society where women have fought to gain rights over their legal positions, social status and their bodies, they are not simplistic objects for the 'male gaze'. With their naturalised characterisations these women stand out from the characters in the later 'women in danger' films[10] in the classical era of the slasher film.[11] The dangers that the protagonists are exposed to stem from a deranged killer, controlling boyfriends and an incompetent police force.

An overlooked danger in this film comes from the lack of solidarity in the feminine microcosm. The sorority house is depicted as a refuge from the masculine world, rather than a site of sisterhood. This is shown most prominently by the group retreating to their own personal spaces in a time of crisis, which leads to each of their deaths. More damning evidence against the concept of feminine solidarity is Barb's accusation that 'you can't rape a townie'. It is quite clear that this haven only has a facade of safety for this immediate group of women.

Black Christmas (2019) presents different kinds of women, 'women constantly in danger'. The film exists as an early entry in the emerging socially aware era of the slasher subgenre that examines real issues in the text rather than as implications in the subtext. The main issues that *Black Christmas* (2019) depicts are rape culture, institutionalised misogyny and toxic masculinity. These women are in constant danger from the world around them compared to their counterparts from the 1974 version, which limits the textual aggressors to individual men.

The protagonists of *Black Christmas* (2019), Riley, Jesse, Chris and Marty, are introduced slower than their 1974 counterparts and their characterisation retains this pace. Riley is introduced as our point-of-view character. Like Jess, she is not sexualised by the camera or the narrative. In her first sequence, Riley and Fran have a normalised discussion about diva cups as Riley gives Fran a sanitary towel. This is a casual and textually important conversation without the common stigmas associated with menstruation. These women do not shy away from their personal issues and show a bond that is missing from the sorority house of 1974. More importantly, they are not bearers of the 'bleeding wound' as discussed by Barbara Creed.[12] Instead, it is depicted as one of many sources of feminine solidarity in the post-MeToo era. This depiction of solidarity continues, and the sorority house of 2019 is presented as a true safe space for the women within.

Jesse is portrayed as an upbeat and pleasant woman who wants to comfort her sisters. Kris is introduced as an activist who has succeeded in getting the bust of the 'sexist and racist' founder of the university, Calvin Hawthorne, removed from campus. She is a vocal feminist and wants what is best for women everywhere, even when it threatens the women around her. Marty is depicted as another normal yet strong female figure and her relationship, where she has the dominant role, is focused on. This dominance is shown as a strength of modern femininity where women are not as restricted to archaic gender roles.

There is a strong sense of normality in the portrayal of the sorority sisters from the 'women in danger' and the 'women constantly in danger' eras. Neither relies strongly on stereotypes and this results in naturalised characterisations. Unfortunately for the non-stereotypical characters of both 1974 and 2019, this sense of normality is what puts them in danger. Their non-compliance to the 'normality' of the horror genre and male-dominated societies that crave obedient women results in them being targeted by singular psychopaths and institutions.

The most popularised academic theories regarding the slasher film and how characters are chosen to die or survive are based on concepts of punitive morality. Petridis summarises this with the concept of 'normality' punishing youthful transgressors, via the 'other', who partake in sex, drugs and alcohol.[13] Non-textual and non-subtextual arguments are weaved regarding this idea that usually stems from psychoanalytical thought[14] or from the context of a conservative society.[15] Both films present an interesting alternative to the standard narrative of punitive measures taken against social transgressors.

In the opening Christmas party sequences of *Black Christmas* (1974), an obscene phone call is made to the sorority. The women gather around and listen to Billy's sexual taunts, which have disrupted the setting. Billy snorts like a pig, laughs and spouts fragmented phrases such as 'pig cunt', 'let me lick it' and 'suck my fat juicy cock'. A disturbing contrast is created as the camera pans around the shocked and disgusted group of women while 'Hark! The Herald Angels Sing' underscores Billy's vulgar suggestions. This dichotomy undermines the concept of the sorority house as a site of normality. Most of the women are unprepared for the horrors that men want to inflict upon them.

It is made clear that this is not the first obscene call from either Billy or other assailants; Barb states she gets two calls a day in the city. Sexual harassment via the telephone is depicted as a common occurrence that women must endure. Barb shows her desensitisation by challenging Billy verbally. Her response is shown to be both a retaliation against obscene callers and a frustration with the harassment's consistency. Billy responds with 'I'm going to kill you' and what seems to be a hollow threat is realised by the end of the film.

Barb is framed as a transgressor by Billy in this scenario. If we take into consideration the quantity and frequency of these calls, it is assumed that the obscene call is presented as the norm in this setting. We must remember that this is also indicative of the real-world obscene call. Barb strikes back and Billy assumes justification to kill, despite defence not being a transgressive act. This is a pastiche of reality, shown by the male reaction against feminist acts and movements throughout the history of North America.[16] For most of human history, women have had to endure such indignities, but in a society that has seen the second wave of feminism, women now have the tools to fight back. This is clearly not enough, as retaliation is met with the destruction of the film's feminine microcosm.

The women of *Black Christmas* (2019) are shown to be less passive by performing a subversive song-and-dance routine that deals with the concept of 'frat boy rape culture', at a fraternity talent show. The routine begins as a reference to *Mean Girls* (2004), a film where the protagonist objectifies herself to climb the social hierarchy, but quickly transitions to a song about fraternities drugging and raping unsuspecting women. The song 'Up in the Frat House' references the concept of 'he said, she said' arguments, gaslighting victims and accusations of women leading men on. The women are booed during their exposé of the men in the crowd, like Brian who raped Riley three years earlier and Phil who attempted to rape Helena that night. Each of the protagonists have either been raped, spiked or are close to someone who has been attacked. This is a sad reflection on the horrors that women endure and it is presented in a manner that avoids Otherising the attackers or romanticising the victims. Sexual violence is depicted as an act committed by and against real people. Rape and sexual harassment are built into the environment that these women live in, but these sorority sisters decide to fight back.

After the performance, the protagonists rush out of the fraternity house. Before leaving, Riley proudly states 'maybe that'll teach Brian Huntley not to rape another girl'. The performance is the inciting incident for the murders that follow. The fraternity use the routine, the rape accusations and Riley's confidence in speaking out against their leader as justification to destroy the sorority. Billy has been replaced by a disturbing institution. Despite the presentation of a modern evil, the idea of feminine defence being perceived as an attack remains. Women that fight back, 'disobedient women', need to be punished by an archaic institution that prides itself on masculine superiority. This gendered declaration of war is in fact revenge against the redistribution of power among the sexes. This concept has proliferated throughout the twentieth century[17] and led to the modern angry, white male.[18]

The women of 2019 endure the violence against them and triumph over the masculine microcosm that fosters dangerous views on consent and dominance. Textually, Riley and Kris understand that this is not a one-off event. Despite the destruction of the Calvin Hawthorne bust – an act that removes the power from the fraternity by a literal smashing of patriarchy – the ideology lives on. Even if misogyny can be removed completely from Hawthorne University, there is a hostile world awaiting them.

Both films provide a political approach to their character portrayals and the 'normality' of women. Since these texts are slasher films, there will be a body count and vivid violence depicted against women.[19] Slasher films of the classical era tend to show violence against both sexes equally, with an emphasis on either brutality or sensuality. This trend continued steadily, leading to the emerging socially aware era, but with the balance between brutality and sensuality becoming disrupted with a stronger focus on the brutal aspects. Both *Black Christmas* films have narratives framed around feminine microcosms; therefore this violence is aimed almost exclusively at women.[20]

The murders of the 1974 film are quite simple in their execution. Billy waits for the opportune moment to strike, descends from the attic and viciously attacks the protagonists. Clare, the first victim, is packing to go home while Billy is hiding in her closet. Billy suffocates her with a clear plastic garment cover as the diegetic sound merges the mix of Billy's mimicry, Clare's gasps and sounds from the party below. The brevity and viciousness of this kill leaves a lingering impression as it fully separates Billy from the Gothic villains of classical horror. Barb is the third victim of the film and has an asthma attack after seeing Billy entering her room. Believing this to be a nightmare, she goes back to sleep after Jess has calmed her. Billy's return heralds the most striking sequence of the film. The following scene is intercut between the murder of Barb and a choir of children singing 'Oh Come, All Ye Faithful', creating another disturbing dichotomy between the visual purity of children and salacious murder. Barb's murder is the most graphic sequence in the film due to the combination of suggestive imagery and the angelic underscore.

The framing of the sequence would suggest that this act is more akin to a rape: Billy plunges a crystal unicorn's horn into Barb, she lays in bed attempting to fend him off and her asthmatic gasps could be mistaken for moans. The initial shots switch between point of view and close ups of the weapon. Billy previously shows referentiality as he quotes Peter's private comments. The attack on Barb is enough to suggest that he overheard the comment about how 'townies can't be raped'. This is an example of Billy's twisted sense of humour rather than the repressed sexual urges discussed by Robin Wood.[21] Barb was not raped, literally or symbolically, instead the imagery mimics a consistent tool of suppression used against women.

Phyl's murder occurs off-screen, but its presence is still felt. Viewing the previous murders allows the audience to comprehend Billy's methodology. The absence of violence combined with the sudden appearance of Phyl's corpse later allows our imagination to take over. Phyl checks on Barb and we hear Billy whisper 'Agnes' as the door slams shut. This death, while not being as viscerally brief as Clare's nor as vividly brutal as Barb's, retains a terrifying power as it forces the audience to create their own horror.

The politics behind the murder of these women comes into play after their deaths have occurred. Billy is not content to leave the corpses littering the house, instead he objectifies them via modelling. After Clare's murder, Billy takes her corpse back to the attic, his Gothic space. Clare is placed on a rocking chair in front of a window with the garment bag still wrapped around her head. Later in the film, her abject corpse is seen cradling a decaying doll as Billy rocks the chair while muttering. Billy is not only modelling the corpses; he also appears to be playing a demented game of house. After Barb and Phyl's murders, he models the corpses on Barb's bed. This piece of imagery is reminiscent of pin-up girls posing, Phyl's arm is arched with her hand behind her head and Barb lays across her. This abjectified shot is a gruesome pastiche of objectified femininity.

Billy abjectifies, or Otherises, these women in life and he objectifies them in death. A feminine microcosm appears to stir his rage and it will not settle until these women conform to his ideal. Unfortunately, his ideal is a docility that can be achieved only during the transformation from strong non-stereotypical women to cold and silent playthings. This is a hyperbolic example of reactionary masculinity of the late twentieth century.[22] The murders of the 2019 film are disparate to that of the original. A lesser focus is placed on them as societal horrors and non-fatal violence take centre stage. The sorority sisters are still murdered, but horror is now reserved for the living. Fran's murder is a parallel to Clare's but happens much later in the narrative. She searches for Claudette and is strangled from behind as a crash zoom draws the audience in. After a brief struggle, the shot cuts to her sorority sisters in a less satisfying manner than the original film, as the peaceful transition to the purchasing of a Christmas tree does not instil the same effect. Fran's corpse is the only one that is left as an abject object like in the original film, nor is she there due to a perverse sense of humour. The forgotten corpse is a logistical issue, which recalls the hurried nature of the modern spree killer.[23]

Jesse's death results from a need to remove herself from her friend's arguments. She is stabbed off-screen with a mirror shard. This sequence is rather unremarkable and functions as a method of whittling down the cast members for a more manageable finale. Marty, on the other hand, dies to maintain the solidarity of the sisterhood. Marty approaches the killer with an axe and mentions that he has a chance to flee before the police arrive. This shows a clear understanding of the legal process. Men are believed;

women are not. Her understanding of gender roles and legal disparity results in Marty's axe being turned on her and forced into her stomach. This appears to be a direct attack on femininity, referencing Gelson's lecture on the transition from feminine belly magic to masculine head magic.

There are two strong thematic issues on agency and the body left to discuss: pregnancy and rape. Both issues reinforce the idea that horror is for living women, particularly in the post-MeToo era. Jess, from the 1974 film, has a subplot focusing on an unwanted pregnancy that she intends to abort. Jess confronts her boyfriend Peter, and he reacts in an obsessive and controlling manner. Rather than supporting Jess, he attempts to undermine his girlfriend's agency by insisting on marriage. This subplot is culturally important as *Black Christmas* (1974) was released after the decision of *Roe v. Wade* (1973) and four years after the legalisation of abortion in Canada.[24] This develops the subtextual themes of suppression and the hostility that aims to keep women docile and obedient. Visually, this is hinted at in the introductory party sequence as Jess's jumper has a design that could easily be mistaken for a pair of hands, this is noticeable long before Peter's introduction. The implication here is that this has been a long running feature of the relationship, rather than emerging due to Jess' revelation. Peter's attempts to control Jess rival Billy's urge to destroy her. Both are attempting to remove Jess' agency and objectify the women in their sights. This results in Peter's death. Regardless of whether Jess thought that Peter was the killer or not, this was an act symbolising the restoration of her agency.

Rape is consistent between the 1974 and 2019 *Black Christmas* films. A local woman was raped, Barb's murder references this attack, and Riley was raped prior to the events of the film. Much of the later film is Riley's reclamation of the agency taken from her by Brian. Riley is a strong feminine figure within the sorority, but she appears to shrink outside of it. The confident woman introduced to us becomes quiet when men approach at work and confront her in institutional settings. The first step to recovery is the performance. This is a *de facto* confrontation with her rapist that allows Riley to process the trauma inflicted upon her. This performance is reminiscent of the utilisation of social media platforms to give women a voice against their attackers in the past decade.

Two instances in the film present trauma as a tool of masculine control and both are retribution for the talent show performance. They imply threats of rape and sexual subjection. The first occurs when one of the killer's pins Riley against a door frame. The killer cuts her cheeks and spreads the blood, like rouge, and then forces a kiss on her under the mistletoe. The threat of sexual assault is being used as a method of control, Riley is simultaneously reminded of the past and threatened with repetition in response to undermining masculine pride via exposition of the truth. The second instance is when Riley is held captive at the fraternity. She is forced to submit alongside mocking taunts such as 'bow bitch' and 'your body, your choice'. Derogatory comments alongside the humiliation that she is subjected to forces her to snap and act against her would-be oppressors.

Malicious Men

Considering that the women of *Black Christmas* 1974 and 2019 are portrayed in a naturalised manner, it is initially strange to realise that the men are not given the same treatment. On a textual level this is problematic, but it makes perfect sense in the films' subtext. The 'women in danger' and the 'women constantly in danger' are not under threat from women, men threaten them. Both films highlight this fact by placing men into two categories: malicious and incompetent. The real danger stems from the malicious men and is ignored by the incompetent men. The earlier text shows that malicious men are solitary and abnormal, whereas institutions are incompetent, but the latter text inverts this concept.

The 1974 film features two male antagonists that fall into the malicious category, Billy and Peter. Billy is obviously malicious; he is a murderous psychopath that devastates the feminine microcosm of the film. It is less clear why Peter is categorised as malicious, but a close reading of the text gives us numerous reasons to include him, such as his attempts to undermine his girlfriend's agency and his worrying obsessive tendencies. Both the killer and the creep need to be addressed to fully understand the malicious men of 1974. As analysis of these two characters relating to violence and female autonomy are already entwined with the prior examination, this discussion on Billy and Peter will focus on the environments that they create.

Billy is an enigma, his motivations, history and psychology are completely unknown to us. Rather than being characterised, Billy is shown to be a malicious force of nature that lacks nuance. We do not need to psychoanalyse Billy; only his textual actions are important. As stated earlier, Billy invades the insular feminine microcosm. It is made clear in the opening sequences that there are restrictions placed on when men can be present, and later sequences show that no men cross the threshold without a feminine escort. Lt Fuller is welcomed in by the sorority sisters, male partners and relatives are invited in at specific times, and the search party is kept at the threshold by Jess and Phyl. This is a male-free zone that Gothicises masculinity by making the men adhere to classical horror rules about thresholds and personal space. The male characters on the periphery of the feminine microcosm are kept at bay by this invisible barrier of consent, much like classical vampires.

These men respect the concept of the threshold, which creates a false sense of security. A contemporary evil that the women are unprepared for penetrates the microcosm. The chaotic elements of Billy are highlighted in his first appearance, as the shot shifts from a steady camera to an uneven point-of-view shot underscored with congested breathing. The harmony of the sorority house depicted by its sturdy walls, soothing rendition of 'Silent Night' and the scenic manor aesthetic are put under instant conflict by Billy's appearance. They may be able to defend against obscene phone calls and incompetent institutions, but they do not fare well against the unrestrained reality of evil in the era of apocalyptic horror.

Billy scales the side of the sorority house and enters through the attic, bypassing the threshold by invading through an elevated space. The attic has two functions in the text: an unexpected hideout for a deranged killer and a Gothic space that slowly engulfs the setting. The mismatched items cluttering the area, the dirt and the lighting inspires comparisons to German expressionism. This presents the setting as unreal and uncanny, fortifying Billy's Gothic space when contrasted against the organised, clean and bright area of the living spaces of the house inhabited by the female cast. Billy's Gothic space is depicted as the source of malicious masculinity in this text.

Billy's invasion into the living areas from his Gothic space begins during the Christmas party. This invasion is heralded by both point-of-view shots of Billy's movements and the prominence of shadows during his attacks. Before Clare's murder, the living areas are mostly bright with minimalistic darkness. The shadows slowly conquer the light throughout the film and expressionism prevails by the end. This is depicted by the sorority house itself growing dimmer as each scene passes and the dwindling use of Billy's point-of-view shots. These semiotic depictions of Billy's success eventually Gothicise the entire building.

The murders reflect this increasing darkness and Gothicising of the narrative. Clare's murder is shown in full lighting, once again depicting the new normality for the horror film and the lack of preparation for a chaotic threat. As Billy carries Clare from the scene of the crime to the Gothic space, we are shown his movements, cast in silhouette, against a wall. This creates another reference to classic horror creating a link between monsters from films such as *The Mummy's Hand* (1940) and *The Creature from the Black Lagoon* (1954). Later, Barb's murder would be cast in harsh shadows that conceal Billy and leave Barb exposed in the shortage of light. This cuts to static shots of Barb's bloody hand and Billy's stabbing motions against a pitch-black backdrop. Phyl walks into Barb's shadow-drenched room and the kill is omitted, emphasising this idea of kills being shot in increasing darkness. This leads to Jess's confrontations with Billy and Peter, which are set in varying degrees of darkness, culminating in her entering the neglected Gothic space of the film, the basement.

Peter's maliciousness has been shown in the film with his growing obsessiveness and attempts to control Jess. The slow revelation of Peter's maliciousness occurs alongside his invasion of the feminine microcosm. The first invasion was calculated, as he waits until the house empties. He enters and waits for an unsuspecting Jess, which leads to Peter telling Jess that they are getting married and living the life that is expected of them. When Jess reveals that she wants her own agency back, Peter makes vague threats and flees. His second invasion occurs at the film's climax, when Jess has escaped Billy and locked herself in the basement.

The basement functions as the secondary Gothic space, as it creates a strong parallel with the attic and presents an inhospitable setting for the finale. Peter breaks in, confronts Jess and is murdered in self-defence. There is a strong significance in these Gothic spaces being invaded by two different men. One is unseen, unknowable and unhinged; the other is visible, known to the audience and growing unhinged as his subplot unfolds. Peter is a red herring to confuse the audience over Billy's identity, but this is not a satisfying aspect of the text. The two do not appear to be aurally or visually similar and there is a clear disconnect between them.

The positioning of their Gothic spaces helps to unravel the baffling idea that Peter could be mistaken for Billy. The main danger of the narrative descends from above to strike in the middle. The victim in the middle descends below for sanctuary and must defend herself from the lowest invader. The danger aloft is barely personified, he is rage manifested sans identity. Billy is a stand-in for institutionalised misogyny, despite being depicted as a solitary rogue male. The misogyny that pollutes the environment corrupts Peter with its reactionary politics. We see the lines between

Peter and Billy blend together regarding the constant harassing phone calls bombarding the house. Peter's wailing is aurally like Billy's pleading for help and to be stopped prior to his last kill. This makes Peter's death more noteworthy, as it implies that the misogyny of the common man can be overcome, but the institutionalised aggression against women is borderline omnipotent, shown by Billy's final descent from the attic.

Malicious masculinity in the 2019 film is not depicted as being a one-off event or the actions of a solitary man. Instead, it is depicted as an institutional problem. The hierarchy is in place and men reside at the top, like Billy in his attic. The first hint at this subtext stems from the establishing shot of the university campus and the transition to Professor Gelson's lecture. The Gothic spaces in the sorority house have been removed and replaced by Gothic institutions.

The university is depicted as a Gothic space in its own right, prior to the associations with masculinity or archaic ideologies. The university has a dull colour scheme consisting of shades of black and grey. The exterior shots cut to close ups of gargoyle-like figures indented in the walls. These shots are contrasted against the vibrant colours on campus, as each student around the exterior wears brighter colours, making them stand out from the dull building surrounded by snow. These contrasts continue as we transition into Gelson's lecture. Gelson's colour palate is an extension of the university's structures, with his dark-grey suit contrasted against the vibrant students displaying bright primary colours. This, alongside his lecture on the shift from belly magic to head magic, creates a binary of the modern/archaic. The institution and Gelson are depicted as outdated, while the students present a cultural shift towards personal expression rather than suppression. Later, Gelson is revealed to be a Robert Bly-styled figure[25] that radicalises the young men with tales of masculine supremacy.

Gelson is akin to a prophet of radicalised masculinity, as the real threat is posed by the long-dead founder of the university. Hawthorne's bust is revealed to be a magical artefact. This magic takes the form of black goo, a visual metaphor for toxic masculinity, that is used to create an army of absent-minded but dedicated masculine soldiers intent on destroying disobedient women.

Billy has been replaced by the modern Deek Army, his chaos now militarised. This shift in focus can be seen in recent history, the fascination with solitary rogue males such as Ted Bundy, a serial killer that terrorised a sorority house in 1978, to large ideological and unorganised groups of men angry at the world, such as white supremacy groups, the online incels and conservative political groups aiming to return the world to a pre-feminist normality.[26] The 'Deek Army' is another group that aims to terrorise those that are perceived as disrupting male supremacy.

Calvin Hawthorne also has a real life parallel; this is not just reserved for the Bly-like Gelson or the misogynist 'Deeks'. He established Hawthorne University in 1819 – Kris refers to him as a 'sexist and racist' – and he held a vast amount of power. Thomas Jefferson founded the University of Virginia in 1819, owned slaves and raped the female slaves, and was the third president of the United States of America. This parallel strengthens the subtextual concept, in the classical and socially aware era of slasher films, that misogyny is engrained in more than 200 years of North American history.

The fraternity itself is not framed as a Gothic space like the sorority house of 1974. Gothicism drips from the hazing room, but the rest of the fraternity is a normalised living space. Their increasing maliciousness is shown through their actions. The fraternity participate in and help to perpetuate 'frat boy rape culture'. The members of the fraternity can take advantage of women with zero repercussions, until the finale when they are burned alive for their horrific transgressions.

Brian Huntley, the former president of the fraternity, raped Riley prior to the events of the film. The audience believes Riley completely, but the narrative is against her. Sexual assault survivors are set up to fail at every hurdle, especially considering the only hope of prosecuting their attacker is through the masculine institutions that protect men, such as universities and the police force. Riley is failed by these institutions that strive to protect the masculine ideal. This is another real-world parallel that has become more apparent in the post-MeToo world.

Phil attempts to rape Helena on the night of the performance but is interrupted by Riley. Before Phil leaves, he tells Riley that 'Brian would never have done what [Riley] said he did'. This is initially taken as a sign of masculine solidarity, a mirroring of the sorority sisters, but is quickly undermined by Phil's smile. His expression reveals that he is fully aware of the criminality of himself and his brothers. 'Frat boy rape culture' is real and the perpetrators conceal it. Winking at their victims, smiling throughout their lies, and their complete immunity is where the true horror of this film lays. The masked killers are not terrifying when compared to the societal horrors without weakness. The real horrors are the human elements of the film, inverting the 1974 text that centralises its horror in the chaotic Billy.

The other category of masculinity presented in both texts is the incompetent men. In the 1974 film this is shown through the police force and their investigation into the disappearance of Clare, the obscene phone calls and the missing high school girl. The police force has an ancillary adversarial role in the narrative. Lt Fuller personifies the concept of the incompetent police force. Despite attempts at distancing himself from the 'boys club', he is still the highest-ranking representative of the law. During his search of Clare's room, he examines objects as if they were clues to discredit her character and resolve her disappearance. Lt Fuller asks if Clare drinks a lot, if she has emotional problems, what boys she sees and tries to trip up Jess and Phyl's previous statements. This encounter appears to be an interrogation rather than an investigation and will be familiar to women who seek help from the law. Lt Fuller's efforts to tie Peter to the disappearance of Clare and the obscene calls leads him to disappear from the narrative when the law is needed most. During this time frame, Phyl and the police officer watching the house have been killed and Jess has been tormented by Billy. Peter was killed prior to Lt Fuller directing the officers to hurry to the sorority house, as the final call has been traced back to the second phone line. Billy remains active in the attic, while the incompetent male figures below arrive at their conclusions blaming Peter. The lack of investigation has led to the case unravelling and a psychopath's rage continuing unfettered.

The finale of the film shows us the most damning element of masculine incompetency. All the surviving men of the narrative gather in Jess's room after her sedation. The surrounding men make assumptions about the attacks and slowly leave, despite deciding to remain. The sorority house has not been fully investigated, the Gothic space has not been discovered and the additional bodies remain undisturbed. As the house empties, the camera scans the bedrooms showing the cleared crime scenes, yet the abject atmosphere remains. Billy descends from the attic once more as Jess lays vulnerable. The camera pans out to the exterior of the house as the phone rings one last time. After Billy's initial call, the sequential calls succeed Billy's murders. The implication being that Jess has been murdered off-screen. She should have been saved by the incompetent men that allowed the narrative to unfold, but they offer no support and their inaction has led to the complete destruction of the feminine microcosm.

The incompetency of the masculine institutions of 1974 is inverted in 2019 to show the incompetency of the solitary male. Gil, the campus security guard, continues Lt Fuller's incompetency by disbelieving Riley. He is told about Lindsay's disappearance and the insidious direct messages, yet Gil attempts to do as little as possible. Instead, he suggests alternate possibilities such as her being with a boyfriend, enquiring about Riley trusting strange men, and finishes by stating that 'boys will be boys', relating to the fraternity's actions. Once the women begin to fight back against the predatory fraternity, Gil arrives at the secondary sorority. He points his gun at the victims but is killed before he can take any action.

Gil and his real-world counterparts resort to blaming victims as an easier solution than solving the case and protecting those that need it most, rather than those that will be shielded by the legal system due to the status granted to them by their gender. This is a parallel to the reality of campus investigations that do not involve legal representatives and exist to protect the reputation of the university, rather than their female students. If women are not believed, cases cannot go forward and reputations cannot be tarnished.

As we can see from the analysis above, there are strong thematic and ideological links between *Black Christmas* (1974) and *Black Christmas* (2019). The idea that the latter is not a remake is based on textual elements rather than the film's construction, subtext and impact. Reviews of *Black Christmas* (1974) have mostly been lost to time, but contemporary reviews that can be found online paint a similar picture to the remake. A. H. Weiler states that '*Black Christmas* . . . is a whodunit that begs the question of why it was made'.[27] Gene Siskel stated that 'the picture has only one kind of cheap thrill. Its women repeatedly walk slowly into certain death, and the director plays out the suspense for more than it's worth'.[28]

Black Christmas made $4 million at the box office, which is equivalent to about $20 million today. The film was a success by Canadian standards[29] and became a cult classic after its re-release a decade later. If we look at the figures for the 2019 film, it made $18.5 million. In Hollywood terms, both films are box-office flops with barely a difference in the grosses. Both texts had similar contemporary reviews and profit margins. It is tough to disbelieve Michael Kennedy when he says that the attacks on *Black Christmas* (2019) are based on sexist mentalities[30] fostered by our institutions and cinematic canon.

This chapter has shown that the 2019 film is definitely a remake of the original, as it takes the 1974 film and updates the themes, subtext and narrative elements for the post-MeToo era where we finally understand that horror does not stem from rogue agents or incoherent psychopaths, instead it comes from institutions that encourage violence as revenge for the decrease of social disparity. *Black Christmas* (2019) should take its place as both a strong successor to the most socially important slasher film and as a powerful text that encourages women to stand up against the systems that oppress them. Blumhouse has produced additional slashers of the socially aware era, most notably *Halloween* (2018). They are leading the attempt to rejuvenate the slasher for an audience that can appreciate the immense social potential of the subgenre.

Notes

1. B. Kenigsberg, '*Black Christmas* Review: Horror for a New Era of Campus Debates', *New York Times* (12 December 2019), *www.nytimes.com/2019/12/12/movies/black-christmas-review.html* (accessed 17 June 2020).
2. O. Gleiberman, '*Black Christmas*: Film Review', *Variety* (12 December 2019), *www.variety.com/2019/film/reviews/black-christmas-review-imogen-poots-1203434053* (accessed 17 June 2020).
3. J. M. Anderson, '*Black Christmas*', *Common Sense Media*, *www.commonsensemedia.org/movie-reviews/black-christmas* (accessed 30 June 2020).
4. B. Lee, '*Black Christmas* Review – Woke Slasher Remake is an Unholy, Unscary Mess', *Guardian* (13 December 2019), *www.theguardian.com/film/2019/dec/12/black-christmas-review-remake-unscary-mess* (accessed 17 June 2020).
5. I. Freer, '*Black Christmas* (2019) Review', *Empire* (13 December 2019), *www.empireonline.com/movies/reviews/black-christmas-2019/* (accessed 17 June 2020).
6. R. Reed, '*Black Christmas* is a Crummy Excuse for a Horror Film', *Observer* (18 December 2019), *www.observer.com/2019/12/black-christmas-review-imogen-poots-rex-reed/* (accessed 30 June 2020).
7. M. Kennedy, 'Why *Black Christmas*' Reviews Are so Negative', *Screen Rant* (14 December 2019), *www.screenrant.com/black-christmas-2019-movie-reviews-bad-reason/* (accessed 30 June 2020)
8. Richard Nowell, *Blood Money: A History of the First Teen Slasher Film Cycle* (New York: Continuum, 2011), p. 71.
9. S. Constantineau, '*Black Christmas*: The Slasher Film was Made in Canada', *CineAction*, 82–83 (2010), 58.
10. *Sneak Previews*, 'Women in Danger Films' (23 October 1980), *www.youtube.com/watch?v=fxPWTGcxsus* (accessed 26 June 2020).
11. Sotiris Petridis, *Anatomy of the Slasher Film: A Theoretical Analysis* (Jefferson NC: McFarland, 2019), p. 10.

12. Barbara Creed, *The Monstrous-Feminine: Film, Feminism, Psychoanalysis* (New York: Routledge, 1993), p. 122.

13. Petridis, *Anatomy of the Slasher Film*, p. 19.

14. Carol J. Clover, *Men, Women, and Chain Saws: Gender in the Modern Horror Film* (Princeton NJ: Princeton University Press, 2015), pp. 33–4.

15. Vera Dika, *Games of Terror: Halloween, Friday the 13th, and the Films of the Stalker Cycle* (Toronto: Farleigh Dickinson University Press, 1990), p. 45.

16. Michael Kimmel, *Manhood in America: A Cultural History* (4th edition) (Oxford: Oxford University Press, 2017).

17. Kimmel, *Manhood in America*, pp. 233, 242.

18. Michael Kimmel, *Angry White Men: American Masculinity at the End of an Era* (New York: Nation Books, 2017).

19. Dika, *Games of Terror*, p. 9.

20. Constantineau, '*Black Christmas*', 60.

21. R. Wood, 'Return of the Repressed', in B. K. Grant (ed.), *Robin Wood on the Horror Film: Collected Essays and Reviews* (Detroit MI: Wayne State University Press, 2018), pp. 59–62.

22. Kimmel, *Manhood in America*.

23. Kimmel, *Angry White Men*.

24. M. Monagle, 'The Politics of Slasher *Black Christmas*', *Austin Chronicle* (13 December 2019), *www.austinchronicle.com/screens/2019-12-13/the-politics-of-slasher-black-christmas* (accessed 20 June 2020).

25. Robert Bly, *Iron John: A Book about Men* (London: Random House, 2001), p. 16.

26. Kimmel, *Angry White Men*.

27. A. H. Weiler, 'Screen: Murky Whodunit', *New York Times* (20 October 1975), 45.

28. G. Siskel, '*Black Christmas*', *Chicago Tribune* (6 October 1974), B6.

29. Nowell, *Blood Money*, pp. 61–2, 76.

30. Kennedy, 'Why *Black Christmas*' Reviews are So Negative'.

13

What Lies Behind the White Hood

Looking at Horror Through a Realistic Lens in Spike Lee's *BlacKkKlansman*

Allison Schottenstein

FROM *PARANORMAL ACTIVITY* (2009) to *The Purge* (2013), Blumhouse Productions has produced films that represent our most fantastical nightmares. *BlacKkKlansman* (2019), a Blumhouse and MonkeyPaw production, pushes the horror genre into reality – as director Spike Lee reveals in the film, real life is just as scary. While *Get Out* (2017), an earlier Blumhouse production, may have provoked the audience to see the intersection between horror and social commentary, Lee's film warns the audience that this story is scarier because it 'is based on some fo' real fo' real shit'. Lee's monster is the Ku Klux Klan (KKK). His predator hides beneath a white cloak, secretly lurking among the shadows for his two prey – the Blacks and the Jews.

Lee proclaimed to the *Jewish Telegraph Agency* that the 'Jewish people are No. 2 on the list as far as the Klan goes'.[1] Although the tension between the two groups has existed off and on throughout history, in Lee's perspective, this feud is unimportant compared to the real horror that they share. Lee subtly persuades his American-Jewish viewership not to fear the Black Power salute, but what lies behind the robes of white supremacy. Lee utilises *BlacKkKlansman* to tell Jews and Blacks to stop thinking of themselves as being on opposing sides, but on the same side against one horrific monster – the KKK. Through the characters of Flip Zimmerman (a Jewish undercover cop) and Ron Stallworth (an African-American undercover cop), Spike Lee dismantles the tension between Jews and African Americans by shedding light on the horrors of white supremacy as well as the mistakes that America, and by default, the American Jews, made in their perceptions of the Black Power Movement.

Profound tensions brewed between the two groups during and after the Civil Rights Movement.[2] Some of the problems between Jews and African Americans centred on African Americans wanting to gain control over their communities while de-emphasising white control. The Black Power Movement empowered black identity and America's understanding of race as opposed to the traditional Civil Rights' goal of integration. An outgrowth of the Civil Rights Movement, Black Power promoted racial pride, African-American political institutions, and African-American rights.[3] During the 'March Against Fear' in 1966, Stokely Carmichael and Willie Ricks spoke to a group of sharecroppers – farmers who worked for a landowner in exchange for a scrap of land – in the Delta region in Mississippi calling for 'Black Power'.[4] Other Black Power groups emerged to fight against white supremacy. Huey Newton and Bobby Seale headed the Black Panthers, which Carmichael later joined to help 'organize poor blacks in the urban north'.[5] The Black Power Movement paved the way for movements like Black Feminism, university-level Black Studies and Africana Studies, and the Black Arts Movement. Black Power 'dismantled white supremacy' like no other African-American movement before and proved that the power lies in the masses. This movement also served to inspire Blaxploitation films as it spurred film directors such as Van Peebles and Gordon Parks to portray African Americans in prominent roles, like Shaft. It also allowed directors to reorientate the audience by creating African-American heroes rather than subjugating them to disempowered sidekicks. BlacKkKlansman not only pays homage to the Black Power Movement, but Lee celebrates the characterisation of a Blaxploitation figure in the character of Ron. As Isaac Hayes sings in the Blaxploitation film Shaft, 'who is the man that would risk his neck for his brother man . . . Shaft . . . Can you dig it?' Ron is the quintessential Shaft.[6]

In 1967, James Baldwin's New York Times Magazine article 'Negroes Are Anti-Semitic Because They're Anti-White' is why African Americans had animosity towards Jews because they saw them as white. Jews epitomised whiteness because they ran stores in black areas and lived in better neighbourhoods. From Baldwin's perspective, white Jews assimilated into white American culture, leaving African Americans behind.[7] Black Power leaders wanted to remove white support, which created tension among pro-civil rights Jews. This issue was further complicated because 'young Jews who did not see the white community as their own . . . felt as if they had been exiled from the organization they helped to build'.[8] The relationship became complicated for many American Jews after the Six-Day War of 1967, heightening the Arab-Israeli conflict. Jay Rosenberg proclaimed Jews who supported Black Power, were no better than a 'Jewish Uncle Tom'.[9]

Black Power opposed Israel because it aligned itself with the First World – the white oppressor.[10] The broader Black Power Movement demonised Israel by creating a strategy of non-white Third World solidarity.[11] From here, we can see how some African Americans came to equate Zionism with white imperialism, Nazism, Western colonialism and Black and Arab oppression.[12] The Jewish-supported civil rights organisation the SNCC (or the Student Non-violent Coordinating Committee)[13] opened a Pandora's Box in June of 1967 when it published an anti-Zionist newsletter in the aftermath of the Six-Day War. As a result, there was a media firestorm that began with the *New York Times*. A conflation of anti-Zionism with anti-Semitism would be a problem within the Black Power Movement among such figures as Carmichael from SNCC and the Black Panthers.[14]

Time Magazine featured 'Black vs. Jew' on the 31 January 1969 cover. After the teacher strike at Oceanville-Brownsville, *Time Magazine* signalled to the general public that this iconic pair's relations were severed. Jewish presses also commented on the problems with the Black Power Movement.[15] However, in 1972 – the period in which Lee's *BlacKkKlansman* takes place – was the pinnacle of the Black Power Movement. The Black Political Convention in Gary, Indiana, of 1972, was one the 'most important political, cultural, and intellectual gatherings of the Black Power era'.[16] It called for a political change among African Americans. However, this event's primary focus changed when the media blew out of proportion the Black Power Movement's support of the Palestinian homeland, dividing Jews and African Americans. Reports came out associating the Convention both with anti-Zionism and anti-Semitism.[17]

The *New York Times* media frenzy had created profound concerns in the Jewish community as well. The National Jewish Community Relations Advisory Council, in a memo, on 21 March 1972, summarised how the

Gary Convention equated Israel with 'white racism'.[18] Out of reaction, African-American newspapers such as the *New York Amsterdam News* tried to dismantle the controversy by distancing itself from the situation.[19] Still, it was too late; the divide was there. Mainstream media demonised Black Power and represented it as oppositional towards the American-Jewish community. *BlacKkKlansman*'s purpose is not to recreate this relationship, but instead to call attention to the 'invisible empire' – the KKK. By Lee not rehashing this history between these two minorities, the viewer can focus on the historical enemy.

Ironically, Lee, became known in Hollywood for creating divisions between Jews and Blacks through his films, such as in *Mo' Better Blues* (1990) and *Get on the Bus* (1996). However, he changed and became the voice of unity in *BlacKkKlansman*. Lee had a history of depicting negative images of Jews in films. As journalist Jacob Arns says, Lee characterised Jews as 'scapegoats, turncoats, victims, allies, bystanders, exploiters, and friends'. Through these images, Lee has attempted to illustrate the complexity and struggle that Jews have balancing their whiteness with their ethnic identity. In Lee's *BlacKkKlansmen*, *his* perspective on Jews has altered dramatically due to the altercations in Charlottesville. In Charlottesville, the United States witnessed the rise of right-wing protests, specifically the Neo-Nazi's who chanted anti-Semitic and anti-Black rhetoric. Lee suddenly questioned if Jews fit into white America. After all, white supremacy and anti-Semitism were in full display in Charlottesville? Could this mean, in 2017, that Jews have a connection with African Americans not because their experiences are the same, but because they are both hated by the same group?

In *BlacKkKlansman*, Lee does not provide a solution as to how to stop this monster/KKK – as seen in other horror films – instead, he wants his movie to be a warning to America, African Americans and Jews. America had lived through this nightmare since Reconstruction when the KKK invisibly emerged to scare African Americans and Radical Republicans. However, no one has successfully stopped this spread of hatred as the Klan repeatedly appears throughout the country. Lee illustrates the longevity of this hatred by looking at several historical periods. At the same time, he wants to end this persistent oppression; Lee wants white Americans to stop fearing African-American empowerment.

At the beginning of the film, Lee juxtaposes two historical periods – the Civil War and the Civil Rights Movement – which historians have seen parallels with both periods embattled by the 'African American problem'.[20]

The Confederacy proselytised white supremacy and castigated African Americans as slaves. During the civil rights period, African Americans remained second-class citizens, lacking the same rights as white Americans. The opening scene of *BlacKkKlansman* focuses on Scarlett O'Hara – who represents white southern female gentility – as she gazes upon a sea of injured Confederate soldiers. This moment glorifies the Confederacy and downplays that women like Scarlett O'Hara contributed to the cruel institution of slavery. In Lee's version, Scarlett O'Hara shouts: 'God, help us. God save the Confederacy'. He uses this image to criticise Hollywood, who promoted romantic images of the Confederate South due to the infamous film *Birth of a Nation*, which rewrote history, enabling the past horrors of the KKK to vanish.

In Lee's perspective, the Confederacy was 'saved' because hatred towards African Americans remained in the south's consciousness. Indeed, it was the Vice President of the Confederacy, Alexander H. Stephens, who declared 'new governments . . . cornerstone rests, upon the great truth that the negro is not equal to the white man; that slavery subordination to the superior race is his natural and normal condition'.[21] Lee wants to press upon his viewer not to buy into the glamour of the Confederate South, especially when co-creators of the *Game of Thrones* attempted to create the alternative history series *Confederate*, which would have glorified the Confederate South and diminished the cruelties of slavery. Lee positions himself as the symbolic offspring of Oscar Devereaux Micheaux, who used the medium of film to speak out against the horrors of racism in *Within Our Gates* (1920), a commentary on *Birth of a Nation* (1915). *BlacKkKlansman* wants the audience to squirm, so they are forced to confront their prejudices.

Lee segues into a televised programme from the 1950s to show that oppression towards African Americans persists, especially in the media. He features an inarticulate racist, named Dr Kennebrew Beauregard, to illustrate the dangers of the Confederacy, which morphed into white supremacy. This white-centric movement is not exclusive to hatred of African Americans, but also includes hatred of Jews in its web. This scene functions as setting up the historical background for *BlacKkKlansman*. Lee wants to explain that white supremacy has transcended from the time of the Confederacy to the 1950s and beyond. Lee visually and verbally illustrates the horrors of white supremacy through Beauregard.

Lee uses two powerful images in this scene with Beauregard: a Confederate Flag and the film *Birth of a Nation*. The viewer cannot help focusing on the perturbing well placed Confederate flag, as Beauregard spouts virulent hate speech. He wants the audience to feel fear of this flag as though it was a Nazi Swastika. The flag does not merely represent the Civil War but is a reminder of white supremacy. Lee compounds this evocative image with the footage of *The Birth of Nation*. This film not only enforced a revisionist interpretation of the Civil War and the Reconstruction era – in which the Klan emerged as the saviours of the south – but also caused the creation of a new hatred instilled in the Klan, who also victimised Jews. The premier of the *Birth of Nation* also influenced a rise in lynchings.[22] The new KKK was no longer specific to the south, but haunted all fifty states, finding homes behind the shadows even in western America.

Beauregard's film spews not only hate but also a choking fear that he could provoke others to harm Blacks and Jews. He incites fear of integration and the desegregation of school systems. Beauregard mentions Little Rock High School in 1957 – one of the earliest acts of desegregation post-*Brown v. Board of Education* (1954) – as a tactic to create divisions between whites and Blacks. Beauregard presents himself as the voice of reason as he calls attention to America's infraction on white American civil rights, which was a reality in the 1950s. He paints desegregation as a terrorist action. He fiercely proclaims that the Jews are the source behind the unravelling of white America. Beauregard's fear tactics were real and dangerous, considering that white supremacists bombed many synagogues between 1954–9 and beyond. He describes Jews as monsters: 'the Jewish-controlled puppets on the US Supreme Court compelling white children to go to school with an inferior race is the final nail in a coffin . . . in a black coffin towards America becoming a mongrel nation'. His goal was to convince white Americans to fear African Americans and, by default, Jews, for occupying America. Beauregard's manipulation is similar to the way that anti-Semites incited fear across Europe towards Jews in the nineteenth and twentieth centuries. Beauregard even goes as far as to call the transformation of an integrated America as an 'international Jewish conspiracy'. Such a phrase provokes the viewer to recall the *Protocols of the Elders of Zion*, a text that, for over a century, had the sole purpose to make people fear Jews.

Beauregard demonises civil rights activists: 'Martin Luther coons of this world and their army of commies started their civil rights assault against our holy white Protestant values'. Beauregard purposefully uses the word 'commies' to refer to Jews whom white supremacists linked to communism because of their open support for civil rights. The emphasis of

'Protestant values' highlights how the Klan approved only of white Protestants. Lee does this to remind white Jews that they hide behind their skin colour, but it does not fully protect them from white supremacy. Beauregard hypnotically repeats over and over again, 'we had a great way of life' to reiterate to 'whites' that the past was better before Jews and African Americans began to speak out.

Lee creates the character Beauregard as a larger-than-life figure, but a stumbling, fantastic speaker. Beauregard's ideas are incoherent and all over the place, showing the haphazardness of the language of hate. As it says in Proverbs 4:19, the 'way of the wicked is like deep darkness, they do not know what makes them stumble'. Initially, Beauregard is featured in a black and white background, setting the mood of darkness. As he becomes more entrenched in a fit of rage, the background turns red – a sign of danger – calling attention to his viewers that as Beauregard fills with more rage, he is more akin to the devil. Lee purposely sets up this scene to provoke Americans to wake up, stand up against white supremacy and destroy it at its roots. Lee then transitions to the 1970s – the height of Black Power and the end of Black-Jewish relations – to show how the beast of white supremacy did not vanish decades after Beauregard. Indeed, the American monster behind the hood never dies.

Lee switches his focus away from the 1950s south to 1972 Colorado Springs. Ron, a cop who looks like he came out of a Blaxploitation film, arrives at the Colorado Spring police station in 1972. Ron meets with both the African-American recruitment agent Mr Turrentine and Chief Bridges. They ask him his opinions on the Vietnam War – a war that African Americans negatively associated with womanising, nightclubs and drugs. Although Mr Turrentine is Black, he is surprised that Ron had not acted like other stereotypical 'soul brothers'. Mr Turrentine questions Ron on how he would react if someone called him a 'N*****'. Ron is shocked by his new reality but agrees to take the position, even though he has no idea what he is walking into or what danger to expect from his colleagues. Ron says, if they 'treat me right, I treat them right'. Turrentine tells him that he needs to think of himself as 'Jackie Robinson', the first professional Black baseball player for the Brooklyn Dodgers. After all, he will be the first 'Black cop in this city' and must expect to experience racism. Ron agrees that if he has to deal with it, he will. Chief Bridges promises to have Ron's 'back', but with limitations: 'I can only do so much.' Ron wants acceptance among his fellow cops, he is even willing to 'chop' his Afro and appear 'clean-shaven' for more opportunities.

At the station, the police treat Ron as a second-class cop. Chief Bridges puts him to work in the records department where cops constantly berate him with racist statements, such as calling him 'officer toad' and every black prisoner a 'toad', a derogatory slur against African Americans. Ron is determined not to let his race dictate his future. The viewer is afraid for Ron because he has placed himself into a toxic environment. Ron does not have the support of his colleagues, even though they are all cops. He fights to gain a chance to go undercover. The only reason Chief Bridges gives him the opportunity is because 'the Black radical, Stokely Carmichael, is giving a speech' in Colorado Springs, and they need a Black person to infiltrate and gather information. During this time, the police feared groups such as the Black Student Union and speakers like Carmichael. Chief Bridges says, 'And as far as I'm concerned, FBI Director J. Edgar Hoover was dead right when he said the Black Panthers are the greatest internal threat to the security of these United States'. Lee wants to stress how misguided Americans were of who was the 'internal threat'. In real life, the FBI watched Black Power leaders closely, but Lee wants the audience to question whether these tactics were needed or was this fear misplaced? Although the FBI would begin to investigate the Klan in the 1970s – which caused Klan members to become anti-government – Lee demands that his viewers do not equate Black Power with terrorist groups like the white supremacists.[23]

Carmichael's speech sets the tone for an alternative perspective of Black Power. He does not appear as a villain but as a leader. He implores the Black audience to 'stop running away from being Black' and not be afraid. He tells African Americans not to destroy themselves to emulate the whites: 'We are Black, and we are beautiful'. Carmichael wants to stop the cycle of self-loathing, which the viciousness of racism propels. African Americans must see themselves as individuals that are part of a group, not a *monolithic* black identity. To emphasise this, Lee superimposes individual African-American heads to underscore it. Carmichael feels that 'black self-love' is necessary because of an experience he had as a child. He expressed how ashamed he felt when as a young boy, he watched the film, *Tarzan*, cheering on Tarzan to 'kill the savages'. Without realising that he had opposed himself, he explained that racism had caused him to believe he was not worthy of living as a Black man. Carmichael claimed that 'it was as though a Jew saw Nazis take Jews to a concentration camp and cheered them on'.

He asks them to protest against the white racist cops that kill African Americans and oppose the 'illegal' 'racist' Vietnam War. African

Americans spoke out against the Vietnam War, calling the 'participation' of African-American soldiers as 'American seasonal bloodletting', primarily since the army recruited so many lower-income African Americans.[24] He described the police treatment towards African Americans as being 'shot down like dogs'. He would rather an African American kill a 'white racist cop than a Vietnamese' because at least 'he is doing it for a reason'. This sentimentality helps the viewer realise the risk that Ron took joining the police force.

Carmichael sets the stage for cop duo Ron and Flip, who find unity in their fight against the enemy – the KKK. Carmichael found inspiration in a quote from Rabbi Hillel the Elder and applied it to Black Power: 'If I am not for myself, who will be for me . . . And if not now, when?' Carmichael utilises Hillel's wisdom to encourage his young African-American peers to fight racism. He demands the Black Student Union 'pick up a gun an arm yourself because a war is coming against Whites and Blacks'. His message is not about purposefully killing whites, but a call for self-defence. Beauregard and Carmichael are opposites in their philosophy; one promotes terror towards minority groups, the other fosters self-defence against terror.

After the event, Patrice, President of the Black Student Union, and Carmichael become subject to police abuse. The incident shows that Carmichael was right about protecting oneself from the police. The policeman, Landers – a known racist cop – tells them to take their 'Black asses and Black elbows and spread them'. They only thing they did wrong was *driving while Black*. The police refer to Carmichael on several occasions as a 'n*****'. They did not know what would happen to them. Lee demonstrates that members of the police were unwilling to protect everyone equally. Carmichael's message was clear; the law does not equally protect Black citizens. They must defend themselves. Ron tries to convince Chief Bridges – after explaining that Carmichael was not a threat – that the police were obliged to investigate certain police officers' unlawful acts in the force.

Ron joins the intelligence unit. On his first day, he looks through the newspaper to discover a KKK advertisement with a number to call. Ron pretends to be white to make contact. He uses ethnic slurs against Jews and African Americans to build trust with the Klan leader, Walter. Ron declares that the only worthy people are those who have 'pure White Aryan blood running through their veins'. The police in the intelligence unit are shocked that he brazenly called the President of the local Klan. Ron makes plans to meet Walter. He hatches a plan to create 'two Ron

Stallworths' – the Black man on the phone and the white man in person. Chief Bridges questions Ron's ability to convince Walter because he is afraid that Ron sounds Black on the phone compared to a white male. Ron says he is fluent in both 'Jive' and the 'King's English' to imply to the chief that he has stereotypical images of Black people.

Ron does not realise that his partner in this heist is Jewish until the cop Jimmy tells Flip to 'lose that Jewish necklace around your neck'. Flip says, 'Jimmy, it's not a Jewish necklace. It's the Star of David, Okay'. Ron says to him, 'Flip, you're Jewish'. Flip is flippant about his Jewish identity and does not proudly acknowledge it to Ron: 'I don't know, am I?' Flip's dismissal of his Jewish identity brings up 'passing'. Can Jews hide behind their whiteness?

The viewer is immediately worried about whether Flip will pass when he meets Walter and the Klan. At a KKK-friendly bar, Walter explains that they call themselves the 'organisation' to appear mainstream, be 'invisible' and change the 'feel' of the Klan, which was the goal of David Duke. Walter complains that African Americans 'are taking over' everywhere. One of the members proposes violence, but Walter downplays that they are 'non-violent', attempting to show superiority to other groups, like Black Power, which the FBI associates with violence.

Felix, another Klan member, is suspicious of Flip and asks him if he is Jewish. Flip has only met them once, and already Felix is questioning his whiteness. After all, Flip has dark hair, dark eyes and a large nose, which makes him fit the stereotypical Jewish look.[25] Felix desperately wants Flip to admit that he is Jewish to have power over him. Felix states that Jews are responsible for the death of Christ and provides him with enough justification to kill Flip if proven 'Jewish'. Flip turns the tables: 'are you trying to offend me . . . Of course, I am no stinkin Kike'. The fact that Ron and Flip continue this ruse with the Klan illustrates their belief that Flip's skin colour would protect him from harm. Ron can hide his Blackness, and Flip can show his whiteness. However, Lee professes that they are both vulnerable, but in different ways. They can pretend, but if the Klan finds out both of their identities, their lives will be in danger.

Ron meets with Sergeant Trapp to discuss the Klan investigation. Sergeant Trapp explains that the Klan is trying to become more 'mainstream' to gain acceptance. They want to bring the Klan into the White House. As Trapp says, 'politics is another way to sell hate' to everyday Americans. Ron cannot believe that America would elect a figure like David Duke. Trapp tells Ron that he is 'naïve' for a Black man. In this conversation, Lee wants us to see the potential for institutionalised hatred towards Blacks and Jews. He also wants to make the greater point that when hate enters the White House, the entire country becomes unsafe for Blacks and Jews.

Flip attends a meeting at Felix's house while Ron watches and listens from a distance. Felix again, questions Flip's 'pure whiteness'. He takes out his gun and calls it the 'Jew Killer' to threaten Flip. He wants Flip to have a 'Jew lie detector test'. Felix wants 'to make sure there is no Jew in him'. Walter defends Flip and tells Felix he is not a Jew. Walter insists that Flip could not be Jewish because he does not wear a 'yarmulke' or a 'Star of David'. They also discuss the Holocaust. Felix believes that the Holocaust is a 'hoax' and the 'biggest Jewish conspiracy'. Flip tries to convince him that the Holocaust was real and 'beautiful' as it destroyed a 'whole race of leeches'. Such a statement does not satisfy Felix's desire to kill him in cold blood. He wants to degrade Flip by asking to see his penis: 'I hear you Jews do something funny with your dicks. Some weird Jew shit'. Felix points a gun at Flip's head, trying to intimidate him into admitting his Jewishness. Flip fights back by calling Felix a 'faggot' for wanting to see his penis. Ron senses that Felix could kill Flip, and he risks his own life, getting out his car and throwing a brick through the window to cause a distraction. In this scene, the hero is an African American, not a white man, changing the traditional narrative, especially for horror films. Although Flip admits he was an 'ass hair away' from death, he was reluctant to admit it was because of his Jewish identity.

Flip does not want to 'risk' his life for this mission. He claims that for Ron, this is a 'crusade', and for him, 'it's a job. It's not personal, nor should it be'. Flip is in denial of his Jewish identity. Ron questions him: 'Why haven't you bought into this?' Flip says to Ron, 'Why should I?' Ron says: 'Because you're Jewish, brother . . . You've been passing for a WASP . . . Doesn't that hatred you been hearing the Klan say doesn't that piss you off?' Lee is telling the viewer – and, largely, the American-Jewish community – to wake up to reality. White supremacists, Nazis and racists vehemently hate Jews. Their white skin cannot protect them from hate crimes and death.

Ron pushes Flip, 'why you acting like you ain't got skin in the game, brother?' He wants him to realise they are both playing a risky game for the sake of a greater cause – to end white supremacy in Colorado. Flip faces challenges dealing with the fact that he is both white and Jewish. He defensively proclaims, 'It's my fucking business', while Ron clarifies, 'It's our business'. When Ron says that it 'our business', he is expressing that the Klan is not only a Black problem, but also a Jewish problem.

Ron is determined to wake Flip up to the reality of the Klan. He first starts with calling attention to Flip about the policeman Landers who attacked Patrice and Carmichael. The viewer does not know if Landers ever expressed hatred towards Jews or has an affiliation with the Klan; however, we know that he attacks Blacks for no just cause. He questions Flip, 'why do you tolerate it?' Flip answers they are 'family' and we stick together. Ron points out that the police are imitating the Klan. The question of security is a problem in *BlacKkKlansman*'s universe. Not only are the police unwilling to protect Black lives, but the Colorado Klan has members that are 'army trained'. The FBI is aware that some of the Colorado Klan were top security officials in the US government/NORAD. Lee wants to point out that the difference between Black Power and White Power is that the latter has the 'power'. Lee strongly points out that the police and the US government's refusal to *purge* these white supremacists once and for all, justifies the legal persecution of minorities – Blacks and Jews. The government has become the quintessential bystander to horror.

As Flip transforms more into a Klansman, he begins to think about the reality of what it means to be Jewish in America, regardless of practice, in a country in which the Klan exists. Flip confronts his identity with Ron: 'I'm Jewish, yes, but I wasn't raised to be . . . I never thought much about being Jewish . . . I didn't have a Bar Mitzvah. I was just another white kid. And now I am in some basement denying it out loud . . . Now I'm thinking about it all the time . . . Is that passing? . . . then I have been passing.' He refuses the Klan membership because it symbolises his passing and the evil that it represents: 'I don't want that.' Even though Jews are not a race, the legacy of what it means to be 'Jewish' remains burnt in the hearts of anti-Semites.

In traditional horror films, the monster randomly attacks in a dream, at a party, at the front door or in an abandoned house; however, the Klan brazenly sends flyers to the Black Student Union, stating 'you can sleep tonight knowing the Klan is watching you'. They are watching you and waiting for the perfect moment to come and kill you. The emphasis of 'sleep' shows that the Klan can appear at any time like the bogeyman. There is not enough time to seek shelter for protection. Since we know that parts of the police share the same hatred as the Klan, no one is there to protect them. In every classic horror film, the monster's victims have no choice but to take matters into their own hands or risk death. The Black Student Union stands up to their monster by allowing their event to occur and not taking refuge, despite Ron's warning of a possible attack. The viewer knows something is up, even from the beginning, because of the constant discussion of cross burnings or an 'explosion', which the character Ivanhoe, a fellow Klansman, perpetually mentions. Ivanhoe says the reason for cross burnings is to 'freak out the Jew media and keeps the n****** on their n***** toes'.

The most disturbing scene is when Connie and Felix discuss in bed their goals for the elimination of Blacks and Jews from *their* America. Their dream is to 'cleans[e] the country: first, the Spokes, then the Kikes'. Without a doubt, they devise a genocidal plan. Lee points out that Jews and African Americans cannot escape their history. As long as white supremacy exists, Klan, like Connie and Felix, will transform the world to represent a new confederacy, eliminating both Jews and African Americans. Felix and Connie plan their attack on the Black Student Union.

Lee dramatically juxtaposes two scenes, one at the Black Student Union where civil rights activist Jerome Turner is the keynote speaker, and the other at Flip's Klan initiation with the Grand Wizard, Duke presiding. Turner recounts the lynching of seventeen-year-old mentally impaired Jesse Washington, who the residents of Waco accused of murdering and raping Lucy Fryer in 1916. Washington was brutally lynched after a four-minute trial – he was stabbed, battered, castrated, doused in coal and oil, mutilated and burnt. People took photographs and allowed their children to view this horrific spectacle.

As Turner tells the story of Washington, Duke arrogantly declares the white race is 'scientifically' superior – an idea that contributed to Washington's death. However, Duke does not include all whites. Flip must pledge that he is a 'white non-Jewish American'. The Klan has a strict definition of who constitutes 'white' and 'American'. Duke imitates the practice of baptism – but instead of a priest sprinkling holy water on the new believers in Christ – Duke splashes water on those willing to bathe themselves in the ever-flowing waters of hatred. After Flip's inauguration, everyone watches *The Birth of a Nation* to remind those in attendance of the Klan's powerful legacy. Connie calls the actors playing the Klan an 'inspiration'. They shout 'White Power' while raising their arms in salute.

Turner discusses the frightening impact of *The Birth of a Nation*, which caused the second wave of the KKK. President Woodrow Wilson permitted the viewing of this film in the White House. He quotes Wilson's infamous quote that *The Birth of Nation* was 'like writing history with lightning. My only regret is that it is all so terribly true'. Whether or not

Wilson made this statement, Lee wanted to highlight the lack of action on behalf of the government to contain white supremacy. The real horror is how Connie and Felix interpret this film as giving them a license to murder Blacks and Jews to preserve the 'white race'. Lee wants his audience to question whether the Klan will evolve and continue to appear in every decade of American history? As pop culture mythologist Nathan Robert Brown articulates, 'the boogeyman never dies – he just changes his appearance'. This is true for the Klan.[26]

Before the event, Chief Bridges assigns Ron to be Duke's bodyguard. While Ron does not witness the Klan initiation, he listens to Duke's praise of white America during the luncheon. Ron convinces Duke to take a Polaroid with him. Unbeknownst to Duke, Ron puts his arm around him as the Polaroid snaps, causing Duke to vehemently say, 'what did you just do, boy?' Out of spite, Ron tells Duke: 'Sir, if you lay a finger on me, I'll arrest your ass for assaulting an officer . . . That's worth at least five years in prison. Try me, see if I'm playing.' Ron wants Duke to believe that his badge offers him some protection. Duke threatens him and says: 'Why don't you come down to Louisiana sometime? See how we play.' It seems doubtful, Ron would make it out of Louisiana alive.

Finally, Felix has proof that Flip is Jewish after Walker, a fellow Klansman, recognises Flip as the cop that sent him to prison. Flip realises he is about to be exposed and follows Ron. Ron discovered that Connie had left the party to set a bomb at the Black Student Union. When her plan goes awry, she drops the bomb near Patrice's car. As Ron attempts to arrest Connie, she calls out 'rape', and the police beat and arrest him without checking his credentials because he appears as the Black villain out to rape *innocent* white women. Flip finally arrives and yells at the police for arresting an undercover cop. The bomb detonates, killing Felix, Walker (the man who wanted to out Flip) and Ivanhoe. Patrice and the Black Student Union are safe.

The viewer hopes the Klan will be defeated. After all, the police arrest Landers and Connie for their crimes. However, change comes to a halt as budget cuts prevent any further investigation into the local Klan. At the point where the viewer thinks Ron ties with the Klan are over, Duke calls Ron to mourn the 'loss of [their] heroic brothers'. Ron has the last laugh when he reveals to Duke that he is not white and lambasts him as a 'racist, peckerwood, red neck, inchworm, needle-dick motherfucker!' Ron's comeback was fruitless as Duke continued spreading hatred through the decades.

In the last scene, Ron and Patrice see a cross burning in the distance. Lee zeroes in on the eyes of one of the Klan members. As we stare into his eyes, Lee transports us from 1972 Colorado Springs to 2017 Charlottesville, Virginia. There is no difference between the Colorado Springs KKK and the white supremacist protesters at Charlottesville. Lee blames Duke for instigating the Charlottesville rampage, culminating into this 'Unite to Right Rally'. After all, a month before Charlottesville, there was a KKK rally in the city. Duke promoted action against the removal of the Confederate statues. He proclaimed, just as Beauregard said, 'we had a great way of life', Duke also wants to reclaim America's old ways when he says that Charlottesville is 'the first step toward taking America back'.

We see a crowd of people holding up lights shouting 'Blood and Soil', a reference to the slogan 'Blut und Boden', that promoted Nazi racism.[27] Their hatred towards Jews is apparent as they chant 'Jews will not replace us'. They also shout 'White Lives Matters' to emphasise the struggle of white America. These white Americans may not drape themselves in hoods, but they are vocalising the same hateful rhetoric. Lee then cuts to the scene in Emancipation Park, where fighting ensues between both protesting groups. We see people holding up Confederate flags next to Nazi flags illustrating their shared ideological hatred. The most frightening scene is with James Alex Fields, a white supremacist who murderously runs over innocent bystanders and kills activist Heather Hayer.

Lee believes there is 'no place for hate'. Blacks and Jews must unite together against the common enemy – white supremacy. They need to put aside their differences and embrace the reality that no one can vanquish the Klan and their 'invisible empire' as it remains united through time. Black Lives Matter is not the villain, the white hooded monster is the real nightmare. Unlike in a horror film where the monster dies or disappears for some time, the bogeyman in the white hood only lives to reappear decade after decade, spreading his hate across the country.

Blumhouse Productions messes artfully with our minds. It brings us to fantastical worlds where we believe that *The Purge* is real, and we cannot *Get Out* of the sunken place. Conversely, Blumhouse takes us to Colorado Springs, where we meet the Klan, hoping that this is not reality. Blumhouse will continue to be the reigning king of horror because it understands that fear is both the monster under the bed and the horrific images that we see on the news. Blumhouse comprehends the complexity of the human psyche for better or for worse. Films such as *Get Out*, *BlacKkKlansman*, *Us* are only the beginning. Blumhouse will continue to disturb our sense of what is real and what is not, because until we find the antidote to racism, all kinds of monsters will continue to reappear – because this 'shit' is 'real'.

Notes

1. N. Pfefferman, 'Spike Lee: The Jewish Character in *BlacKkKlansman* Added a Lot of "Complexity" to the Film', *Jewish Telegraph Agency* (12 February 2019), *www.jta.org/2019/02/12/culture/spike-lee-the-jewish-character-in-blackkklansman-added-a-lot-of-complexity-to-the-film* (accessed 15 May 2020).

2. Cheryl Greenberg, *Troubling the Waters* (Princeton NJ: Princeton University Press, 2006), p. 214.

3. Peniel E. Joseph, *Waiting 'Til the Midnight Hour: A Narrative History of Black Power in America* (New York: Henry Holt and Company, 2006), pp. xvii–xviii.

4. *SNCC Digital Gateway*, 'June 1966: Meredith March', *https://snccdigital.org/events/meredith-march/* (accessed 15 May 2020).

5. Joseph, *Waiting 'Til the Midnight Hour*, p. 207.

6. K. P. Feldman, 'Representing Permanent War: Black Power's Palestine and the End(s) of Civil Rights', *New Centennial Review*, 8/2 (2008), 193–231.

7. Feldman, 'Representing Permanent War', 193–231.

8. P. Buhle and R. D. G. Kelley, 'Allies of a Different Sort: Jews and Blacks in the American Left', in J. Salzman and C. West (eds), *Struggles in the Promised Land: Towards a History of Black-Jewish Relations in the United States* (New York: Oxford University Press, 1997), p. 214.

9. See M. Jay Rosenberg, 'To Jewish Uncle Toms', in Michael E. Staub (ed.), *The Jewish 1960s: An American Sourcebook* (Waltham MA: Brandeis University Press, 2004).

10. Seth Forman, *Blacks in the Jewish Mind: A Crisis of Liberalism* (New York: New York University Press, 1998), p. 139; W. E. Martin Jr, '"Nation Time!": Black Nationalism, The Third World, and Jews', in *Struggles in the Promised Land*, p. 342.

11. Martin, 'Nation Time!' p. 352.

12. G. E. Rubin, 'African Americans and Israel', in *Struggles in the Promised Land*, p. 358.

13. Richard Kazarian and Robert Weisbord, *Israel in the Black Perspective* (Westport CT: Praeger, 1985), p. 2.

14. Huey Newton, *To Die for the People*, Toni Morrison (ed.) (San Francisco CA: City Lights Books, 2009), p. 197.

15. See, *Jewish Telegraphic Agency* beginning in 1967.
16. Joseph, *Waiting 'Til the Midnight Hour*, p. 276.
17. Weisbord and Kazarian Jr, *Israel in the Black Perspective*, p. 48.
18. Weisbord and Kazarian Jr, *Israel in the Black Perspective*, p. 48.
19. See Elijah Anderson and Tukufu Zuberi (eds), *The Study of African American Problems: W. E. B. Du Bois's Agenda, Then and Now* (Thousand Oaks CA: Sage, 2000).
20. Anderson and Zuberi, *The Study of African American Problems*.
21. A. H. Stephens, 'Appendix B – Cornerstone Address', in J. L. Wakelyn (ed.), *Southern Pamphlets on Secession, November 1860–April 1861* (Chapel Hill NC: University of North Carolina Press, 1996), p. 406.
22. See Melvyn Stokes, *D. W. Griffith's The Birth of a Nation: A History of the Most Controversial Motion Picture of All Time* (New York: Oxford University Press, 2008).
23. J. Drabble, 'From White Supremacy to White Power: The FBI, COIN-TELPRO-WHITE HATE, and the Nazification of the Ku Klux Klan in the 1970s', *American Studies*, 48/3 (2007), 49–74.
24. Kimberly Phillips, *War! What is it Good For?: Black Freedom Struggles and the U.S. Military from World War II to Iraq* (Chapel Hill NC: University of North Carolina Press), p. 156.
25. S. A. Glenn, 'Funny, You Don't Look Jewish', in Susan A. Glenn and Naomi B. Sokoloff (eds), *Boundaries of Jewish Identity* (Seattle WA: University of Washington Press, 2011), p. 72.
26. Nathan Robert Brown, *The Complete Idiot's Guide to Zombies* (New York: Penguin, 2010), p. 42.
27. M. Wagner, '"Blood and Soil": Protesters Chant Nazi Slogan in Charlottesville', *CNN* (12 August 2017), *www.cnn.com/2017/08/12/us/charlottesville-unite-the-right-rally/index.html* (accessed 15 May 2020).

Bibliography

Abbott, Stacey, 'When the Subtext Becomes Text: *The Purge* Takes on the American Nightmare' (paper presented at Fear 2000: Horror Media Now, Sheffield Hallam University, Sheffield, 6 April 2018).

— 'James DeMonaco's *The Purge Anarchy* (2014) – Post-Millennial Horror', in Simon Bacon (ed.), *Horror: A Companion* (New York: Peter Lang, 2019), pp. 119–26.

Adams, Cecil, 'To African-Americans, What Does "Signifying" Mean?', *The Straight Dope* (28 September 1984), *www.straightdope.com/columns/read/498/to-african-americans-what-does-signifying-mean/* (accessed 2 April 2020).

Aldana Reyes, Xavier, 'The *[Rec]* Films: Affective Possibilities and Stylistic Limitations of Found Footage Horror', in Xavier Aldana Reyes and Linnie Blake (eds), *Digital Horror: Haunted Technologies: Network Panic and the Found Footage Phenomenon* (New York: I. B. Tauris, 2016), pp. 149–60.

Altman, Rick, 'A Semantic/Syntactic Approach to Film Genre', in Barry Keith Grant (ed.), *Film Genre Reader IV* (Austin TX: University of Texas Press, 2012), pp. 27–41.

Anderson, Elijah, and Tukufu Zuberi (eds), *The Study of African American Problems: W. E. B. Du Bois's Agenda, Then and Now* (Thousand Oaks CA: Sage, 2000).

Anderson, Jeffrey M., '*Black Christmas*', *Common Sense Media*, *www.commonsensemedia.org/movie-reviews/black-christmas* (accessed 30 June 2020).

Andreeva, Nellie, 'Feature Producer Jason Blum Signs First-Look Television Deal with Lionsgate', *Deadline* (14 February 2012), *https://deadline.com/2012/02/*

feature-producer-jason-blum-signs-first-look-television-deal-with-lionsgate-231013/ (accessed 30 January 2021).

Anolik, Ruth Bienstock, *American Gothic Literature: A Thematic Study from Mary Rowlandson to Colson Whitehead* (Jefferson NC: McFarland, 2018).

Arbues, Jennifer 'Found-footage Horror Movies that are Actually Good', *Looper* (16 October 2019), *www.looper.com/170479/found-footage-horror-movies-that-are-actually-good/* (accessed 6 May 2020).

Armitage, Matt, 'Horror in the 2010s – Part 1: The House that Blum Built?', *25 Years Later* (12 September 2017), *https://25yearslatersite.com/2020/07/03/horror-in-the-2010s-part-1-the-house-that-blum-built/* (accessed 1 January 2021).

Armstrong, Megan A., '"A Nation Reborn": Right to Law and Life in *The Purge* Franchise', *Journal of Intervention and Statebuilding*, 13/3 (2019), 377–92.

Bacon, Simon, 'Introduction', in Simon Bacon (ed.), *Horror: A Companion* (New York: Peter Lang, 2019), pp. 1–8.

Balanzategui, Jessica, *The Uncanny Child in Transnational Cinema: Ghosts of Futurity at the Turn of the Twenty-First Century* (Amsterdam: Amsterdam University Press, 2018).

Banet-Weiser, Sarah, *Empowered: Popular Feminism and Popular Misogyny* (Durham NC: Duke University Press, 2018).

Barnes, Brooks, 'Spinning Horror into Gold', *New York Times* (21 October 2013), *www.nytimes.com/2013/10/21/business/media/turning-low-budget-horror-into-gold.html/* (accessed 3 February 2021).

Barfield, Charles, 'Jason Blum Calls *Whiplash* a "Disaster Theatrically" and Says the Days of Low-Budget Dramas in Theaters are Over', *The Playlist* (20 June 2019), *https://theplaylist.net/jason-blum-whiplash-theatrical-disaster-20190620/* (accessed 7 February 2020).

Bekmambetov, Timur, 'Rules of the Screenmovie: The *Unfriended* Manifesto for the Digital Age', *Movie Maker* (22 April 2015), *www.moviemaker.com/unfriended-rules-of-the-screenmovie-a-manifesto-for-the-digital-age/* (accessed 31 January 2021).

Benjamin, Eric, 'Buy Low, Sell High: How Blumhouse Does Horror Films the Right Way', *The Daily Orange* (11 April 2018), *http://dailyorange.com/2018/04/buy-low-sell-high-blumhouse-horror-films-right-way/* (accessed 7 February 2020).

Berardinelli, James, 'Paranormal Activity 4', *Reelviews* (19 October 2012), *www.reelviews.net/reelviews/paranormal-activity-4* (accessed 21 June 2020).

Berns, Fernando Gabriel Pagnoni, and Canela Ailén Rodriguez Fontao, 'New Paternal Anxieties in Contemporary Horror Cinema: Protecting the Family against (Supernatural) External Attacks', Laura Tropp (ed.), *Deconstructing*

Dads: Changing Notions of Fatherhood in Popular Culture (Lanham MD: Rowman and Littlefield, 2016), pp. 165–79.

Bhattacharji, Alex, 'How Producer Jason Blum is Disrupting Hollywood', *Wall Street Journal Magazine* (16 July 2018), *www.wsj.com/articles/how-producer-jason-blum-is-disrupting-hollywood-1531750907/* (accessed 7 February 2020).

Blake, Linnie, and Xavier Aldana Reyes, 'Introduction: Horror in the Digital Age', in Linnie Blake and Xavier Aldana Reyes (eds), *Digital Horror: Haunted Technologies, Network Panic and the Found Footage Phenomenon* (London: I. B. Tauris, 2016), p. 1–13.

Bloom, Paul, *Descartes' Baby: How the Science of Child Development Explains What Makes Us Human* (New York: Basic Books, 2004).

Blumstein, Daniel T., *The Nature of Fear: Survival Lessons from the Wild* (Cambridge MA: Harvard University Press, 2020).

Bly, Robert, *Iron John: A Book about Men* (London: Random House, 2001).

Bohn, Sarah, and Eric Schiff, *The Great Recession and Distribution of Income in California* (San Francisco CA: Public Policy Institute of California, 2011).

Bolling, Gaius, 'Jason Blum Thinks Moviegoing Will be Very Different After the Coronavirus', *JoBlo* (24 March 2020), *www.joblo.com/movie-news/jason-blum-thinks-moviegoing-will-be-very-different-after-the-coronavirus/* (accessed 7 April 2020).

Bonner, Hannah, '#Selfveillance: Horror's Slut Shaming Through Social Media, Sur- and Selfveillance', in Samantha Holland, Robert Shail and Steven Gerrard (eds.), *Gender and Contemporary Horror in Film* (Bingley: Emerald Publishing, 2019), pp. 85–99.

Boutwell, Brian B., Mathias Clasen and Jens Kjeldgaard-Christiansen, '"We Are Legion": Possession Myth as a Lens for Understanding Cultural and Psychological Evolution', *Evolutionary Behavioral Sciences*, 15/1 (2021), 1–9.

Bowen, Sesali, 'How Jason Blum Makes Horror Movies with a Message', *Nylon* (20 September 2019), *www.nylon.com/jason-blum-interview* (accessed 6 May 2020).

Box Office Mojo, '*Get Out*', *www.boxofficemojo.com/release/rl256280065/* (accessed 15 May 2020).

Bradley, Laura, 'This was the Decade Horror Got "Elevated"', *Vanity Fair* (17 December 2019), *www.vanityfair.com/hollywood/2019/12/rise-of-elevated-horror-decade-2010s/* (accessed 30 January 2021).

Bradshaw, Peter, 'Paranormal Activity', *Guardian* (25 November 2009), *www.theguardian.com/film/2009/nov/25/paranormal-activity-review* (accessed 21 June 2020).

Bray, Mark, *Antifa: The Anti-Fascist Handbook* (Melbourne: Melbourne University Publishing, 2017).

Brown, Bridget, *They Know Us Better than We Know Ourselves: The History and Politics of Alien Abduction* (New York: New York University Press, 2007).

Brown, Nathan Robert, *The Complete Idiot's Guide to Zombies* (New York: Penguin, 2010).

Buckmaster, Luke, 'Paranormal Activity 4 Movie Review: Milking the Digicam Cash Cow', *Crikey Inq* (29 October 2012), *https://blogs.crikey.com.au/cinetology/2012/10/29/paranormal-activity-4-movie-review-milking-the-digicam-cash-cow/* (accessed 22 June 2020).

Buckwalter, Ian, 'Shorter is Scarier: Why Horror Anthologies Need to Make a Comeback', *The Atlantic* (8 October 2012), *www.theatlantic.com/entertainment/archive/2012/10/shorter-is-scarier-why-horror-anthologies-need-to-make-a-comeback/263312/* (accessed 25 June 2020).

Buhle, Paul, and Robin D. G. Kelley, 'Allies of a Different Sort: Jews and Blacks in the American Left', in Jack Salzman and Cornel West (eds), *Struggles in the Promised Land: Towards a History of Black-Jewish Relations in the United States* (New York: Oxford University Press, 1997), pp. 197–229.

Bukszpan, David, 'Here's Why R-Rated Horror Movies are Making a Comeback on the Big Screen', *CNBC* (28 October 2017), *www.cnbc.com/2017/10/28/heres-why-r-rated-horror-movies-are-making-a-comeback-on-the-big-screen.html/* (accessed 7 February 2020).

Bumbray, Chris, 'Review: *Paranormal Activity 4*', *Jo Blo* (19 October 2012), *www.joblo.com/movie-news/review-paranormal-activity-4* (accessed 21 June 2020).

Burleson, Donald R., 'The Alien', in S. T. Joshi (ed.), *Icons of Horror and the Supernatural: An Encyclopedia of Our Worst Nightmares* (Westport CO: Greenwood Press, 2007), pp. 1–30.

Business World, 'Horror on a Shoestring: The Blum Manifesto', (19 September 2017), *www.bworldonline.com/horror-shoestring-blum-manifesto/* (accessed 7 February 2020).

Butler, Judith, *Frames of War: When is Life Grievable?* (London: Verso, 2009).

Campbell, John Edward, 'Alien(ating) Ideology and the American Media: Apprehending the Alien Image in Television through *The X-Files*', *International Journal of Cultural Studies*, 4/3 (2001), 327–47.

Cantor, Joanne, 'Fright Reactions to Mass Media', in Jennings Bryant and Dolf Zillmann (eds), *Media Effects: Advances in Theory and Research* (second edition) (Mahwah NJ: Lawrence Erlbaum Associates, Publishers, 2002), pp. 287–306.

Caponi, Gena Dagel, *Signifyin(g), Sanctifyin', & Slam Dunking: A Reader in African American Expressive Culture* (Amherst MA: University of Massachusetts Press, 1999).

Carleton, R. Nicholas, 'Fear of the Unknown: One Fear to Rule them All?' *Journal of Anxiety Disorders*, 41 (2016), 5–21.

Cassidy, Sarah, 'The Online Generation: Four in 10 Children are Addicted to the Internet', *Independent* (9 May 2014), *www.independent.co.uk/life-style/gadgets-and-tech/news/the-online-generation-four-in-10-children-are-addicted-to-the-internet-9341159.html* (accessed 25 June 2020).

Cavanagh, Patrick, '*Happy Death Day* Director Addresses the Franchise's Possible Future', *ComicBook* (15 August 2019), *https://comicbook.com/horror/news/happy-death-day-3-details-christopher-landon-sequel-details/* (accessed 4 November 2019).

Cavanaugh, Shannon E., and Paula Fomby, 'Family Instability in the Lives of American Children', *Annual Review of Sociology*, 45 (2019), 493–513.

Cherry, Brigid, *Horror* (New York: Routledge, 2009).

Chesnais, François, *Finance Capital Today: Corporations and Banks in the Lasting Global Slump* (Leiden: Brill, 2016).

Childs, Ben, '*Chronicle*'s Found-Footage Fetish Weakens Its Superhero Powers', *Guardian* (27 January 2012), *www.theguardian.com/film/filmblog/2012/jan/27/chronicle-found-footage-superhero-powers* (accessed 21 May 2020).

Church, David, *Post-Horror: Art, Genre and Cultural Elevation* (Edinburgh: Edinburgh University Press, 2021).

Cieply, Michael, 'Film on a Tiny Budget Earns Big Money', *New York Times* (26 October 2009), C2.

— 'Thriller on Tour Lets Fans Decide on the Next Stop', *New York Times* (20 September 2009), *www.nytimes.com/2009/09/21/business/media/21paranormal.html/* (accessed 30 January 2021).

Clark, Jerome, *Extraordinary Encounters: An Encyclopedia of Extraterrestrials and Otherworldly Beings* (Santa Barbara CA: ABC-CLIO, 2000).

Clarke, Meredith, 'The First Purge is the Perfect Political Commentary on the Trump Era', *NBC News* (7 July 2018), *www.nbcnews.com/think/opinion/first-purge-perfect-political-commentary-trump-era-ncna889511/* (accessed 20 January 2021).

Clasen, Mathias, 'Monster Evolve: A Biocultural Approach to Horror Stories', *Review of General Psychology*, 16/2 (2012), 222–9.

— *Why Horror Seduces* (New York: Oxford University Press, 2017).

— and Todd K. Platts, 'Evolution and Slasher Films', in Dirk Vanderbeke and Brett Cooke (eds), *Evolution and Popular Narrative* (Boston: Brill, 2019), pp. 23–42.

Clover, Carol J., 'Her Body, Himself: Gender in the Slasher Film', *Representation*, 20, 187–228.

— *Men, Women, and Chainsaws: Gender in the Modern Horror Film* (Princeton NJ: Princeton University Press, 2015).

Cohen, Ralph, 'History and Genre', *New Literary History*, 17/2 (1986), 203–18.

Collis, Clark, 'Jamie Lee Curtis Says the new *Halloween* is a #MeToo Movie', *Entertainment Weekly* (27 September 2018), *https://ew.com/movies/2018/09/27/ jamie-lee-curtis-halloween-metoo/* (accessed 15 January 2021).

Connell, R. W., *Masculinities* (Cambridge: Polity Press, 2005).

Conrich, Ian, 'Puzzles, Contraptions and the Highly Elaborate Moment: The Inevitability of Death in the Grand Slasher Narratives of the *Final Destination* and *Saw* Series of Films', in Wickham Clayton (ed.), *Style and Form in the Hollywood Slasher Film* (London: Palgrave Macmillan, 2015), pp. 105–17.

Constantineau, Sara, '*Black Christmas*: The Slasher Film was Made in Canada', *CineAction*, 82–83 (2010), 58–63.

Cooper, Marianne, and Allison J. Pugh, 'Families Across the Income Spectrum: A Decade in Review', *Journal of Marriage and Family*, 82/1 (2020), 272–99.

Corrigan, Timothy, 'Auteurs and the New Hollywood', in Jon Lewis (ed.), *The New American Cinema* (Durham NC: Duke University Press, 1999), pp. 38–63.

Creed, Barbara, *The Monstrous-Feminine: Film, Feminism, Psychoanalysis* (New York: Routledge, 1993).

Cronin, Claire, 'Transcendental Repair: The Ghost Film as Family Melodrama', *Horror Studies*, 10/1 (2019), 27–43.

Crook, Simon, '*Paranormal Activity* Review', *Empire* (22 October 2009), *www.empireonline.com/movies/reviews/paranormal-activity-review/* (accessed 21 June 2020).

Crucchiola, Jordan, 'The New Master of Horror', *Vulture* (3 March 2017), *www.vulture.com/2017/03/get-outs-jason-blum-is-the-new-master-of-horror.html/* (accessed 30 January 2021).

— 'Let's Recap the Twisted Mythology of *The Purge*', *Vulture* (2 July 2018), *www.vulture.com/2018/07/lets-recap-the-twisted-mythology-of-the-purge.html/* (accessed 20 January 2021).

D'Alessandro, Anthony, 'Blumhouse has Plenty to Smile about as *Happy Death Day* Scares Up $26M+ Opening', *Deadline* (15 October 2017), *https://deadline.com/2017/10/happy-death-day-blade-runner-2049-weekend-box-office-the-foreigner-jackie-chan-1202187771/* (accessed 10 November 2019).

D'Alessandro, David, 'How Miramax & Blumhouse Brought *Halloween* Back from the Dead', *Deadline* (22 October 2018), *https://deadline.com/2018/10/ halloween-jamie-lee-curtis-john-carpenter-box-office-reboot-blumhouse-miramax-1202486748/* (accessed 1 January 2021).

Derry, Charles, *The Suspense Thriller: Films in the Shadow of Alfred Hitchcock* (Jefferson NC: McFarland, 2001).

Dika, Vera, *Games of Terror:* Halloween, Friday the 13th, *and the Films of the Stalker Cycle* (Toronto: Farleigh Dickinson University Press, 1990).

Dixon, Wheeler Winston, *A History of Horror* (New Brunswick NJ: Rutgers University Press, 2010).

Donaldson, Mike, 'What is Hegemonic Masculinity?', *Theory and Society*, 22/5 (1993), 643–57.

Donnelly, Mike, 'Blumhouse Productions Hit with Layoffs, Pay Cuts for Senior Leadership (EXCLUSIVE)', *Variety* (10 April 2020), *https://variety.com/2020/film/news/blumhouse-productions-layoffs-coronavirus1234577187/* (accessed 31 August 2020).

Drabble, John, 'From White Supremacy to White Power: The FBI, COINTELPRO-WHITE HATE, and the Nazification of the Ku Klux Klan in the 1970s', *American Studies*, 48/3 (2007), 49–74.

Driscoll, Catherine, *Teen Film: A Critical Introduction* (New York: Berg, 2011).

Dumas, Chris, 'Horror and Psychoanalysis: A Primer', in Harry M. Benshoff (ed.), *A Companion to the Horror Film* (London: Wiley-Blackwell, 2014), pp. 21–37.

Edwards, Griffin Sims, and Stephen Rushin, 'The Effect of President Trump's Election on Hate Crimes', *Social Science Research Network* (14 January 2018), *https://papers.ssrn.com/sol3/papers.cfm?abstract_id=3102652* (accessed 12 May 2020).

Eisenberg, Eric, 'How Horror Studio Blumhouse Decides Whether or Not a Movie Will Be R-Rated', *Cinema Blend* (12 January 2018), *www.cinemablend.com/news/2063170/how-horror-studio-blumhouse-decides-whether-or-not-a-movie-will-be-r-rated/* (accessed 7 February 2020).

Elberse, Anita, 'Jason Blum's Blumhouse Productions', *Harvard Business Review* (18 May 2018).

Ellis, Joseph J., *His Excellency: George Washington* (New York: Vintage Books, 2005).

Everhart, Spencer, 'Framework of Fear: The Postmodern Aesthetic of *Paranormal Activity 2*', *Cinethesia*, 1/1 (2012), 1–9.

Fagan, Jay, and Glen Palm, *Fathers and Early Childhood Programs* (Clifton Park NY: Delmar Learning, 2004).

Fanon, Frantz, *Black Skin, White Masks* (New York: Grove Press, Inc., 1967).

Fear, David, 'What Do *The Purge* Movies Say About Us?', *Rolling Stone* (2 July 2018), *www.rollingstone.com/movies/movie-features/what-do-the-purge-movies-say-about-us-666940/* (accessed 20 January 2021).

Feldman, Keith P., 'Representing Permanent War: Black Power's Palestine and the End(s) of Civil Rights', *New Centennial Review*, 8/2 (2008), 193–231.

Fisher, Mark, *Capitalist Realism: Is There No Alternative?* (Winchester: Zero Books, 2009).

Fitzgerald, Lauren, 'Female Gothic and the Institutionalisation of Gothic Studies', in Diana Wallace and Andrew Smith (eds), *The Female Gothic: New Directions* (New York: Palgrave Macmillan, 2009), p. 13–25.

Fleming Jr, Mike, 'Universal Makes First-Look Deal with Jason Blum of *Paranormal Activity* and *Insidious*', *Deadline* (29 June 2011), *https://deadline. com/2011/06/universal-in-first-look-deal-with-paranormal-activity-and-insidious-producer-jason-blum-144401/* (accessed 30 January 2021).

— 'Blumhouse Launches Multi-Platform Arm BH-Tilt', *Deadline* (9 September 2014), *https://deadline.com/2014/09/blumhouse-launches-multi-platform-arm-bh-tilt-831985/* (accessed 7 February 2020).

— 'Universal, Blumhouse Extend to Decade-Long Film, TV Production Pact', *Deadline* (20 July 2014), *https://deadline.com/2014/07/universal-blumhouse-extend-to-decade-long-production-pact-806978/* (accessed 30 January 2021).

— 'Blumhouse Launches Indie TV Studio With ITV; *The Purge* becomes Series, Roger Ailes Fox News Series Lands at Showtime', *Deadline* (4 April 2017), *https://deadline.com/2017/04/blumhouse-the-purge-roger-ailes-fox-news-tv-series-showtime-itv-1202060793/* (accessed 30 January 2021).

— 'How Jason Blum Honed His Micro-Budget Blockbuster Formula – *Deadline* Disruptors', *Deadline* (16 May 2017), *https://deadline.com/2017/05/jason-blum-blumhouse-jordan-peele-disruptors-interview-news-1202094624/* (accessed 1 January 2021).

Fletcher, Rosie, 'How Jason Blum Changed Horror Movies', *Den of Geek* (3 March 2020), *www.denofgeek.com/movies/how-jason-blum-changed-horror-movies/* (accessed 4 May 2020).

Fleury, James, Bryan Hikari Hartzheim and Stephen Mamber, 'Introduction: The Franchise Era', in James Fleury, Bryan Hikari Hartzheim, Stephen Mamber (eds), *The Franchise Era: Managing Media in the Digital Economy* (Edinburgh: Edinburgh University Press, 2019), p. 1–28.

Forman, Seth, *Blacks in the Jewish Mind: A Crisis of Liberalism* (New York: New York University Press, 1998).

Foutch, Haleigh, 'Jason Blum on *The First Purge*, the Future of the Franchise and *Halloween*'s R Rating', *Collider* (2 October 2018), *https://collider.com/jason-blum-interview-first-purge-halloween/* (accessed 7 February 2020).

Frederick, Candice, 'How *The Purge* Became the Most Unexpectedly Important Horror Franchise of the Decade', *Slash Film* (4 July 2018), *www.slashfilm.com/evolution-of-the-purge/* (accessed 7 February 2020).

Freer, Ian, '*Black Christmas* (2019) Review', *Empire* (13 December 2019), *www.empireonline.com/movies/reviews/black-christmas-2019/* (accessed 17 June 2020).

Freud, Sigmund, 'The Uncanny', in Vincent B. Leitch *et al.* (eds), *Norton Anthology of Theory and Criticism* (New York and London: W. W. Norton & Company, 2001), pp. 929–52.

Garrahan, Matthew, 'Master of Thrills on a Shoestring', *Financial Times* (31 May 2011), *www.ft.com/content/bc7bc3e6-8baf-11e0-a725-00144feab49a/* (accessed 30 January 2021).

Gates Jr, Henry Louis, 'The "Blackness of Blackness": A Critique of the Sign and the Signifying Monkey', *Critical Inquiry*, 9/4 (1983), 685–723.

— *The Signifying Monkey: A Theory of African-American Literary Criticism* (Oxford: Oxford University Press, 1988).

Gilbey, Ryan, 'Commission Us: "Found footage" – the Discovery that Disappeared Again', *Guardian* (14 October 2010), *www.theguardian.com/film/film-blog/2010/oct/14/found-footage-blair-witch-project* (accessed 25 June 2020).

Gilchrist, Todd, '*Paranormal Activity*, *The Purge*'s Jason Blum on Fixing a Film Series – Even When it's a Hit', *Forbes* (7 April 2014), *www.forbes.com/sites/toddgilchrist/2014/04/07/paranormal-activity-purge-jason-blum-blumhouse-marked-ones-blu-ray/#2816694f67bc/* (accessed 7 February 2020).

Giles, Jeff, '*Happy Death Day* is Familiar but Fun', *Rotten Tomatoes* (12 October 2017), *https://editorial.rottentomatoes.com/article/happy-death-day-is-familiar-but-fun/* (accessed 10 November 2019).

Giroux, Jack, 'You Should Have Left Producer Jason Blum on the Future of Movie Theaters and which Filmmakers Fit the Blumhouse Mold [Interview]', *Slash Film* (25 June 2020), *www.slashfilm.com/jason-blum-interview/* (accessed 30 January 2021).

Gleiberman, Owen, 'As *Blair Witch* Flops, is the Found-Footage Horror Film Over?', *Variety* (18 September 2016), *https://variety.com/2016/film/columns/blair-witch-is-the-found-footage-horror-film-over-1201864069/* (accessed 10 April 2019).

— '*Black Christmas*: Film Review', *Variety* (12 December 2019), *www.variety.com/2019/film/reviews/black-christmas-review-imogen-poots-1203434053* (accessed 17 June 2020).

Glenn, Susan A., 'Funny, You Don't Look Jewish', in Susan A. Glenn and Naomi B. Sokoloff (eds), *Boundaries of Jewish Identity* (Seattle WA: University of Washington Press, 2011), pp. 64–90.

Gordon, Alex 'Making America Gory Again: How the *Purge* Films Troll Trumpism', *Guardian* (4 July 2018), *www.theguardian.com/film/2018/jul/04/how-the-purge-trolls-trumps-america-jason-blum-first-purge/* (accessed 20 January 2021).

Grant, Barry Keith, *Monster Cinema* (New Brunswick NJ: Rutgers University Press, 2018).

Graser, Marc, 'Hollywood Rethinks Its Scare Flair . . .', *Variety* (30 July–5 August 2007), 1, 37.

Greenberg, Cheryl, *Troubling the Waters* (Princeton NJ: Princeton University Press, 2006).

Grindon, Leger, 'Cycles and Clusters: The Shape of Film Genre History', in Barry Keith Grant (ed.), *Film Genre Reader IV* (Austin TX: University of Texas Press, 2012), pp. 42–59.

Guerrasio, Jason, 'How the Company Behind 2 of the Year's Biggest Movies is Blowing Up the Hollywood Playbook', *Business Insider* (1 March 2017), *www.businessinsider.com/blumhouse-productions-get-out-split-2017-2/* (accessed 7 February 2020).

— 'Horror Movie Juggernaut Blumhouse is Jumping into Podcasting with a Series for iHeartRadio', *Business Insider* (10 October 2019), *www.businessinsider.com/blumhouse-making-original-horror-podcasts-for-iheartradio-details-2019-10/* (accessed 30 January 2021).

— '*Us* and *BlacKkKlansman* Producer Jason Blum's Plan to Take Over Hollywood is Simple: Stay Independent', *Business Insider* (16 April 2019), *www.businessinsider.com/jason-blum-on-staying-independent-in-hollywood-2019-4/* (accessed 7 February 2020).

Guerrero, Ed., 'A Circus of Dreams and Lies: The Black Film Wave at Middle Age', in Jon Lewis (ed.), *The New American Cinema* (Durham NC: Duke University Press, 1999), pp. 328–52.

Guthrie, Marisa, and Tatiana Siegel, 'From *American Horror Story* to *Walking Dead*: How Horror Took Over Hollywood', *Hollywood Reporter* (9 October 2013), *www.hollywoodreporter.com/news/american-horror-story-walking-dead-645007* (accessed 4 May 2020).

Hamad, Hannah, *Postfeminism and Paternity in Contemporary U.S. Film: Framing Fatherhood* (New York: Routledge, 2013).

Hamblin, Jon, '*Paranormal Activity* Reviews', *Rotten Tomatoes, www.rottentomatoes.com/m/Paranormal_Activity/reviews* (accessed 15 January 2021).

Hart, Adam Charles, 'Millennial Fears: Abject Horror in a Transnational Context', in Harry M. Benshoff (ed.), *A Companion to the Horror Film* (London: Wiley-Blackwell, 2014), pp. 329–45.

— *Monstrous Forms: Moving Image Horror Across Media* (New York: Oxford University Press, 2020).

Harcourt, Bernard, *Exposed: Desire and Disobedience in the Digital Age* (Cambridge MA: Harvard University Press, 2015), pp. 1–28.

Harvey, Dennis '*Dark Skies*', *Variety* (4 March 2013), 18.

Heiland, Donna, *Gothic and Gender: An Introduction* (Malden MA: Blackwell, 2004).

Hertz, Barry, 'Producer Jason Blum is Revolutionizing Horror Movies – for Better or Worse', *Globe and Mail* (5 June 2017), *www.theglobeandmail.com/arts/film/producer-jason-blum-is-revolutionizing-horror-movies-for-better-or-worse/article25400806/* (accessed 7 May 2020).

Hess, Amanda, 'The Shaming of Izzy Laxamana', *Slate* (12 June 2015), *https://slate.com/technology/2015/06/izabel-laxamana-a-tragic-case-in-the-growing-genre-of-parents-publicly-shaming-their-children.html* (accessed 27 June 2020).

Hill, Annette, *Paranormal Media: Audiences, Spirits and Magic in Popular Culture* (New York: Routledge, 2010).

Hill, Evan, *et al.*, 'How George Floyd Was Killed in Police Custody', *New York Times* (31 May 2020), *www.nytimes.com/2020/05/31/us/george-floyd-investigation.html* (accessed 5 July 2020).

Hills, Matt, and Steven Jay Schneider, '"The Devil Made Me Do It!" Representing Evil and Disarticulating Mind/Body in the Supernatural Serial Killer Film', in Martin F. Norden (ed.), *The Changing Face of Evil in Film and Television* (New York: Rodopi, 2007), pp. 71–87.

Hoerl, Kristen, 'Cinematic Jujitsu: Resisting White Hegemony through the American Dream in Spike Lee's *Malcolm X*', *Communication Studies*, 59/4 (2008), 355–70.

Hong, Sun-ha, *Technologies of Speculation: The Limits of Knowledge in a Data-Driven Society* (New York: New York University Press, 2020).

Horn, John, 'The Haunted History of *Paranormal Activity*', *Los Angeles Times* (20 September 2009), *www.latimes.com/zap-haunted-history-paranormal-activity-story.html/* (accessed 30 January 2021).

— 'Shifting Gears', *Los Angeles Times* (12 September 2013), D1, D6.

— 'Trying to Make a Killing for Less', *Los Angeles Times* (6 June 2013), D1, D10–D11.

Hough, Peter, *Understanding Global Security* (third edition) (New York: Routledge, 2013).

Humphreys, James, 'The Haunted House That Blum Built – How an Indie Producer Saved Horror and Changed Hollywood', *Cineramble* (20 October 2018), *http://cineramble.com/2018/10/the-haunted-house-that-blum-built-how-an-indie-producer-saved-horror-and-changed-hollywood/* (accessed 7 February 2020).

Hunter, Rob, '*Black Christmas* Review: Good Intentions, Questionable Execution', *Film School Rejects* (14 December 2019), *https://filmschoolrejects.com/black-christmas-2019-review/* (accessed 20 June 2020).

Hutchings, Peter, *The Horror Film* (New York: Pearson, 2004).

Ito, Robert, 'A Slasher Film for #MeToo', *New York Times* (15 December 2019), AR17.

Jackson, Kimberly, *Gender and the Nuclear Family in Twenty-First-Century Horror* (New York: Palgrave Macmillan, 2016).

Joho, Jess, 'Why 2018's *Halloween* is the Slasher Movie Made for the #MeToo Era', *Mashable* (26 October 2018), *https://mashable.com/article/2018-halloween-reinvents-final-girl-feminist-horror-trope/* (accessed 15 January 2021).

Jones, Steve, *Torture Porn: Popular Horror After Saw* (New York: Palgrave Macmillan, 2015).

Joseph, Peniel E., *Waiting 'Til the Midnight Hour: A Narrative History of Black Power in America* (New York: Owl Books, 2011).

Kahn, Paul W., *Finding Ourselves at the Movies: Philosophy for a New Generation* (New York: Columbia University Press, 2013).

Kawin, Bruce F., *Horror and the Horror Film* (London: Anthem Press, 2012).

Kazarian, Richard, and Robert Weisbord, *Israel in the Black Perspective* (Westport CT: Praeger, 1985).

Kelley, Sonaiya, 'An Oral History of *The Purge* Franchise: From Micro-Horror Breakout to Trump-Era Cautionary Tale', *Los Angeles Times* (4 July 2018), *www.latimes.com/entertainment/movies/la-et-mn-the-purge-series-oral-history-20180704-story.html/* (accessed 20 January 2021).

Kellner, Douglas, 'Poltergeists, Gender, and Class in the Age of Reagan and Bush', in David E. James and Rick Berg (eds), *The Hidden Foundation: Cinema and the Question of Class* (Minneapolis MN: University of Minnesota Press, 1996), pp. 217–39.

Kendrick, James, 'The Terrible, Horrible Desire to Know: Post-9/11 Horror Remakes, Reboots, Sequels and Prequels', in Terence McSweeney (ed.), *American Cinema in the Shadow of 9/11* (Edinburgh: Edinburgh University Press, 2016), p. 249–68.

Kenigsberg, Ben, '*Black Christmas* Review: Horror for a New Era of Campus Debates', *New York Times* (12 December 2019), *www.nytimes.com/2019/12/12/movies/black-christmas-review.html* (accessed 17 June 2020).

Kennedy, Michael, 'Why *Black Christmas*' Reviews Are so Negative', *Screen Rant* (14 December 2019), *www.screenrant.com/black-christmas-2019-movie-reviews-bad-reason/* (accessed 30 June 2020).

— 'Every Insidious Movie Ranked, Worst to Best', *Screen Rant* (12 January 2020), *https://screenrant.com/insidious-movies-ranked-best-worst/* (accessed 31 January 2021).

Kim, Jonathan, 'How the *Purge* Horror Franchise became a Successful, Unlikely Political Allegory', *Medium* (29 June 2018), *https://medium.com/rethinkreviews/how-the-purge-horror-franchise-became-a-successful-unlikely-political-allegory-5cb2100f8247/* (accessed 20 January 2021).

Kimmel, Michael, *Angry White Men: American Masculinity at the End of an Era* (New York: Nation Books, 2017).

— *Manhood in America: A Cultural History* (fourth edition) (Oxford: Oxford University Press, 2017).

Kirk, Neal, 'Networked Spectrality: *In Memorium, Pulse* and Beyond', in Linnie Blake and Xavier Aldana Reyes (eds), *Digital Horror: Haunted Technologies, Network Panic and the Found Footage Phenomenon* (London: I. B. Tauris, 2016), pp. 54–65.

Kit, Borys, '*Get Out* Producer Jason Blum on Hollywood's Leadership Crisis and Missing Out on *La La Land*', *Hollywood Reporter* (16 March 2017), *www.hollywoodreporter.com/heat-vision/get-producer-jason-blum-hollywoods-leadership-crisis-missing-la-la-land-985861/* (accessed 7 February 2020).

Konda, Kelly, 'Box Office: Blumhouse's Secret to Success is Astonishingly Simple, yet Nearly Impossible to Emulate', *We Minored in Film* (17 October 2017), *https://weminoredinfilm.com/2017/10/17/box-office-blumhouses-secret-to-succcess-is-astonishingly-simple-yet-nearly-impossible-to-emulate/* (accessed 7 February 2020).

Kord, T. S., *Little Horrors: How Cinema's Evil Children Play on Our Guilt* (Jefferson NC: McFarland, 2016).

Kupers, Terry A., 'Toxic Masculinity as a Barrier to Mental Health Treatment in Prison', *Journal of Clinical Psychology*, 61/6 (2005), 713–24.

Kvaran, Kara M., '"You're All Doomed!" A Socioeconomic Analysis of Slasher Films', *Journal of American Studies*, 50/4 (2016), 953–70.

Lackner, Eden Lee, 'Grays', in Michael M. Levy and Farah Mendlesohn (eds), *Aliens in Popular Culture* (Santa Barbara CA: ABC-CLIO, 2019), pp. 135–7.

LaRossa, Ralph, *The Modernization of Fatherhood: A Social and Political History* (Chicago IL: University of Chicago Press, 1997).

Leadbeater, Alex, '*The Purge* Timeline Explained: 2014–2040', *Screen Rant* (6 July 2018), *https://screenrant.com/purge-movie-timeline-explained/* (accessed 20 January 2021).

Lee, Benjamin, 'Why Horror Super-producer Jason Blum has Turned to Publishing', *Guardian* (1 July 2017), *www.theguardian.com/books/2017/jul/01/jason-blum-horror-publishing-get-out-purge-feral/* (accessed 30 January 2021).

— '*Black Christmas* Review – Woke Slasher Remake is an Unholy, Unscary Mess', *Guardian* (13 December 2019), *www.theguardian.com/film/2019/dec/12/black-christmas-review-remake-unscary-mess* (accessed 8 May 2020).

Leeder, Murray, *Horror Film: A Critical Introduction* (New York: Bloomsbury Academic, 2018).

Leonard, Suzanne, *Fatal Attraction* (Malden MA: Blackwell, 2009).

Lincoln, Ross, 'Blumhouse and the Calculus of Low Budget Horror – Produced

By', *Deadline* (30 May 2015), *https://deadline.com/2015/05/blumhouse-panel-produced-by-conference-1201435034/* (accessed 7 February 2020).

Loewen, James W., *Sundown Towns: A Hidden Dimension of American Racism* (New York: Touchstone, 2005).

Luther, Catherine A., Carolyn Ringer Lepre and Naeemah Clark, *Diversity in U.S. Mass Media* (Hoboken NJ: Wiley-Blackwell, 2017).

Lyon, David, 'Surveillance Studies: Understanding Visibility, Mobility and the Phonetic Fix', *Surveillance and Society*, 1/1 (2002), 1–7.

Lyons, Suzanne, *Indie Film Producing: The Craft of Low Budget Filmmaking* (Burlington MA: Focal Press, 2012).

MacFarquhar, Neil, Alan Feuer and Adam Goldman, 'Federal Arrests Show No Sign that Antifa Plotted Protests', *New York Times* (11 June 2020), *www.nytimes.com/2020/06/11/us/antifa-protests-george-floyd.html/* (accessed 20 January 2021).

Mann, Craig Ian, 'Death and Dead-End Jobs: Independent Horror and the Great Recession', in Pete Bennett and Julian McDougall (eds), *Popular Culture and the Austerity Myth: Hard Times Today* (New York: Routledge, 2017), pp. 175–88.

Martin Jr, Waldo E., '"Nation Time!": Black Nationalism, The Third World, and Jews', in Jack Salzman and Cornel West (eds), *Struggles in the Promised Land* (New York: Oxford Press, 1997), pp. 341–55.

Martina, Michael, Jarrett Renshaw and Tim Reid, 'How Trump Allies Have Organized and Promoted Anti-Lockdown Protests', *Reuters* (22 April 2020), *www.reuters.com/article/us-health-coronavirus-trump-protests-idUSKCN2233ES/* (accessed 20 January 2021).

Masters, Kim, 'Jason Blum's Crowded Movie Morgue', *Hollywood Reporter* (7 March 2014), *www.hollywoodreporter.com/news/jason-blums-crowded-movie-morgue-683212/* (accessed 7 February 2020).

— 'Blumhouse Plans Film Shoot on Universal Lot Despite Insurance Risks', *Hollywood Reporter* (18 May 2020), *www.hollywoodreporter.com/news/blumhouse-plans-film-shoot-universal-lot-insurance-risks-1294936* (accessed 30 January 2021).

McAndrew, Francis T., and Sara S. Koehnke, 'On the Nature of Creepiness', *New Ideas in Psychology*, 43 (2016), 10–5.

— 'The Psychology, Geography, and Architecture of Horror: How Places Creep Us Out,' *Evolutionary Studies in Imaginative Culture*, 4/2 (2020), 47–62.

McClintock, Pamela, 'Mega-Profits for Micro-Pic', *Daily Variety* (26 October 2009), 1, 23.

— 'Trio's New Alliance', *Daily Variety* (5 February 2010), 1, 12.

— '*Insidious* is the Most Profitable Film of 2011', *Hollywood Reporter* (26 April 2011), *www.hollywoodreporter.com/news/insidious-is-profitable-film-2011-182335/* (accessed 1 January 2021).

McCollum, Victoria, 'Introduction', in Victoria McCollum (ed), *Make America Hate Again: Trump-Era Horror and the Politics of Fear* (New York: Routledge, 2019), pp. 1–19.

McGirr, Lisa, *Suburban Warriors: The Origins of the New American Right* (Princeton NJ: Princeton University Press, 2001).

McMurdo, Shellie, *Blood on the Lens: North American Found Footage Horror Cinema and Cultural Trauma* (Edinburgh: Edinburgh University Press, forthcoming).

McNary, Dave, '"Deli" on Plate with Pic Pair', *Daily Variety* (8 May 2006), 1, 13.

Ménard, A. Dana, Angela Weaver and Christine Cabrera, '"There are Certain Rules that One Must Abide by": Predictors of Mortality in Slasher Films', *Sexuality and Culture*, 23/2 (2019), 621–40.

Mendelson, Scott, 'Box Office: After *Split* and *Get Out*, *Happy Death Day* may get a Blumhouse Bump', *Forbes* (9 October 2017), *www.forbes.com/sites/scottmendelson/2017/10/09/box-office-after-split-and-get-out-happy-death-day-may-get-blumhouse-bump/#6fe7ace36051/* (accessed 7 February 2020).

— 'Box Office: Why *Insidious* is Hollywood's Most Underrated Horror Franchise', *Forbes* (29 October 2020), *www.forbes.com/sites/scottmendelson/2020/10/29/patrick-wilson-will-direct-insidious-5-for-blumhouse/?sh=4a18fe695942* (accessed 16 January 2021).

Meslow, Scott, '12 Years After *Blair Witch*, When Will the Found-Footage Horror Fad End?', *Atlantic* (6 January 2012), *www.theatlantic.com/entertainment/archive/2012/01/12-years-after-blair-witch-when-will-the-found-footage-horror-fad-end/250950/* (accessed 20 April 2020).

Meta Critic, 'Critic Reviews for *Get Out*', *www.metacritic.com/movie/get-out/critic-reviews* (accessed 15 May 2020).

Meyers, Helene, *Femicidal Fears: Narratives of the Female Gothic Experience* (Albany NY: State University of New York Press, 2001).

Michasiw, Kim Ian, 'Some Stations of Suburban Gothic', in Robert Martin and Eric Savoy (eds), *American Gothic: New Interventions in a National Narrative* (Iowa City IA: University of Iowa Press, 1998), pp. 237–57.

Milan, Atif, and Amir Sufi, *House of Debt: How They (and You) Caused the Great Recession and How We Can Prevent It from Happening Again* (Chicago IL: University of Chicago Press, 2015).

Miller, Cynthia J., 'Coming Home to Horror in *Insidious: The Last Key*', in Cynthia J. Miller and A. Bowdoin Van Riper (eds), *Horror Comes Home: Essays on Hauntings, Possessions and Other Domestic Terrors in Cinema* (Jefferson NC: McFarland, 2020), pp. 206–18.

Mohr, Ian, 'Par Drawing a Blum Role,' *Daily Variety* (20 May 2005), 1, 26.

Monagle, Matthew, 'The Politics of Slasher *Black Christmas*', *Austin Chronicle* (13 December 2019), *www.austinchronicle.com/screens/2019-12-13/the-politics-of-slasher-black-christmas* (accessed 20 June 2020).

Moore, Roger, '*Dark Skies* is Light on Originality', *Pittsburgh Post* (25 February 2013), C8.

Morgan, Kenneth, 'George Washington and the Problem of Slavery', *Journal of American Studies*, 34/2 (2000), 279–301.

Morrison, Cary, 'Creature Conflict: Man, Monster and the Metaphor of Intractable Social Conflict', in Paul L. Yoder and Peter Mario Kreuter (eds), *Monsters and the Monstrous: Myths and Metaphors of Enduring Evil* (Oxford: Inter-Disciplinary Press, 2004), pp. 167–75.

Mulvey, Laura, *Visual and Other Pleasures* (New York: Palgrave Macmillan, 2009).

Murphy, Bernice M., '"It's Not the House That's Haunted": Demons, Debt, and the Family in Peril Formula in Recent Horror Cinema', in Murray Leeder (ed.), *Cinematic Ghosts: Haunting and Spectrality from Silent Cinema to the Digital Era* (New York: Bloomsbury, 2015), pp. 235–51.

Nemiroff, Perri, '*Insidious Chapter 2* Producer Talks Micro-Budget Horror & *Amityville: Lost Tapes*', *Screen Rant* (9 September 2013), *https://screenrant.com/insidious-2-interview-jason-blum-amityville-lost-tapes/* (accessed 1 January 2021).

Neubeck, Kenneth, *When Welfare Disappears: The Case for Economic Human Rights* (New York: Routledge, 2006).

Newby, Richard, 'Why *Truth or Dare* Feels Like a Step Back for Blumhouse', *Hollywood Reporter* (15 April 2018), *www.hollywoodreporter.com/heat-vision/truth-dare-movie-is-a-step-back-blumhouse-1102803/* (accessed 7 February 2020).

Newton, Huey, *To Die for the People*, Toni Morrison (ed.), (San Francisco CA: City Lights Books, 2009).

Ng, Andrew Hock Soon, *Women and Domestic Space in Contemporary Gothic Narratives: The House as Subject* (New York: Palgrave Macmillan, 2015).

Ní Fhlainn, Sorcha, 'Sweet Bloody Vengeance: Class, Social Stigma and Servitude in the Slasher Genre', in Marlin C. Bates (ed.), *Hosting the Monster* (New York: Rodopi, 2008), pp. 179–96.

Nicholas, Alexandra Heller, *Found Footage Horror Films: Fear and the Appearance of Reality* (Jefferson NC: McFarland, 2014).

Nowell, Richard, *Blood Money: A History of the First Teen Slasher Film Cycle* (New York: Bloomsbury, 2011).

Nyren, Erin, 'Jason Blum Booed, Removed at L.A.'s Israel Film Festival after Anti-Trump Comments', *Variety* (6 November 2018), *https://variety.com/2018/film/news/jason-blum-booed-israel-film-festival-anti-trump-comments-1203021778/* (accessed 17 June 2020).

O'Malley, Sheila, '*Paranormal Activity: The Marked Ones*', *Roger Ebert* (4 January 2014), *www.rogerebert.com/reviews/paranormal-activity-the-marked-ones-2014* (accessed 21 June 2020).

Öhman, Arne, and Susan Mineka, 'Fears, Phobias, and Preparedness: Toward an Evolved Module of Fear and Fear Learning', *Psychological Review*, 108/3 (2001), 483–522.

Oleksinski, Johnny, 'How the *Purge* Team Created Its Terrifying Masks', *New York Post* (5 July 2018), *https://nypost.com/2018/07/05/how-the-purge-team-created-its-terrifying-masks/* (accessed 20 January 2021).

Olsen, Mark, '*Dark Skies* Above Suburbia', *Los Angeles Times* (23 February 2013), D8.

Olson, Christopher J., and CarrieLynn D. Reinhard, *Possessed Women, Haunted States: Cultural Tensions in Exorcism Cinema* (Lanham MD: Lexington Books, 2017).

Orr, Christopher, 'V/H/S: Is There Life Left in Found-Footage Horror', *The Atlantic* (5 October 2012), *www.theatlantic.com/entertainment/archive/2012/10/v-h-s-is-there-life-left-in-found-footage-horror/263272/* (accessed 21 May 2020).

Palley, Thomas, 'America's Flawed Paradigm: Macroeconomic Causes of the Financial Crisis and Great Recession', *Empirica*, 38/1 (2011), 3–17.

Parsons, Ben, 'The Blumhouse Model: Factory Filmmaking or Artist's Dream?', *The Boar* (20 September 2020), *https://theboar.org/2020/04/the-blumhouse-model-factory-filmmaking-or-artists-dream/* (accessed 6 May 2020).

Pascoe, C. J., and Tristan Bridges, 'Exploring Masculinities: History, Reproduction, Hegemony, and Dislocation', in C. J. Pascoe and Tristan Bridges (eds), *Exploring Masculinities: Identity, Inequality, Continuity, and Change* (New York: Oxford University Press, 2016), pp. 1–34.

Patches, Matt, 'Blumhouse has Never Produced a Theatrically Released Horror Movie Directed by a Woman – but Hopes to', *Polygon* (18 October 2018), *www.polygon.com/2018/10/17/17984162/halloween-blumhouse-female-director* (accessed 21 June 2020).

Patterson, Cleaver, *Don't Go Upstairs! A Room-by-Room Tour of the House in Horror Movies* (Jefferson NC: McFarland, 2020).

Peck, Jamie, Nik Theodore and Neil Brenner, 'Neoliberalism Resurgent? Market Rule after the Great Recession', *South Atlantic Quarterly*, 111/2 (2012), 265–88.

Peikert, Mark, 'Why Jason Blum Loves Making Horror', *Backstage* (22 October 2015), *www.backstage.com/magazine/article/jason-blum-loves-making-horror-9432/* (accessed 21 June 2020).

Petridis, Sotiris, *Anatomy of the Slasher Film: A Theoretical Analysis* (Jefferson NC: McFarland, 2019).

Pfefferman, Naomi, 'Spike Lee: The Jewish Character in *BlacKkKlansman* Added a Lot of "Complexity" to the Film', *Jewish Telegraph Agency* (12 February 2019), *www.jta.org/2019/02/12/culture/spike-lee-the-jewish-character-in-blackkklansman-added-a-lot-of-complexity-to-the-film* (accessed 15 May 2020).

Phillips, Kimberly, *War! What is it Good For?: Black Freedom Struggles and the U.S. Military from World War II to Iraq* (Chapel Hill NC: University of North Carolina Press).

Phillips-Fein, Kim, 'Conservatism: A State of the Field', *Journal of American History*, 98/3 (2011), 723–43.

Pinedo, Isabel Cristina, *Recreational Terror: Women and the Pleasures of Horror Film Viewing* (Albany NY: State University of New York Press, 1997).

— 'Postmodern Elements of the Contemporary Horror Film', in Stephen Prince (ed.), *The Horror Film* (New Brunswick NJ: Rutgers University Press, 2004), pp. 85–117.

Platts, Todd K., 'The New Horror Movie', in Brian Cogan and Thom Gencarelli (eds), *Baby Boomers and Popular Culture: An Inquiry into America's Most Powerful Generation* (Denver CO: Praeger, 2015), pp. 147–63.

— 'A Comparative Analysis of the Factors Driving Film Cycles: Italian and American Zombie Film Production, 1978–82', *Journal of Italian Cinema and Media Studies*, 5/2 (2017), 191–210.

— 'Unmade Undead: A Post-Mortem of the Post-9/11 Zombie Cycle', in James Fenwick, Kieran Foster and David Eldridge (eds), *Shadow Cinema: The Historical and Production Contexts of Unmade Films* (New York: Bloomsbury, 2020), pp. 251–66.

— 'Cut-Price Creeps: The Blumhouse Model of Horror Franchise Management', in Mark McKenna and William Proctor (eds), *Horror Franchise Cinema* (New York: Routledge, forthcoming).

— and Mathias Clasen, 'Scary Business: Horror at the North American Box Office, 2006–2016', *Frames Cinema Journal*, 11 (2017), *https://framescinemajournal. com/article/scary-business-horror-at-the-north-american-box-office-2006-2016/* (accessed 30 June 2020).

Pomerantz, Dorothy, 'The Triumph of Paranormal Activity', *Forbes* (18 October 2012), *www.forbes.com/sites/dorothypomerantz/2012/10/18/the-triumph-of-paranormal-activity/#5ebb1bc37b68* (accessed 25 June 2020).

Prigge, Matt, 'Blumhouse Head Jason Blum Says He's Definitely Not Making Any Virus Horror Movies After the Pandemic Ends', *Uproxx* (11 April 2020), *https://uproxx.com/movies/jason-blum-moviegoing-coronavirus/* (accessed 31 August 2020).

Ramella, Brynne, 'Blumhouse is on the Brink of Changing Horror Movies', *Screen Rant* (20 May 2020), *https://screenrant.com/blumhouse-horror-movie-changes-small-budget-after-coronavirus/* (accessed 30 January 2021).

Raymos, Dino-Ray, 'Get Out Director Jordan Peele on Divisiveness, Black Identity and the "White Savior"', *Deadline* (22 October 2017), *https://deadline.com/2017/10/jordan-peele-get-out-film-independent-forum-keynote-speaker-diversity-inclusion-1202192699/* (accessed 10 May 2020).

Recode Staff, '*Get Out* Producer Jason Blum Talks about Netflix, Low-Budget Movies and the Oscars', *Vox* (15 March 2018), *www.vox.com/2018/3/15/17118460/get-out-producer-jason-blum-talks-about-netflix-low-budget-movies-and-the-oscars/* (accessed 7 February 2020).

Redmon, Mike, 'Blumhouse Founder Jason Blum Believes the Coronavirus Will Have a Permanent Effect on How We Watch Movies', *Uproxx* (24 March 2020), *https://uproxx.com/movies/jason-blum-coronavirus-vod-movie-theater-release-window/* (accessed 31 August 2020).

Reed, Rex, '*Black Christmas* is a Crummy Excuse for a Horror Film', *Observer* (18 December 2019), *www.observer.com/2019/12/black-christmas-review-imogen-poots-rex-reed/* (accessed 30 June 2020).

Reeves, Aaron, Martin McKnee and David Stuckler, 'Economic Suicides in the Great Recession in Europe and North America', *British Journal of Psychiatry*, 205/3 (2014), 246–7.

Rester, Daniel, 'Ranked Insidious Films', *We Live Entertainment* (13 October 2020), *https://weliveentertainment.com/welivefilm/ranked-insidious-films-halloween-horror-month/* (accessed 31 January 2021).

Robinson, Chauncey K., '*The First Purge*: A Horror Movie Terrifyingly Close to Reality', *People's World* (3 July 2018), *www.peoplesworld.org/article/the-first-purge-a-horror-movie-terrifyingly-close-to-reality/* (accessed 20 January 2021).

Rockoff, Adam, *Going to Pieces: The Rise and Fall of the Slasher Film, 1978–1986* (Jefferson NC: McFarland, 2002).

Rosenberg, Jerry M., *The Concise Encyclopedia of the Great Recession 2007–2010* (second edition) (Lanham MD: Scarecrow Press, 2012).

Rosenberg, M. Jay, 'To Jewish Uncle Toms', in Michael E. Staub (ed.), *The Jewish 1960s: An American Sourcebook* (Waltham MA: Brandeis University Press, 2004), pp. 232–6.

Rubin, Gary E., 'African Americans and Israel', in Jack Salzman and Cornel West (eds), *Struggles in the Promised Land* (New York: Oxford Press, 1997), pp. 357–70.

Rubin, Rebecca, 'How Blumhouse Got Everything Right About Making a *Halloween* Sequel', *Variety* (22 October 2018), *https://variety.com/2018/film/box-office/halloween-box-office-analysis-horror-1202987761/* (accessed 30 January 2021).

Ryan, Chris 'Scare Tactics', *The Ringer* (2 November 2016), *www.theringer.com/2016/11/2/16077310/blumhouse-new-hollywood-success-paranormal-activity-the-purge-74dc38852ac5/* (accessed 7 February 2020).

Salemme, Danny, 'Jason Blum Has Plans to Create a Shared Universe for Blumhouse', *Screen Rant* (2 February 2019), *https://screenrant.com/blumhouse-shared-universe-jason-blum-plans/* (accessed 2 November 2019).

Sayad, Cecilia, 'Found-Footage Horror and the Frame's Undoing', *Cinema Journal*, 55/2 (2016), 43–66.

Schaefer, Sandy, 'Jason Blum: *Happy Death Day 3* isn't Likely to Happen', *Screen Rant* (2 November 2019), *https://screenrant.com/jason-blum-happy-death-day-3-not-happening/* (accessed 2 November 2019).

— '*Blair Witch* and the Evolution of the Found-Footage Genre', *Screen Rant* (17 September 2016), *https://screenrant.com/blair-witch-found-footage-discussion/* (accessed 21 June 2020).

Scheck, Frank, '*Paranormal Activity 2*: Film Review', *Hollywood Reporter* (22 October 2010), *www.hollywoodreporter.com/review/paranormal-activity-2-film-review-32162* (accessed 21 June 2020).

Schocket, Andrew, *Fighting Over the Founders: How We Remember the American Revolution* (New York: New York University Press, 2015).

Sconce, Jeffrey, *Haunted Media: Electronic Presence from Telegraphy to Television* (Durham NC: Duke University Press, 2000),

Scrivner, Coltan, John A. Johnson, Jens Kjeldgaard-Christiansen and Mathias Clasen, 'Pandemic Practice: Horror Fans and Morbidly Curious Individuals are More Psychologically Resilient during the COVID-19 Pandemic', *Personality and Individual Differences*, 168/1 (2021).

Shaviro, Steven, 'The Glitch Dimension: *Paranormal Activity* and the Technologies of Vision', in Martine Beugnet, Allan Cameron and Arlid Fetveit (eds), *Indefinite Visions: Cinema and the Attractions of Uncertainty* (Edinburgh: Edinburgh University Press, 2017), pp. 316–33.

Shields, Mike, 'Jason Blum-backed Crypt TV Thinks the Next Freddy Krueger Will be Launched on Mobile Phones', *Business Insider* (31 October 2017), *www.businessinsider.com/jason-blum-backed-crypt-tv-sees-next-freddy-krueger-launched-on-mobile-2017-10/* (accessed 30 January 2021).

Shiller, Robert J., *The Subprime Solution: How Today's Global Financial Crisis Happened, and What to Do About It* (Princeton NJ: Princeton University Press, 2008).

Siegel, Tatiana, and Borys Kit, 'New *Dracula* Movie in the Works as Universal

Remakes Its Monsterverse (Exclusive)', *Hollywood Reporter* (10 March 2020), *www.hollywoodreporter.com/heat-vision/new-dracula-movie-works-as-universal-remakes-monsterverse-1283635/* (accessed 7 April 2020).

Sipos, Thomas M., *Horror Film Aesthetics: Creating the Visual Language of Fear* (Jefferson NC: McFarland, 2010).

Siskel, Gene, '*Black Christmas*', *Chicago Tribune* (6 October 1974), B6.

Smuts, Aaron, 'Cognitive and Philosophical Approaches to Horror', in Harry M. Benshoff (ed.), *A Companion to the Horror Film* (London: Wiley-Blackwell, 2014), pp. 3–20.

SNCC Digital Gateway, 'June 1966: Meredith March', *https://snccdigital.org/events/meredith-march/* (accessed 15 May 2020).

Sneak Previews, 'Women in Danger Films', (23 October 1980), *www.youtube.com/watch?v=fxPWTGcxsus* (accessed 26 June 2020).

Snelson, Tim, 'The (Re)possession of the American Home: Negative Equity, Gender Inequality, and the Housing Crisis Horror Story', in Diane Negra and Yvonne Tasker (eds), *Gendering the Recession: Media and Culture in an Age of Austerity* (Durham NC: Duke University Press, 2014), pp. 161–80.

Sobczynski, Peter, '*Paranormal Activity: The Ghost Dimension*', *Roger Ebert* (23 October 2015), *www.rogerebert.com/reviews/paranormal-activity-the-ghost-dimension-2015* (accessed 21 June 2020).

Spiderbaby, Lianne, 'Wan on Wan', *Fangoria* (April 2011), 39.

Stephens, Alexander H., 'Appendix B – Cornerstone Address', in Jon L. Wakelyn (ed.), *Southern Pamphlets on Secession, November 1860–April 1861* (Chapel Hill NC: University of North Carolina Press, 1996), pp. 402–12.

Stevens, Dana, '*Paranormal Activity*', *Slate* (30 October 2009), *https://slate.com/culture/2009/10/paranormal-activity-reviewed.html* (accessed 21 June 2020).

Stewart, Andrew, 'Sony Scores in Pickup Game', *Daily Variety* (7 December 2010), 16.

Stewart, Sara, 'Elisabeth Moss gives it her all, but this *Invisible Man* isn't a must-see', *New York Post* (26 February 2020), *https://nypost.com/2020/02/26/elisabeth-moss-gives-it-her-all-but-this-invisible-man-isnt-a-must-see/* (accessed 30 June 2020).

Stewart, Scott, 'Commentary with Writer/Director Scott Stewart, Producer Jason Blum, Executive Producer Brian Kavanaugh-Jones and Editor Peter Gvozdan', *Dark Skies*, Blu-ray (Toronto: eOne, 2013).

Stokes, Melvyn, *D. W. Griffith's The Birth of a Nation: A History of the Most Controversial Motion Picture of All Time* (New York: Oxford University Press, 2008).

Stone, James D., 'Horror at the Homestead: The (Re)Possession of American Property in *Paranormal Activity* and *Paranormal Activity II*', in Kirk Boyle and

Daniel Mrozowski (eds), *The Great Recession in Film, Fiction, and Television: Twenty-First Century Bust Culture* (Lanham MD: Lexington Books, 2013), pp. 51–65.

Summers, Nick, 'Timeless Wisdom from a Chiseling Skinflint', *Forbes* (April 2014), 64–5.

Sutton, Candice, 'Covid 19 Coronavirus Backlash: US Citizens Protest Lockdown in "Zombie Hordes"', *New Zealand Herald* (17 April 2020), *www.nzherald. co.nz/world/covid-19-coronavirus-backlash-us-citizens-protest-lockdown-in-zombie-hordes/WMMLDL5VFWRVDSYV4BV7VGMXDE/* (accessed 20 January 2021).

Swanson, Alexander, 'Audience Reaction Movie Trailers and the Paranormal Activity Franchise', *Transformative Works and Cultures*, 18 (2015), 1–27.

Szabo, Sarah, 'Small Details You Missed in The First Purge', *Looper* (9 July 2018), *www.looper.com/128083/small-details-you-missed-in-the-first-purge/* (accessed 20 January 2021).

Tallerico, Brian, 'Review of *Halloween*', *Roger Ebert* (19 October 2018), *www.roger ebert.com/reviews/halloween-2018/* (accessed 20 January 2021).

Taylor, Drew, '*Happy Death Day 2U* Producer Jason Blum Wants to Make 10 More *Halloween* Movies', *Moviefone* (13 February 2019), *www.moviefone. com/2019/02/13/happy-death-day-2u-jason-blum-interview/* (accessed 7 February 2020).

Telotte, J. P. 'Faith and Idolatry in the Horror Film', in Barry Keith Grant (ed.), *Planks of Reason: Essays on the Horror Film* (London: Scarecrow Press, 1984), pp. 20–35.

Thompson, Sophie, 'Insidious has been Named the Scariest Horror Film of All Time', *Pop Buzz* (29 September 2020), *www.popbuzz.com/tv-film/news/insidious-scariest-movies-all-time-ranking/* (accessed 30 January 2021).

Thurman, Trace, 'The 10 Best Blumhouse-Produced Horror Films!', *Bloody Disgusting* (17 September 2015), *https://bloody-disgusting.com/editorials/3361660/best-blumhouse-horror-films/* (accessed 25 June 2020).

Tobias, Scott, '*Paranormal Activity 4*', *The A.V. Club* (19 September 2012), *https://film.avclub.com/paranormal-activity-4-1798174682* (accessed 21 June 2020).

Tram, Jamie, 'Digital Disquietude in the Screencast Film', *Senses of Cinema*, 92 (2019), *www.sensesofcinema.com/2019/cinema-in-the-2010s/digital-disquietude-in-the-screencast-film/* (accessed 31 January 2021).

TV Tropes, 'Magical Negro', *https://tvtropes.org/pmwiki/pmwiki.php/Main/Scary-BlackMan* (accessed 14 May 2020).

Ugwu, Reggie, 'The Hashtag that Changed the Oscars: An Oral History', *New York Times* (11 February 2020), *www.nytimes.com/2020/02/06/movies/oscars-sowhite-history.html* (accessed 14 May 2020).

Ukockis, Gail, *Misogyny: The New Activism* (Oxford: Oxford University Press, 2019).

Vaidhyanathan, Siva, *Antisocial Media: How Facebook Disconnects Us and Undermines Democracy* (Oxford: Oxford University Press, 2018).

Variety, 'Jason Blum: Variety Cover Shoot', *YouTube* (12 June 2018), *https://youtu.be/a2wTuT3WL-8a* (accessed 27 June 2020).

Virtue, Graeme, 'Is *Get Out* a Horror Film, a Comedy . . . or a Documentary?', *Guardian* (17 November 2017), *www.theguardian.com/film/filmblog/2017/nov/17/get-out-golden-globes-race-horror-comedy-documentary-jordan-peele* (accessed 16 May 2020).

— 'Why Smart Horror is Putting the Fear into Sequel-Addicted Hollywood', *Guardian* (12 April 2018), *www.theguardian.com/film/2018/apr/12/horror-quiet-place-get-out-hollywood/* (accessed 30 January 2021).

Wagner, Meg, '"Blood and Soil": Protesters Chant Nazi Slogan in Charlottesville', *CNN* (12 August 2017), *www.cnn.com/2017/08/12/us/charlottesville-unite-the-right-rally/index.html* (accessed 15 May 2020).

Wallace, Diana, *Female Gothic Stories: Gender, History and the Gothic* (Cardiff: University of Wales Press, 2013).

Warren, Matt, 'How to Fix Found Footage in Three Easy Steps', *Film Independent* (20 October 2016), *www.filmindependent.org/blog/fix-found-footage-three-easy-steps/* (accessed 13 May 2020).

Weaver, Angela D., Dana Ménard, Christine Cabrera and Angela Taylor, 'Embodying the Moral Code?: Thirty Years of Final Girls in Slasher Films', *Psychology of Popular Media Culture*, 4/1 (2015), pp. 31–46.

Weaver, Courtney, 'Trump Blames "Antifa" for Protests Despite Lack of Evidence', *Financial Times* (4 June 2020), *www.ft.com/content/04ba905f-f965-4f7b-80ab-cccb0f912ddc/* (accessed 20 January 2021).

Webb, Beth, 'Horror Specialist Blumhouse has Quietly become 2020's Most Exciting Film Studio', *NME* (14 May 2020), *www.nme.com/features/horror-specialist-blumhouse-has-quietly-become-2020s-most-profitable-film-studio-2668647* (accessed 21 May 2020).

Wee, Valerie, *Japanese Horror Films and Their American Remakes: Translating Fear, Adapting Culture* (London: Routledge, 2014).

Weiler, A. H., 'Screen: Murky Whodunit', *New York Times* (20 October 1975), 45.

Wijaszka, Zofia, '*Black Christmas*: Smashes the Patriarchy with Strong Women', *Film Inquiry* (18 December 2019), *www.filminquiry.com/black-christmas-2019-review/* (accessed 30 June 2020).

Wikipedia, 'List of Accolades received by *Get Out*', *https://en.wikipedia.org/wiki/List_of_accolades_received_by_Get_Out* (accessed 15 May 2020).

Wilchins, Riki, *Queer Theory, Gender Theory: An Instant Primer* (Los Angeles CA: Alyson Books, 2004).

Williams, Jason, 'Donald Trump and Race', *Social Justice* (11 January 2017), *www.socialjusticejournal.org/donald-trump-and-race/* (accessed 20 January 2021).

Wilson, D. Harlan, *They Live* (New York: Wallflower Press, 2015).

Wood, Robin, *Hollywood from Vietnam to Reagan . . . and Beyond* (New York: Columbia University Press, 2003).

— 'An Introduction to American Horror Film', in Jeffrey Andrew Weinstock (ed.), *The Monster Theory Reader* (Minneapolis MN: University of Minnesota Press, 2020), pp. 108–35.

—'Return of the Repressed', in Barry Keith Grant (ed.), *Robin Wood on the Horror Film: Collected Essays and Reviews* (Detroit MI: Wayne State University Press, 2018), pp. 57–62.

Woodward, Adam, '*Paranormal Activity* Reviews', *Rotten Tomatoes*, *www.rottentomatoes.com/m/Paranormal_Activity/reviews* (accessed 15 January 2021).

Yagci, Alper H., 'The Great Recession, Inequality and Occupy Protests around the World', *Government Opposition*, 52/4 (2017), 640–70.

Yamato, Jen, 'With *Searching*, *Unfriended* and beyond, Timur Bekmambetov Seeks a New Cinematic Language that Mirrors Our Digital Lives', *Los Angeles Times* (17 August 2018), *www.latimes.com/entertainment/movies/la-ca-mn-timur-bekmambetov-searching-unfriended-dark-web-screenlife-20180817-story.html* (accessed 25 June 2020).

Zaretsky, Natasha, *No Direction Home: The American Family and the Fear of National Decline, 1968–1980* (Chapel Hill NC: University of North Carolina Press, 2007).

Zimmer, Catherine, 'Caught on Tape? The Politics of Video in the New Torture Film', in Aviva Briefel and Sam J. Miller (eds), *Horror After 9/11: World of Fear, Cinema of Terror* (Austin TX: University of Texas Press, 2012), pp. 83–106.

Zinoman, Jason, *Shock Value: How a Few Eccentric Outsiders Gave Us Nightmares, Conquered Hollywood, and Invented Modern Horror* (London: Penguin Books, 2012).

Žižek, Slavoj, *Enjoy Your Symptom!: Jacques Lacan in Hollywood and Out* (third edition) (New York: Routledge, 2008).

Index